Cultural Studies and Finance Capitalism

While many discussions of the economic crisis of 2007-2008 have sought to explain the causes of the financial collapse, this volume looks to supplement these accounts by exploring possible alternatives for the post-crisis world in which we now live. However, rather than offering a strictly economic approach, *Cultural Studies and Finance Capitalism* argues that the crisis was as much cultural as economic, and that any way forward must understand the complex relationship between media, culture and the economy. The chapters in this volume deal with a wide range of themes including celebrity culture, media coverage of the economy, examinations of economic theory and financial markets. They bring together research that combines an historical perspective with a view towards the future of critical cultural and political analysis. In a period marked by anxiety and economic austerity, this volume offers the reader tools for understanding the place and importance of cultural research in the post-crisis era.

This book was originally published as a special issue of the journal *Cultural Studies*.

Mark Hayward is Assistant Professor in the Department of Global Communications at the American University of Paris, France. His research focuses on television, cultural policy and representations of the economy in popular culture. He has published essays in *Modern Italy* and *Cultural Studies* as well as translating several texts from Italian and French.

Cultural Studies and Finance Capitalism

The Economic Crisis and After

Edited by

Mark Hayward

Routledge
Taylor & Francis Group
LONDON AND NEW YORK

First published 2012
by Routledge
2 Park Square, Milton Park, Abingdon, Oxon, OX14 4RN

Simultaneously published in the USA and Canada
by Routledge
605 Third Avenue, New York, NY 10017

Routledge is an imprint of the Taylor & Francis Group, an informa business

This book is a reproduction of *Cultural Studies*, volume 24, issue 3. The Publisher requests to those authors who may be citing this book to state, also, the bibliographical details of the special issue on which the book was based.

British Library Cataloguing in Publication Data
A catalogue record for this book is available from the British Library

ISBN13: 978-0-415-68681-5 (hbk)

Typeset in Garamond
by Taylor & Francis

Publisher's Note
The publisher would like to make readers aware that the chapters in this book may be referred to as articles as they are identical to the articles published in the special issue. The publisher accepts responsibility for any inconsistencies that may have arisen in the course of preparing this volume for print.

Contents

Notes on Contributors

John Clarke is a professor of Social Policy at the Open University in the UK. His work has addressed the struggles to remake welfare states and public services. Three recent books explore these issues: *Changing Welfare, Changing States: New Directions in Social Policy* (Sage, 2004); *Creating Citizen-Consumers: Changing Publics and Changing Public Services* (with Janet Newman, Nick Smith, Elizabeth Vidler and Louise Westmarland, Sage, 2007); and *Publics, Politics and Power: Remaking the Public in Public Services* (with Janet Newman, Sage, 2009).

Steve Cross is Senior Lecturer in Media and Cultural Studies at London College of Communication, University of the Arts London. He has taught at Goldsmiths College, London School of Economics and at the Universities of Lodz, Essex and Middlesex.

Matthew Dunn is a doctoral candidate in Human Communication Studies at the University of Denver. His research explores the articulation of communication ethics and psychoanalysis.

Lawrence Grossberg is the Morris Davis Distinguished Professor of Communication Studies at the University of North Carolina at Chapel Hill, as well as Distinguished Adjunct Professor of American Studies, Anthropology and Geography. He is, coincidentally, the co-editor of this journal. His new book, *We All Want to Change the World: The Intellectual Labor of Cultural Studies* will be published in 2010 by Duke University Press.

Stefano Harney is a Chair in Strategy, Culture, and Society at the School of Business and Management, Queen Mary, University of London.

Jayson Harsin is Assistant Professor of Global Communications at The American University of Paris. His reasearch interests include economic rights and political imaginaries; and convergence culture, rumor, and political branding. His most recent work appears in the edited collections *Cultural Studies: An Anthology* (Blackwell, 2009) and *The Diffusion of Social Movements* (Cambridge University Press, forthcoming 2010).

Mark Hayward teaches in the Department of Global Communication at the American University of Paris.

Darrin Hicks is an Associate Professor in Human Communication Studies at the University of Denver. His current research focuses on affective dimensions of collaborative governance as well as the genealogy of conviction.

Jo Littler is Senior Lecturer in Media and Cultural Studies at Middlesex University, London, UK. She is author of *Radical Consumption: Shopping for Change in Contemporary Culture* (Open University Press, 2009), co-editor (with Roshi Naidoo) of *The Politics of Heritage: The Legacies of 'Race'* (Routledge, 2005) and editor of *Mediactive 2: Celebrity* (L&W, 2005; downloadable at http://www.lwbooks.co.uk). She is currently writing a book on celebrity.

Randy Martin is Professor and chair of Art and Public Policy at New York University and author, most recently, of *An Empire of Indifference: American War and the Financial Logic of Risk Management* (Duke University Press, 2007).

Mark Hayward

THE ECONOMIC CRISIS AND AFTER

Recovery, reconstruction and cultural studies

This introductory article engages with possibilities for cultural studies during the economic crisis of 2008 and its aftermath. It begins by considering the nature of the crisis and the recovery that follows. It goes on to explore the relationship between cultural studies and economic discourse, arguing that the cultural studies of the economy and the 'economic' has always taken place in reference to a specific set of contextual and conjunctural factors. In conclusion, the relationship between the politics of recovery and the possibilities of reconstruction are developed as a possible way of understanding current and future contributions by cultural studies researchers to discussions about the economy.

The crisis consists precisely in the fact that the old is dying and the new cannot be born; in this interregnum a great variety of morbid symptoms appear.

Antonio Gramsci, Prison Notebooks

There is nothing more crucial than Gramsci's recognition that every crisis is also a moment of reconstruction; that there is no destruction which is not, also, reconstruction; that, historically nothing is dismantled without also attempting to put something new in its place.

Stuart Hall, 'Gramsci and Us'

The economic crisis and after

There has been a great deal written and said about the economic crisis over the past two years.(1) A significant portion of this material has taken the form of explanations and diagnoses of how the meltdown occurred and who exactly was responsible. While some of these writings have taken on the voice of economic and political analysis, other modes of discourse have also circulated [for example, the 'confessions' of guilty consciences implicated in the irresponsible activities of investment banks and regulatory agencies (Cresus 2009, Anderson 2009, Ishikawa 2009)]. What many of these ways of addressing the crisis share is a desire to locate the cause, the source, of the collapse. Usually this has meant delving deep into the arcane logics of derivatives and other financial products, or locating fault in the collective hubris that lead to the overextension of individuals, banks and corporations in the murky waters of credit speculation.

Some authors, however, taking up the burdens of the contemporary crisis, have offered a litany of modest (and not so modest) proposals for the future. While a few seized this moment as the breach through which a frontal attack against capitalism might be waged, less radical voices have taken up the promise of history and demanded that politicians and bankers alike offer us a 'new deal' (Krugman 2009). As is often the case, the most persuasive voices to emerge in this moment of crisis mixed reason with hope, bringing together descriptive and promissory registers of discourse.

The most recent example of the mixture of analysis and hope can be seen in the growing number of experts and public figures who have taken great effort to declare an end to the economic crisis of the past two years. These declarations are instructive because they highlight the complexities of analysing and intervening into a period of crisis and its aftermath. While speaking some kind of 'truth' and certainly having some rhetorical effect, such statements have mostly served to highlight the difference between economic nomenclature and the 'real economy'. Thus, the great recession of 2008 has 'ended' even as unemployment and other measures of the welfare of a significant portion of the population continue to show signs of catastrophic trauma. Or, in the carefully chosen words of US Federal Reserve Chairman Ben Bernanke in September 2009, 'Even though from a technical perspective the recession is very likely over at this point, it's still going to feel like a very weak economy for some time' (Bull & Felsenthal 2009).

Some fear that we are entering a 'jobless recovery' in which the institutions of global finance have been able to save their own skins, but at a cost to the livelihoods of millions of others (Grice & O'Grady 2009, Monfort 2009, Goodman & Healy 2009). Others have suggested that the recovery might remain a primarily statistical phenomenon for years to come, in which most economic indicators show that all is well even as the welfare of the majority show little, if any signs of improvement. Many experts describe it as 'anemic'; one remarked that, 'this is not a normal recovery. It's tepid and weak' (Goldman 2009) and another described it as a 'phantom recovery' (Roubini 2009). Who or what exactly, then, is recovering? Clearly those who took to the streets and passionately declared, 'We won't pay for your crisis!' were right as this recovery (just like the excesses which preceded the crisis) is not enjoyed by all, but rather restricted to a relatively small number of institutions and individuals.

As the effects of the crisis continue to reverberate across the globe, it is becoming clear that it has only served to worsen the forms of marginalization and alienation that characterized the neo-liberal economic order of the past three decades. The global distribution of wealth and welfare continues to be divided according to the racialized and gendered lines of inequality that characterized the pre-crisis global 'geography of livelihoods' (Ross 2009). It is a dire situation. As Hicks and Dunn write in their contribution to this volume, 'beneath the chatter of crisis and redemption make sure to listen for the slaughtering bell'. But, it is not all simply business as usual. At the same time, there is a renewed desire on the part of many people to re-write the rules of the economic order and rein in the excessive power wielded by banks and investors (Schifferes 2009). There is a widespread feeling that suggests that the suffering caused by the crisis should logically entail the reworking of the global financial system or we must all face the inevitability of future collapses and crises on an equal or greater scale to the present moment.

However, in a time of recovery, the desire for a broad rethinking of the global financial system seems to lose its energy and purpose as the suffering of multitudes is accommodated as part of the status quo. As John Clarke writes in this volume, 'States of anxiety, insecurity, outrage, scepticism and more have been mobilized, managed, negotiated, contained and directed - with few signs of success.' After all, as many critics have noted, there has been little change in the operations at the major lending institutions and investment houses at the centre of the near collapse (Berenson 2009, Reich 2009). Calls for financial reform and regulation multiply, but very little change has taken place (Whitelaw 2009). Everything is different, yet nothing is changing. What, then, is there to be said about the economic crisis of 2008 and its aftermath? And, speaking directly to our purpose here, what is there to say in Cultural Studies about the crisis and recovery?

The failure of claims that we have come to the 'end' of the crisis to either ring true or effect immediate change should make clear to us the uncertainty of the present moment. Yes, the economic crisis has passed and the recovery has started. However, the recovery should not be seen as a fait accompli, marked by a turnaround in economic growth in the G8 countries. Let us start by acknowledging that any recovery from the crisis will come about not merely through the natural workings of the economy (for there is no such thing) or even the intervention of states and international organizations exclusively, but through an intentional and expansive programme that will engage with the institutions and the activities that define contemporary finance capitalism as well as the ideas and affective investments which all of us have in the current configuration of the economy. After all, the affective ties which linked the circulation to capital to development of the self that Randy Martin explored in *Financialization of Daily Life* (Martin 2002), cannot so easily be undone at the first sign of trouble. Thus, the recovery must be understood as a project on the part of financial and political elites to re-establish and fortify an economic and social order that was on the brink of collapse and discredit.

While the global financial system returns to 'normal', many individuals have been left traumatized by recent events; they have changed their spending and saving habits as well as their general attitude towards the global economic system, its institutions as much as its promises. Sometimes these changes have been forced by the personal experience of unemployment or the loss of housing or other forms of economic dispossession, but in many cases people have made these adaptations in their worldview and behaviours according to their perception of the dangers and risk posed by the present situation. In this sense, the generalization of the experience of precarity in Western Europe and North America (particularly the United States and Britain) will be one of major long-term consequences of the crisis. Therefore, any 'recovery' which shores up the current global financial system will be more than economic; it will also involve the hearts and minds of individuals, convincing and coaxing them into believing that it is once more safe to swim in the waters of investments and credit. This is the project at the centre of the current recovery, a recovery that is building itself up on the economic indicators of 'trust' and 'confidence' of individuals in institutions.(2)

As Hall (1988) reminds us in the epigraph, every period of crisis is accompanied by a project for reconstruction. For this reason, the months and years to come are crucial, as the struggle over significant changes in the global financial system will be settled, hopefully with the interests of people rather than financial institutions at its centre. However, as in any struggle over hegemony, this is easier said than done. If opinion polls are useful for discerning the general sentiment of large numbers of people, it is clear that this is a moment in which contradictory ideas and emotions are at the forefront of people's thoughts about the economy. On the one hand, there remains the anger, distrust, and resentment towards financial institutions and the failure of state regulation. Many surveys show that the majority of individuals still fear future crises due to failure on the part of both the state and the banks to change their ways. At the same time, there is a desire for things to return to the way they were before. Thus, the contemporary crisis has also given rise to a variety of forms of nostalgia. In everyday life, this has ranged from candy to Yorkshire pudding (Aston 2009). In the words of an Australian marketing researcher, 'The youth market's love of nostalgia is a direct reflection of better time that existed pre-GFC (global financial crisis) and climate change' (Fahmy 2009). But this has also entailed a variety of political and economic nostalgia, from Keynsianism (Skidelsky 2009) to a populist desire for regressive forms of economic governance.

Often the desire for radical forward-looking change and nostalgia for the way things used to be are interwoven. Nowhere is the tension between these two desires more apparent than in contemporary declarations about the end of the crisis and the beginning of the recovery. In their attempt to respond and quell fears and anxieties, they often follow a discourse in which the return to the old ways and the new ways demanded by many, sit uncomfortably alongside one another. It is this uneasy juxtaposition that highlights the importance of cultural studies work on the crisis and recovery. As the essays collected here show, the crisis was more than simply 'economic' in nature. They show how the 'economy' is better understood as a complex assemblage of institutions and practices that continually escapes claims that it is merely a space for the exchange and allocation of resources. Thus the recovery must also engage with a similarly complex collection of sites, practices and institutions.

Cultural studies and the economic

In this regard, these essays build upon earlier work in cultural studies that has taken up the question of the economic (as category) and the economy (as object) as theoretically informed engagements with particular moments.

Looking back at cultural studies engagement with the economy and the economic, we might describe this work as evolving around three thematics. Acknowledging these previous points of engagement, it is therefore a mistake to say - as some critics in more 'serious' disciplines have accused - that cultural studies has failed to engage with the economy. Or, that its primary intellectual contribution has been the development of a sophisticated, and deceptive, justification for complicity with contemporary capitalism. Rather, these three themes have served to rethink and rework received notions of the 'economic' and the 'economy' in the humanities and social sciences. Indeed, in light of these concerns, it is possible to re-read the history of cultural studies as being grounded in an analysis of a variety of economic contexts as well as of received knowledge about the nature and significance of the economy.

The first of these, deeply rooted in the projects of cultural studies since their inception, involves an engagement with the assumed relations between the economic, political and cultural. Fundamental to this critique was the pioneering work of Raymond Williams, Stuart Hall, James Carey and others, who challenged the inherited view of culture found in reductively 'economistic' versions of Marxist thought (Hall 1996, Williams 1978, Carey 1988). The critique of 'economism' that was central to a great deal of early cultural studies work is sometimes read as a plea for greater attention to culture, but this was not the end in itself. Rather, this critique can be seen as part of a larger project which entailed expanding our understandings of the 'material,' a term which had been often primarily associated with the economic in the Marxian tradition. This is a concern that extends from early work on ideology and through the engagement with post-Fordism in the 1980s. Today, just as the use of the concept of culture has proliferated into many sites previously thought to be outside the scope of its relevance, we might also trace through this work a simultaneous destabilization of the category of the 'economic' as clearly distinguishable from other social phenomena.

Another set of engagements, implicitly present in early cultural studies work but becoming more pronounced in recent years, has engaged with the economy as discourse, internal to the practices and processes of representation. The work of Timothy Mitchell on the construction of the 'economy' in his work on Egypt (Mitchell 1998) and David Ruccio's call for greater study of 'economic representations' (Ruccio 2008) stand as two models for work in this vein. The goal of both these traditions is to re-read and re-situate the relationship between culture and the economy in a way that contributes to the establishment of a more egalitarian social order. This is a body of work that benefited a great deal from the influence of Michel Foucault, and the interest in cultural policy as taken up by Tony Bennett and others (Bennett 1992, Hesmondhalgh 2005, Yudice 2003).

Finally, we might look to work on the economy that has emerged at the intersection of feminist and post-colonial approaches, which have also proven to be among the most persuasive critics of established understandings of the economic and the economy. One might consider the re-reading of Marx's understanding of value offered by Gayatri Spivak as a possible starting point for understanding the way in which the fundamental categories of political economy, even a critical political economy, are open to instability and indeterminancy (Spivak 1988). Similarly, the work of J. K. Gibson-Graham offers a challenging reading of the limits placed upon the possibilities for social change by the discourse of capitalism as found in both economics and its institutional adaptations and evolutions. As they note at the beginning of The End of Capitalism (As we Knew It), 'the project of understanding the beast [capitalism] has itself produced a beast' (Gibson-Graham 1996, p. 1). They go on to explain, 'it is the way capitalism has been "thought" that has made it so difficult for people to imagine its supersession' (Gibson-Graham 1996, p. 4).

Yet, in discussing these approaches to the economy and the economic, we must also pay attention to cultural studies faith in the transformative potential of critical intellectual work, and its claims that it is this engagement that distinguishes it from other related projects more exclusively focused on analysis and description. Cultural studies has long been sensitive to the significance of moments of crisis (economic, moral, cultural) as moments when it is possible to trouble - and perhaps transform - existing systems and structures of inequality and oppression. Indeed, beyond a shared topic, common to all three of the earlier-mentioned engagements with the economic is the fact that they were not merely abstract exercises, or the products of an academic turf war.

In every case, it is important to situate cultural studies' engagement with economy in relation to the conjunctural forces and contradictions that defined their moment of intervention. As Harney notes in his chapter, the struggle over 'economism' needs to be understood as an attempt to structure an intellectual project of social change in the context of various changes in the nature of capitalism after World War II. Similarly, the engagement with the economy as a discursive construct can be read in relation to both a variety of changes in the significance of culture in government action, as well as the growing prominence of neo-classical economics as the dominant explanatory discourse during the neo-liberal revolution of the 1980s and 1990s. Finally, the engagement from post-colonial feminists speaks to struggles around expanding the scope and scale of research beyond the assumed contours of economy spatially and socially. It provided a necessary critique to the complex mobilizations of exclusion that have defined the most recent period of globalization.

If these previous moments are any indication, we can infer than there is indeed a great deal to say about the economic crisis that takes culture seriously. The essays collected here take up and adapt the legacy of this tradition. They do not raise the question of the economy as an abstract, theoretical problem, but engage with the particular context of the current moment. Like a great deal of cultural studies work, the conceptual and theoretical advances regarding thinking about the economy and the economic developed in response and relation to contextual specificities. They remind us that the economic crisis is not merely a crisis of particular economic order, but should be seen as an opportunity to raise questions about the place of the economy within the current conjuncture more generally. Thus, one of the aims of this volume is not simply to instantiate a 'cultural studies of the economy', but to remind scholars working in cultural studies that the economy is, and must remain, a site of constant engagement and experimentation. The economy is, as it always has been, a problematic mutually constituted within and alongside the other problematics that have defined cultural studies.

In the chapters by Lawrence Grossberg and Randy Martin, the relationship between the economy, discourse and affect come to the fore. In Grossberg's chapter, this takes the form of an extended engagement with the problem of how to analyse the current conjuncture, asking what tools are necessary to map the temporalities and geographies of finance capitalism. Arguing that the contemporary crisis should be read as a crisis of modernity, it provides a model of how cultural studies work that takes the specific materialities of the economy and the economic in the era of finance might be done. Grossberg's goal is to develop a better story for mapping the world in which we live. It is an argument that finds echoes in the chapter from Randy Martin, in which he raises the relationship between accounts of the economic crisis and the moralization associated with the parable. Tracing the drift of derivatives out of the economic, he argues that there is a greater need for cultural studies to trace the contours of economic discourse in order to understand the 'ungainly request' finance capital makes on all of us.

The contributions from Jayson Harsin and Darrin Hicks and Matthew Dunn offer complementary analyses of the 1930s and the Great Depression. However, the primary impetus of these pieces is not merely to provide insight into our present moment by means of a series of loose parallels. Instead, Harsin places our current moment in the context of a longer history of economic rights in the United States, arguing that 'we are living in a historical a priori, as Foucault called it, of economic rights (a particular articulation of individual freedom, government, and economics)'. Concluding with a survey of possible transformations in contemporary understandings and deployments of economic rights, Harsin suggests that there is hope (but no guarantee) for a new understanding of the relationship between freedom, economic agency and community. Hicks and Dunn similarly take us back to the years around the great depression, taking us through the debates and proposals that led to the Securities Act of 1933. By highlighting those proposals (ultimately rejected) that demanded greater obligation of the part of securities dealers to their clients, they bring to light the significance of intersubjectivity in our understanding of the failures of the financial system as well as reminding us that other forms of market relations were possible. They make this argument in the context of recent discussions around economic irrationality, discussions of 'animal spirits' in the economy, and make clear that a more developed understanding of economic agency and behaviour continues to be needed.

The contributions from Steve Cross and Jo Littler and Stefano Harney, return us to more familiar territory for cultural studies as constituted around the concept of cultural economy. Cross and Littler's essay returns to the affective terrain of economic life touched upon by Grossberg, Hicks and Martin. By tracing the cultural history of Schadenfreude, the authors ask that we consider the subjective obstacles to equality. Schadenfreude, they argue, describes an affective state 'that desires equality, but is primarily unable to think it as anything other than "leveling through humiliation"'. Harney, in his short piece, takes up some of the issues recently broached in the exchange between Daniel Mato and Toby Miller on the concept of the creative/cultural industries. Through a re-reading of the history of British cultural studies, Harney shows the on-going need to pay greater attention to the question of labour as central to the project of cultural studies work. Both chapters return us to familiar contexts, and offer necessary engagements with our understanding of the economy and the economic as sites of affective and material production.

Finally, John Clarke's chapter asks us to think about a question that has concerned many: what comes next? Rejecting simplistic claims that we are exiting the neo-liberal era, he asks us to reconsider what the crisis was so that we might make sense of what follows. Returning us to the years in which the power of markets to resolve every issue, Clarke highlights the complexity of invocations of the 'new deal' and its relationship to a variety of projects which enlist the public (emotionally and economically) in the recovery. The chapter ends on an ambivalent note. It brings us back to the complexity I have been addressing around the possibilities and promises for recovery.

Recovery and reconstruction

For many, the events of the 1930s and the Great Depression serve as starting point for making sense of our present conjuncture. I do not deny the relevance of this moment, its symbols and institutions as a precedent for the present moment (as the epigraph from Gramsci would indicate). However, unlike those who invoke the faded promise of the 'new deal' as the necessary way forward, these essays are not simply about describing a fixed set of 'solutions'. For this reason, this volume is not simply 'about' the crisis and its aftermath, but instead draws our attention to the transition between a period of crisis and a period of reconstruction (as is also evident in the epigraph from Gramsci). Indeed, it is the concept of reconstruction, rather than recovery (which seems intimately tied to the maintenance of the status quo), that I believe is useful for situating these essays.

In *Black Reconstruction in America*, W. E. B. Du Bois recognizes the potential for change as well as its undoing during periods of reconstruction in his study of the aftermath of the American civil war, a period when an attempt was made to include millions of former slaves in a politically and economically democratic society. He writes:

"One reads the truer deeper facts of Reconstruction with a great despair. It is at once so simple and human, and yet so futile. There is no villain, no idiot, no saint. There are just men; men who crave ease and power, men who know want and hunger, men who have crawled... So slight a gesture, a word, might set the strife in order, not with full content, but with growing dawn of fulfillment. Instead roars the crash of hell..." (Du Bois 1992)

Counterposing the promise of 'abolition democracy' to the litany of global tragedies of which the failure of Reconstruction is but a single piece, Du Bois makes apparent what is at stake in the aftermath of crisis.(3) It is not that the world no longer moves forward in time, but that the promise of the future becomes increasingly dim and the territory becomes crowded with the 'morbid symptoms' of which Gramsci speaks. That Du Bois outlines these consequences in the final chapter of his study, called 'The Propaganda of History' where he engages with how the period is taught to school children barely two generations later, reminds us of the importance (and risks) of intellectual work.

However, analyses of a crisis do not necessarily provide clarity, and they certainly do not provide opportunities for the scholar to save the day (no matter how much such fantasies might flatter our desires). Many of those writing on the economic crisis and its aftermath have marshaled the veridical energies bestowed the discourse of economics in our era to make their argument; relying on the infallibility of economic logic, they implicitly suggest that 'clear-headed' analysis will allow, if not compel, us to make 'clearheaded' decisions about the future. It seems obvious, yet it is precisely at such a moment that many clear heads become muddled.

The essays collected here do not simply offer the 'truth' of the crisis as it happened, nor do they outline the necessary steps through which we might achieve utopia tomorrow. Instead, they are attempts to grapple with the movement between explaining the crisis and proposing a way forward. They show that the movement between these two moments - crisis and reconstruction - is hardly as straightforward as is often assumed. The assumed temporal, material and ontological relations between the present, the past and the future, the proximate and the remote, the material and the virtual are shown to be precisely what is up for grabs. However, in expanding our understanding of the present moment, these essays also seek to expand and intensify the potential for transformation as part of a critical intellectual project. They seek to produce a space in which more radical futures - radical in both their transformative and creative potential - are possible. In this, this volume seeks to move beyond describing, reacting and recovering from the crisis and develop the promise of cultural studies.

Acknowledgements

The author would like to thank Lawrence Grossberg and Kelly Jakes for reading and giving thoughtful feedback on this introduction.

Notes

1 Alongside the voluminous amount of material to be found in newspapers and magazines, a number of books have appeared over the past two years explaining the origins of the crisis. Notable among these are John Bellamy Foster and Fred Magdoff's The Great Financial Crisis: Causes and Consequences (2009), Graeme Turner's The Credit Crunch: Housing Bubbles, Globalisation and the Worldwide Economic Crisis (2008), and George Cooper's The Origin of Financial Crises (2008). To this might also be added an equally large number of television documentaries (like PBS's Inside the Meltdown), online videos [i.e. 'How to Explain the 2008 US Financial Crisis to Your Kids (and most adults)'] and even dramatizations (The Last Days of Lehman Brothers).

2 For example, the Chicago Booth/Kellogg School Financial Trust Index was set up as a way to monitor the trust and confidence of average Americans in their financial system, arguing that, 'Trust is a powerful motivator of economic behavior.' As early as July 2009, the index noted 'a sense of optimism and a reduction in fear and anger toward America's financial institutions.' The data is collected from a random sample of 1000 individuals asked to complete a survey.

3 For further developments on the concept of 'abolition democracy' see Lipsitz (2004) and Davis (2005).

References

Anderson, G. (2009) *Cityboy: Beer and Loathing in the Square Mile*, London, Headline Publishing Group.

Aston, H. (2009) 'Sweet taste of nostalgia helps to comfort us through crunch', *Sunday Express*. Available at: http://www.express.co.uk (accessed 19 September 2009).

Bellamy Foster, J. & Magdoff, F. (2009) *The Great Financial Crisis: Causes and Consequences*, New York, Monthly Review Press.

Bennett, T. (1992) 'Useful culture', *Cultural Studies*, vol. 6, no. 3, pp. 395-408.

Berenson, A. (2009) 'A year later, little change on Wall St.', *New York Times*,
vol. 1.

Bull, A. & Felsenthal, M. (2009) 'Bernanke says recession is 'very likely' over', *Reuters.com*. Available at: http://www.reuters.com (accessed 19 September 2009).

Carey, J. W. (1988) *Communication as Culture: Essays on Media and Society*, London, Routledge.
Cooper, G. (2008) *The Origin of Financial Crises: Central Banks, Credit Bubbles, and the Efficient Market Fallacy*, New York, Vintage Books.
Cresus (2009) *Confessions d'un banquier pourri*, Paris, Fayard.
Davis, A. Y. (2005) *Abolition Democracy: Beyond Prisons, Torture, and Empire*, New York, Seven Stories Press.
Du Bois, W. (1992) *Black Reconstruction in America, 1860-1880*, New York, The Free Press.
Fahmy, M. (2009) 'Weary of modern woes, youth long for the past: survey', *Reuters.com*. Available at: http://www.reuters.com (accessed 19 September 2009).
Gibson-Graham, J. K. (1996) *The End of Capitalism (as we Knew It): A Feminist Critique of Political Economy*, Cambridge, MA: Blackwell Publishers.
Goldman, D. (2009) 'Fed not acting like there's a recovery', CNNMoney.com. Available at: http://www.money.cnn.com (accessed 19 September 2009).
Goodman, P. S. & Healy, J. (2009) 'In unemployment report, signs of a jobless recovery', New York Times, 1.
Grice, A. & O'Grady, S. (2009) 'Britain worries about jobless recovery', Businessweek. Available at: http://www.businessweek.com/print/globalbiz/content/sep2009/gb20090916_487321.htm (accessed 19 September 2009).
Hall, S. (1988) 'Gramsci and us', in *Gramsci's Political Thought: An Introduction*, London, Lawrence and Wishart.
Hall, S. (1996) 'The problem of ideology: Marxism without guarantees', in *Stuart Hall: Critical Dialogues* in *Cultural Studies*, eds D. Morley & K. Chen, London, Routledge, pp. 25-46.
Hesmondhalgh, D. (2005) 'Media and cultural policy as public policy', *International Journal of Cultural Policy*, vol. 11, no. 1, pp. 95-109.
Ishikawa, T. (2009) *How I Caused the Credit Crunch*, London, Icon Books.
Krugman, P. (2009) *The Return of Depression Economics and the Crisis of 2008*, New York, W.W. Norton.
Lipsitz, G. (2004) 'Abolition democracy and global justice', *Comparative American Studies: An International Journal*, vol. 2, no. 3, pp. 271-286.
Martin, R. (2002) *Financialization of Daily Life*, Philadelphia, PA, Temple University Press.
Mitchell, T. (1998) 'Fixing the economy', *Cultural Studies*, vol. 12, no. 1, pp. 82-101.
Monfort, S. (2009) 'Economists eye prospects for jobless recovery', Nasdaq.com. Available at: http://www.nasdaq.com (accessed 19 September 2009).
Reich, R. (2009) 'No downturn for greed', Salon.com. Available at: http://www.salon.com (accessed 13 September 2009).
Ross, A. (2009) *Nice Work if You Can Get It: Life and Labor in Precarious Times*, New York, NYU Press.
Roubini, N. (2009) 'Nouriel Roubini: A Phantom Recovery?', Business Standard. Available at: http://www.business-standard.com/india/news/nourielroubiniphantom-recovery/367421/ (accessed 10 April 2010).
Ruccio, D. F. (ed.) (2008) *Economic Representations: Academic and Everyday*, London, Routledge.
Schifferes, S. (2009) 'Public "backs economic reforms"', BBC News/Business. Available at: http://news.bbc.co.uk (accessed 12 September 2009).
Skidelsky, R. (2009) Keynes: The Return of the Master, Cambridge, MA, Public Affairs.
Spivak, G. C. (1988) *In Other Worlds: Essays in Cultural Politics*, New York, Routledge.
Turner, G. (2008) *The Credit Crunch: Housing Bubbles, Globalisation and the Worldwide Economic Crisis*, London, Pluto Press.
Whitelaw, K. (2009) 'What happened to the push to reform Wall Street?', NPR. Available at: http://www.npr.org (accessed 15 September 2009).

Williams, R. (1978) *Marxism and Literature*, New York, Oxford University Press.
Yudice, G. (2003) *The Expediency of Culture: Uses of Culture in the Global Era*, Durham, NC, Duke University Press.

Lawrence Grossberg

MODERNITY AND COMMENSURATION
A reading of a contemporary (economic) crisis

This piece considers the financial crisis of 2008 through the lens of the derivative, by locating both the derivative and the crisis in the broader context of post-war US conjuncture. Drawing upon the work of Marx, Postone and von Mises, I argue that the derivative can be seen as a response to the collapse of any viable logic of commensuration. Its failure has to be understood, again, in the context of broader conjunctural struggles, constituted in part by a dispersed set of crises of commensuration. In this way, I hope to offer a revised theory of conjunctural analysis as well as the beginnings of a concrete conjunctural study of post-war US society, and to begin to think about how cultural studies might 'articulate' the economic.

Cultural studies and economics

There has been an increasing interest, within cultural studies, in taking on economic matters more directly.[1] The usual and only partly true story is that cultural studies, especially in its British and US lineages, had bracketed economic matters. It is only partly true because there were many within cultural studies, across a range of disciplines and regions, who continued not only to take economic questions seriously but also to seek ways of doing economics that did not reproduce the reductionism and oversimplification that cultural studies criticized in many of the dominant approaches within economics and political economy. Nevertheless, it is true that the challenge of finding better ways of incorporating economic analysis into the conjuncturalist project of cultural studies has become more urgent and more visible in recent years.

The question of what exactly the point of such work is remains. What is a cultural studies of economics/economies supposed to be or do? As I have argued elsewhere,[2] unfortunately, too many of these efforts slip back into forms of reductionism, so that they end up assuming that the economy is, after all, what it is all about, the bottom line. And too often, this becomes simply another occasion to re-inscribe our (usually Marxist) critiques of capitalism or 'neo-liberalism,' or simply power, all of which, at their best, suggest rather predictable 'policy' proposals.

In contrast, I assume that bringing economic events into cultural studies' conjuncturalism is supposed to give us, not only a better – contextual – understanding of some economic matters, but also enable us to better understand the context by expanding our analysis of the articulations that are constituting it.

Part of what it means to have a better understanding of the economic, I believe, requires us to get at the specificity or singularity of the event, in this case the current 'economic' crisis. For cultural studies, this means thinking its specificity conjuncturally, and this in turn requires that we not treat it as a purely and autonomously 'economic' event or simply look at its relations to explicit state policies and struggles. The latter strategies are often predicated on a rather thin historical understanding of the present, in which the crisis is 'explained' as a result of the rise of 'neo-liberalism,' deregulation, globalization and finance markets. In the United States, this is generally traced back to the Reagan revolution and the presidencies of Clinton and G. W. Bush.

My point in this paper is not to invent a new economic theory or even to invent a new economic policy (I leave that to better minds) but to tell a better conjunctural story. That requires us to find other ways of thinking about 'economies,' recognizing that both 'the economic' and economies are both discursively and contextually (materially) constructed. Attempts to understand the specificity of the current crisis in terms only of economic matters (e.g. another iteration of the same old capitalist cycles, or the same old capitalist greed, etc.) are doomed to failure not only from a cultural studies perspective but more importantly, in terms of the possibilities of understanding 'the big picture' as it were, of formulating strategic responses to it and of projecting viable political imaginations of the future. In this sense, I do think that the *radically* interdisciplinary work of conjunctural analysis offers insights and imaginations into what is going on that are simply not available through other disciplinary or less radically interdisciplinary formations in the academy. Further, if we think the crisis is only about economics or political economy, our analyses will start and end by simply repeating what some economists are already saying – whether neo-classical, Keynesian or Marxist – or what the media (of whatever political stripe) are telling us. At that point, I have to believe that we have abandoned our responsibility as intellectuals as well as the project of cultural studies.

Moreover, we have to remember that the assumption that the 'conjuncture' can itself be determinately parsed out as it were into relatively autonomous domains – that the economic exists as a disembedded reality, as Polanyi (1944/2001) would say, is itself an invention of North Atlantic modernity.[3] And since I believe that the contemporary conjuncture is, above all, characterized by struggles over the very possibilities of modernity, we must approach this descriptive logic very cautiously at the very least.

An economic crisis?

The 'event' I want to talk about, or at least to start with, is the 'economic crisis' that began in 2007 and ended . . . somewhere in the future (we hope). This crisis is an articulation of a number of interrelated and apparently 'economic' developments: the collapse of the housing bubble, the collapse of the stock market bubble, the collapse of finance markets, etc., leading into a recession and perhaps worse. The question I want to eventually raise is this: are there not other developments, other trajectories, other contradictions that are constituent elements of this crisis even while they challenge the assumed primacy of the economic?

Of course, part of the crisis is the way it is being lived, which is characterized largely by (a certain populist) anger, fear, uncertainty and a very strong sense not only of incomprehension, but of incomprehensibility since no one seems to actually understand what is going on or what to do about it. But this is actually not a bad starting point: to recognize that we cannot start by assuming that we already understand what is going on or where it is going.[4]

Of course, the media play an important role in constructing our understandings, affects and responses, both popular and governmental, to the crisis. Almost immediately after it became clear that the United States was entering into a seriously stressed economic period, and almost continuously since then, much of the public rhetoric (once you got beyond the actual data as it were), much of the media coverage, including that of many economists, has been nothing short of catastrophic and apocalyptic.[5] Yet even as I write this in the first quarter of 2009, the crisis/recession has not equaled the magnitude of the Great Depression or even, yet, at least in the United States, the recession of the early 1980s. This is not to deny that it has reached levels that are producing real and sustained suffering for many people, that the velocity of declining conditions is extremely rapid, and that, in other parts of the world, the crisis has been devastating, leaving national economies close to collapse (Ireland, Iceland, many developing nations, etc.). It is of course possible that by the time this essay is published, the economy of the United States will be in significantly worse shape than it already is. But still, in the United States, when you look at the actual presentation of data, the relevant comparisons are generally given in terms of the past 10 to 30 years.

This rhetorical inflation evolves either around images of an accelerating rate of collapse, figures of a coming depression, or dire predictions about when a recovery might start (and the likely disappointing velocity of improvement).

So, one might ask, why is the discourse – at least within the national context of the United States (and interestingly enough, the national crisis seems to have made the economies of the developing world even more invisible than usual) – out of all proportion to the event thus far? There are two reasons that have been given – implicitly – to explain these apocalyptic tones: first, it is an 'excuse' for a return to big government and 'socialism;' or second, it is an 'excuse' to transfer large sums of money from the general population to corporations. Perhaps other more reasonable answers might be offered: first, that no one quite understands what is happening (that we are facing a crisis at least as incomprehensible in terms of the dominant economic theories as was stagflation in the late 1970s) and so it is easier to enter into panic mode; and second that the current crisis is, at its core, a crisis of financial capital, a liquidity crisis, which was also the basis of the great panic of 1907 and the Great Depression.

Of course, there is another side to the public and media discourses about the crisis, which claims to comprehend the crisis in its entirety. These are usually stories about business as usual (e.g. business cycles, pendulum swings – a return to regulation will solve all our problems) or sites of blame (e.g. greedy capitalists rather than greedy capitalisms, lax or even dishonest legislators). It is within this second side that I would observe the interesting effort to rescue the very economic theories that are at the same time blamed for the crisis. The economic crisis of the 1970s introduced 'stagflation' into popular discourses, which was then presented as evidence of the inadequacy of the dominant neo-classical synthesis and which facilitated the attack on the Keynesian aspects of the synthesis and the institutional successes of a purer version of neo-classical theory.[6] Ironically, the present crisis, as global as it is, does not have a similar rhetorical function in many of the most influential popular discussions of economics. Yes, deregulated free markets may have failed us in the financial sector (although really because of something other than deregulation itself), but the response often seems to be the continuing need for free and flexible markets elsewhere (especially in labor markets).

So how do we describe the current crisis? I want to begin (not end) by repeating what everyone is saying. It is the perfect wave – caused by the intersection of a number of economic vectors. First, there has been an oversized debt/credit market, which has apparently overwhelmed the commodity market, even as the speculative market had overwhelmed the foreign exchange market. The debt market was estimated to produce 4.8 percent of gross domestic product (GDP), but provided over 30 percent of corporate profits and 10 percent of wages. Even more, the finance and credit market was itself overwhelmed by the complex and enormous market of derivatives, many of which were created using complex algorithms run by computers. According to the Bank for International Settlements, there were

$596 trillion of OTC (over the counter) derivatives as of December 7, and $344 trillion of derivatives sold on the various exchanges as of December 2005. Bryan and Rafferty (2007) estimate that derivatives added approximately $200 trillion to the global money supply, and there were approximately $2.5 trillion in derivates transacted daily. Add to that $12.5 trillion in asset backed securities, plus $60 trillion in collateralized debt swaps (insuring $5 trillion in bonds).[7]

Add to this a heavily inflated stock market, and a housing bubble, which was at least in part based on a 'real' faith in the potential future value of housing and in part necessitated by the declining income of the middle classes, which meant that mortgage equity was used to fund the demands and expectations of middle class lifestyle. Hardt and Negri (2009) describe this as the 'subjective side of the crisis,' and they interpret it as an 'autonomous' alternative form of welfare, with low interest rates providing what was, for all practical appearances, free money. But this housing bubble was fueled in large part by a series of reconfigurations of the mortgage market including an explosion of both the 'originate and distribute' system and subprime lending. And then throw in a run of the mill recession, a cyclical downturn in the economy. Whether this was 'caused' by the liquidity crisis or not, whether it was going to happen without it, it has certainly been amplified and accelerated by it.

The common assumption is that the crisis begins with the collapse of the housing bubble – as if there were not signs of a crisis in corporate and global capitalism before that – and the realization that no one seemed to know the value of many of the financial instruments that banks had created to leverage and securitize their mortgage (and as we are constantly hearing whispered in the background, credit card and corporate) debt. This was assumed to be and was experienced as a breakdown of the relations of credit to collateral. But I want to argue later that this liquidity crisis, when placed at the feet of the instruments themselves, as it were, might be better seen as the result of a failed solution to a real conjunctural problem: the problem of the calculation of value. The explosion of the use of derivatives is connected to other conjunctural changes that have posed real problems and contradictions, not only within what we take to be the economic sector. Confronting an increasingly complex market of incommensurable and changing values, a situation in which no one knows how to measure the value of specific financial assets or how to calculate their comparative value, derivatives seemed to embody an answer, presenting themselves as an impossible yet manageable calculating machine. Until it became clear that the machines were failing! That is to say, what makes contemporary financial assets 'toxic' is not that they are worthless, bundling bad loans as it were, but that no one knows what their worth may be or even how to go about figuring out their worth.[8] But for the moment, let me return to the popular stories of the crisis.

The crisis has been explained in mostly typical and expected ways. My own sense is not that these accounts of the crisis are not true, but that they are all true and yet, even collectively, not true enough to describe, let alone explain, what has happened. First, the crisis is blamed on economic theory (and economists): it is taken to demonstrate the failure of efficient market theory (and of the economists who trumpeted its validity). The collapse of the finance market is the result of the lack of equal and transparent information, resulting in a breakdown of the knowable relation between assets and debt.[9] Second, the crisis is blamed on technology and technologically-based realities: in particular, a mathematical/technological apparatus that not only enabled debt to produce seemingly endless surplus value (profit and growth), but also produced risk beyond what could be calculated.[10] Third, it is blamed on the affectivity of economic behavior (perhaps as an intrusion of what is supposed to be a rational activity?): the crisis is the result of 'irrational exuberance' followed by (an equally irrational?) panic. At the very least, the crisis was brought about by a failure of the trust and faith upon which all market relations are based.[11]

There are at least two accounts that see it as the 'same old same old.' Thus, fourth, it is all the result of greedy capitalists. Some would argue that they have simply been dishonest and perpetrated any number of frauds; others would argue that they have acted in complicity with politicians who have deregulated the markets and institutions of finance to enable them to act in ways that are, at the very least, irresponsible in fiduciary terms. [We might interpret this argument in the light of Polanyi's (1944/2001) double movement of regulation and deregulation.]

Fifth, it is the same old same old, the result of the 'normal' economic or business cycles that define the regularized fluctuations of economic activity. These cycles describe shifts over time between periods of relatively rapid growth of output (recovery and prosperity) and periods of relative stagnation or decline (contraction and recession). Such theories suggest that capitalism moves, as it were, via crises.

There are any number of such cycles: Kitchin inventory cycles (every 3–5 years); Juglar fixed investment cycles (every 7–11 years): Kuznets infrastructural investment cycles (every 15–25 years); and Kondratieff waves (every 45–60 years, as well as multiples of K-waves). The present crisis is often described as the result of either the confluence of a number of these cycles, or the end of another K-wave. These Kondratieff long waves have been identified in the following periods: 1784–1844; 1845–1896; 1896–1949; 1949–(2008?). Each K-wave describes a cycle of seasons; although there is some disagreement about the actual sequence and descriptions, they are generally described as expansion, recession, plateau, and depression. There are also numerous theories about what these waves express (or what causes them, including innovation, capital investment, war and capitalist crisis.

So, however unique and uniquely catastrophic the rhetoric seems to suggest, such explanations have largely returned to the discursive operation of 'economics' as usual. Accounts turn to the search for blame, which is laid at the feet of theory, or technology, or the failure of capitalism, or capitalists' greed (and short-termism), or else, it is inevitable and natural, the simple reassertion of the business (boom–bust) cycles.

There is another kind of explanation of the contemporary crisis, which depends on the claim that the contemporary economy is, in some sense (and different senses have been offered), unlike previous economies. Such accounts of 'the new economy' assume that, for any number of different reasons (depending on who was telling the story and when it was being told), we had supposedly left traditional business cycles, even traditional economic theories, behind. Perhaps the most compelling of such claims, because it came not only from the neo-classical right but also from some sectors of the left, emphasizes the dominance of finance capital in the contemporary economy. This assumed dominance of finance flies in the face of a long tradition of economic thinking that has looked with doubt and suspicion on finance capital and finance economies, especially the credit economy.

In both classical liberal theory and Marxist theory, such financial markets and functions were derided to say the least. Thus, while Marx saw a vital role for credit in the capitalization of commodity production, he also saw the tendency, especially through the rise of stock companies (which in a sense are forms of the social ownership of property), for the emergence of a speculative credit economy, a 'superstructure of credit,' which would claim to constitute new forms of wealth. In such formations, even the capitalist standards of judgment disappear. Thus he writes (Marx n.d., volume 3, chapter 27):

> The two characteristics immanent in the credit system are, on the one hand, to develop the incentive of capitalist production, enrichment through exploitation of the labour of others, to the purest and most colossal form of gambling and swindling, and to reduce more and more the number of the few who exploit the social wealth; on the other hand, to constitute the form of transition to a new mode of production. It is this ambiguous nature, which endows the principal spokesmen of credit from Law to Isaac Pereire with the pleasant character mixture of swindler and prophet.[12]

In fact, Marx distances productive capitalism from such credit economies as based in fictitious or fictive capital (as opposed to the real capital of commodity production). For Marx, money is not real wealth but a claim on real wealth. It is the necessary form of the appearance of value, but it cannot produce or possess real value itself. And hence, the profit of the credit economy is at best a claim on already produced value. In so far as, in credit, money appears as the source of its own productivity, as capital that appears to create itself as its own surplus, it is the purest fetish form of capital.[13] Most Marxist economists would similarly find it hard to imagine the possibility of a viable capitalist formation in which banking (credit) capital was both dominant and determinant.

Similarly, Keynes (cited in Michie 2009) viewed the finance market as a 'casino economy,' describing it as no more than a 'beauty contest,' a concept he elaborated in terms of the growing distance between judgments of value and the actual object of value itself:

> It is not a case of choosing those [faces] which, to the best of one's judgment, are really the prettiest, nor even those which average opinion genuinely thinks the prettiest. We have reached the third degree where we devote our intelligences to anticipating what average opinion expects the average opinion to be. And there are some, I believe, who practice the fourth, fifth and higher degrees.[14]

And many 'mainline' post-Keynesian economists would agree that it is impossible for finance capital to be the truly productive center of capitalism.

At the other extreme, Deleuze and Guattari (1977, p. 249) have hypothesized that 'Capital has no industrial essence functioning other than as merchant, financial and commercial capital, where money would take on functions other than those deriving from its form as the equivalent.' They suggest (1977, p. 232) that financial capital is the true essence or center of capitalist value: 'True economic force . . . the immense deterritorialized flow that constitutes the full body of capital . . . This flow of indefinite debt, an instantaneous creative flow the banks create spontaneously as a debt owing to themselves, a creation ex nihilo that . . . does not enter into income and is not assigned purchase, a pure availability, non-possession and non-wealth.' Or at least, one might say, the means for rendering the debt infinite, partly because everything and anything can be absorbed into the circuit of money.

In between these extremes, some people have hypothesized that the current formation represents the limit possibility of finance capital, in which banking or credit capital is both dominant and determinant, thus creating 'ecumenical' flows of money begetting money, a new sort of mercantilism as it were, a move from capital to money! After all, it is as money, the form of expression of value (rather than capital as the substance of expression of value) that capitalism seems (or at least seemed for a while!) most productive. It is money qua money, in all its complexity,[15] that begins to define or determine not only all finance capital, all liquid instruments, but also the very possibility of profit and hence, of capital although it does not necessarily follow that money somehow has replaced either commodities or capital as the locus of value. At least, that is a story – the romantic story – that has been told.

Derivatives

When the current crisis first came to the public's attention, almost all of the public and media discourses – both the discourses of catastrophe and apocalypse, and those that attempted to either normalize it or to locate the blame for why business as usual had failed, everyone was talking about derivatives. In fact, many of the original descriptions and explanations of the original – financial – dimension of the crisis laid the whole thing at the feet of these 'new' financial instruments. These early stories of the derivative varied almost as much as, and often reproduced, the stories of the crisis itself. Some emphasized the failure of efficient market theory, arguing that the crisis could be precisely located in the uncertainty of the relation between assets and debt (or instruments of debt and security). Others blamed the mathematical-technological apparatuses that were supposed to produce endless surplus but instead, produced increasingly incomprehensible risk. Still others spoke of a classic failure of trust in the financial markets as a result of the failure of the ratings markets, etc.

It is generally taken for granted that derivatives: (1) are about risk and securitization, that they are forms of risk management, whether through hedging or speculation; and (2) their value depends on but remains separable from their underlying asset. This view seems to be held by financial agents, finance economists and most of the social and cultural critics who have written about it, including LiPuma and Lee (2004), Pryke and Allen (2002) and Randy Martin (2007). These authors might disagree about the nature of risk (and whether derivatives represent a new kind of risk) and the relations between derivatives and money; yet all of them in a sense see the derivative as a new incarnation of the commodity form (despite the long history of the derivative) as I will argue.

Let me briefly consider some of LiPuma and Lee's (2004) important contributions, partly to illustrate the most common approach to derivatives among cultural analysts who have taken up the question. LiPuma and Lee begin by emphasizing the circulatory structure of finance or what they call the 'culture of financial circulation,' where circulation quite literally has a life of its own, thus affirming the romantic story of a new paradigm of capitalism built on finance. They usefully define (2004, chapter 5) derivatives as 'transactable contracts' that have the following characteristics: (1) their value depends on but remains separable from – some underlying asset; (2) they have a finite life because they expire, usually after a relatively short term; (3) there is no exchange of actual capital until the derivative is settled, which is often not ever, since they are more often than not rolled over into new derivatives; and (4) they are instruments of leverage that can be used for both hedging and speculation.

The heart of LiPuma and Lee's (2004) analysis, however, limits the romance, in so far as their analysis seems to suggest, without ever stating it directly, that derivatives are simply another example of the commodity form as analyzed by Marx. This becomes obvious, first, in the ways they understand its mystifying properties. Thus, 'the surface level analysis of the risk-bearing derivative offered by the financial community is understandable in the sense that the form suggests the possibility of its misinterpretation' (p. 156). And yet in the end, they do not themselves deviate very much from that surface level analysis in their own assumptions about derivatives as tools of risk management.

More importantly, second, they reproduce, in their analysis of the derivative, quite precisely, Marx's analysis of the logic of the commodity as holding together abstract and concrete labor, and thereby, as I shall argue shortly, they continue to universalize a specific conjunctural logic of value rather than to contextualize it. According to them, derivatives produce value as they work by holding together two modalities and dimensions of risk: abstract and concrete. Consider the following lengthy quotes:

> This mode of objectification creates a two-way street, because it conceptually sutures concrete and abstract dimensions [of risk], making it appear as though the movement from concrete to abstract implicated no human intervention other than the technical assembly and market distribution of the derivative. But something else is happening: the suturing also works in the other direction, creating the impression that the impersonal, asocial and law like characteristics of the abstract dimension are invariably embodied in, and can be read off, the derivative. The plurality of incommensurable types of risk – concrete and specific because they are drawn from real social conditions – are abstracted into a single, homogeneous whole that the financial community may price. (LiPuma & Lee 2004, p. 146)

And again:

> Abstract risk functions systemically because it interconnects the variegated forms of specific concrete risk defining them as quantifiable through the same mathematics, and also because its character is system-wide and abstracted from all sociohistorical contexts. . . . it is ultimately impossible to disembed risks from the contexts of their production and consumption. Nonetheless, it is precisely this process of disembedding these risks that provides the directional dynamic of financial circulation. (LiPuma & Lee 2004, p. 148)

Thus, like Marx's commodity, the derivative embodies (it is, in fact) a (very limited) logic of calculation for comparing and weighing, 'commensurating' as I will call it, the values of different (concrete) terms. Like Marx and most economic theory, LiPuma and Lee (2004) assume that such commensuration is only possible through the mediation of a stable and abstract third term.

Marx's critique of classical economics was that it mistook the appearance for the real, and so naturalized and universalized a concrete particular. On the basis of that critique he offered the possibility of a new political imaginary; I think we need to continue that critique, applied to both economic and cultural analyses that take the appearance of the derivative (risk, insurance, securitization, etc.) for reality. And for all practical purposes, that means taking into account the historical and contextual specificity of the derivative. The derivative has a long history; in fact it has many different histories, and it can be located on any number of historical lines, but it is the singularity of the contemporary practice that needs to be analyzed.[16] I propose, first, that derivatives are not about risk and securitization, although people are certainly using them that way; and second, that derivatives are not built on the separation of the instrument and the asset but on the expansion of a universe of values put into relations of adequation or commensuration. That is, that the derivative offers an other (non-dialectical) logic of calculation or commensuration.

To explain and support this notion, let me turn to the work of Bryan and Rafferty (2006, 2007), on whom I have drawn extensively. They suggest that the specificity of derivatives is that their value is based on their capacity for 'self-transformation.' Derivates are computational: 'they embody systems of calculation that commensurate different forms of capital.' And they do so continuously, not by appealing to a universal, abstract or even common third term, but by creating 'a complex web of conversions, a system of derivatives, in which any 'bit' of capital, anywhere and with any time or spatial profile, can be measured against any other 'bit' of capital, and on an ongoing basis' (2007, p. 141). They call this (2007, p. 140) 'blending' – the derivative's capacity to 'establish pricing relationships that readily convert between ["commensurate"] different forms of assets.' That is, the derivative is a process of capital commensuration.

This makes the derivative, ironically, a universalizing force that breaks down the differences among capital: money (credit), equity (capital) and commodity (assets). The derivative commensurates among all forms of capital, at all locations and across all times. It is a (seemingly) perpetual calculating machine, continuously recalculating the relations, transforming itself even as its 'bits' are changing. Thus the derivative avoids the need for a third term, even as it enables anything to become capital, just as long as it can be commensurated. This theory of the derivative may answer the need to take seriously the challenge of finance capitalism, which might be seen, superficially, as the endless deferral of such comparative measure or commensuration.

Bryan and Rafferty point to a second dimension of the derivative as well, which they call 'binding.' Derivatives are spatio-temporal. They 'establish . . . relationships that bind the future to the present or one place to another'

(2007, p. 140). Similarly, Pryke and Allen (2002) recognize the derivative as the embodiment of a temporal logic. Drawing on Rotman's argument of the derivative as a sign that creates itself out of the future, even out of future states of itself, they argue that derivatives commensurate the present and the future. Derivatives work precisely through establishing such relationships as pricing relationships. That is, it is derivatives themselves, as a (potentially infinite) system and a logic (constantly changing) of commensuration, that establish pricing relationships.

Contextualizing the crisis

I want to begin by reproducing, in very schematic terms, the very limited ways in which the contemporary 'economic' crisis is located contextually and historically, For the sake of time, I will focus on that version of the story as it is told by those who have opposed (or recently, oppose retrospectively) the developments captured in this narrative, a narrative that can be read in part as the history of the spectacular rise and fall into ignominy of the derivative. As I suggested earlier, this is only one of any number of possible histories that could be recounted.

This popular (and critical) history of the contemporary crisis casts it as the culmination of a tumultuous 30–40 years; it is almost always circumscribed as a purely economic narrative that pretty much follows a simple and single straight line. This is a story that has been told, in various ways, many times over the past years. It generally starts with the global crisis of capitalism of the 1970s, a crisis of overproduction and over-accumulation, when the return on real production declined significantly, resulting in a declining rate of profit. (The crisis was in part the result of the changing economies of oil: the price of crude oil increased from $3 to $33 in a very short period of time. The 'fact' that this might require that all sorts of non-economic issues of political struggles and cultural differences be brought into the narrative is conveniently ignored.) Capitalists sought new sites of investment and growth, resulting in a series of bubbles including the various stock markets, dot.com and housing (and also including an increased investment in instability in the third world) (Mackenzie 2008, Henwood 1977). This crisis introduced the notion and the experience of stagflation into economic common sense, which was quickly deployed as an attack on then dominant neo-Keynesian theory and policy.

By the 1980s, with the growing strength of the financial markets on the one hand, and the so-called Washington Consensus (or 'neo-liberal' ideology and structural readjustment policies) on the other hand, the world began to see dispersed and relatively frequent third world debt crises, even as the United States plunged into a severe recession in 1982 (with unemployment reaching

10.8 percent). The restructuring of international relations and global capitalism was further propelled by the policies of Thatcher and Reagan, including the abolition of controls on the flows of 'hot money,' even going so far as the proposed MIA [Multilateral Investment Agreement proposed by the World Trade Organization (WTO)] and the MAI [Multilateral Agreement on Investment, proposed by the Organization for Economic Cooperation and Development (OECD)]. Even while these radical deregulatory measures did not pass, the 1980s saw the opening of financial markets to foreign competition in new and consequential ways. The power of a global finance capitalism fueled a series of other developments, including what critics have called 'short-termism,' with its increasing focus on profit and growth, often through the manipulation of stock prices and the ratios of assets and debt. In addition, this was aided by the 'stockholders' revolution,' which in turn contributed to the growing power of chief executive officers (CEOs) over managers, whose compensation was often defined by bonuses tied to immediate profit and growth, and offered in the form of stocks and stock options.

In 1987, the stock market crashed, followed by the Savings and Loan scandal (with its $200 billion bailout). According to Mackenzie (2008, pp. 186–187), the crisis of 1987 'broke the link that arbitrage established between the stock and futures market . . . the breakdown in arbitrage permitted a substantial gap to open between the prices of index futures and their theoretical values.' Consequently, in 1988, the Group of 10 established the first Basel Accords, which enabled banks to shift their asset risks off the balance sheet, and helped to fuel the boom in securitization, structural investment vehicles, credit default swaps, etc. At the same time, the commitment to finance growth, even in the face of a growing balance of trade deficit, and a growing national debt, in the United States, enabled Federal Reserve Chair Alan Greenspan (who for a while seemed to be the second most recognizable political figure in the United States) to maintain notoriously low interest rates in the name of fighting inflation (and at the cost of full employment some would say), producing a constant flow of cheap credit.

In 1996, the Federal Reserve began to dismantle the boundaries that had been constructed around the banking industry after the Great Depression, allowing commercial banks to get involved in investments (by underwriting securities). In 1999, the Depression-era Glass-Steagall Act was, for all practical purposes, repealed (Gramm-Leach-Bliley Act), opening banks to numerous activities that had been forbidden to them and in effect, creating a new class of functionally unregulated investment banks, and allowing banks in general to operate with a much higher debt to equity ratio. This helped to increase the sources of finance and credit, for example, making General Electric Capital one of the largest 'banks' in the United States. (It should also be at least noted that at least some of these changes – e.g. mark to market accounting and certain openings in the housing markets – were done in part with good intentions and were even judged to be good at the time by more progressive constituencies.)

Still, such accounts too often ignore the role that culture – at least in the form of a limited field of knowledge production and distribution – played in this narrative, since many of these developments are themselves articulated to and through changes in the discipline of economics: first, and most obviously (and in recent months, it has been blamed in numerous discussions), we have to take account of the appearance and development of finance theory. Although finance has been a topic in economics for some time, the current centrality of finance theory – and its very close relation to the actual practice of finance markets – was based on a very significant rethinking of the basic assumptions of the nature and role of finance capital. Moreover, in its contemporary manifestation, which is linked closely with neo-classical economics, the rise of finance theory cannot be separated entirely from the rise of the broader new conservative project and the various alliances through which it was carried forward and which supported and appropriated much of the neo-classical and finance economics view of the world.

It was only in 1938 that Williams challenged the dominant view, which as mentioned earlier, rejected the validity of finance capitalism, by offering instead a 'fundamentalism' asserting that financial instruments reflect the intrinsic value of an asset. In the 1950s, Markowitz challenged fundamentalism by foregrounding the role of risk in finance. This 'simple' reconception had profound implications for the nature of investment and the financial sector, and opened the door to the crisis we are now living through.[17]

Together with Sharpe in the 1970s, Markowitz developed a theory [capital asset pricing model (CAPM), actually a set of derivative equations, but that is largely what finance 'theory' has become] that purported to map the way stock prices reflected a trade off between expected returns and risks (defined largely in terms of the sensitivity of the particular instrument to overall market fluctuations). His theories depended, as Mackenzie (2008, p. 183) puts it, on the assumption that the stock and futures market were 'eternal things in which prices would not be affected significantly by the insurer's purchases or sales.'

The Black–Scholes–Merton (BSM) theory of option pricing followed, arguing that the value of an instrument depended on the volatility of the underlying asset, and this enabled new forms of insuring investment portfolios. According to Mackenzie (2008, p. 33), while the BSM model seemed to fit the patterns of market prices for a while, the relation deteriorated sharply after the crash of 1987 [reaching its low point with the Long Term Capital Management (LTCM) failure in 1998, a fund built precisely on this model]. The Modigliani–Miller 'irrelevance propositions' argued, counter-intuitively, that the market value of any firm is independent of its capital structure, which in turn enabled a major overhaul of the way corporations conceived of their own economic health – and wealth, and financed themselves.

Most commentators on the development of finance theory add that all this work depends largely on the efficient (or perfect) market hypothesis, which argues that 'prices in mature capitalist markets always effectively instantaneously take into account all available price-relevant information' (Mackenzie 2008, p. 29). That is, such markets 'work' because they operate with complete and transparent information: all information is shared and, somewhat incredibly, it is interpreted similarly. Moreover neo-classical finance theory assumes that information has no transaction costs, even in the maximally competitive markets that are assumed to exist.[18]

But not all of the economic story is about the ascendance of finance capital and finance theory. Other developments were also crucial. Here I will only point to two broad developments: First, we have to acknowledge the rapid rise to dominance of a combination of Austrian and neo-classical theories defined in strong opposition to the liberal Keynesian paradigm, and second, its surprisingly public visibility and its enormous popular success, partly through the creation of a series of conservative and libertarian think tanks, which enabled it to have an usually large impact on public discourses, public policy and common sense. In fact, we do not yet have anything like a good understanding of how Austrian and neo-classical economics (and their 'neo-liberal' public face) were so successful at occupying the spaces of common sense and the popular logics of calculation of economic and political possibilities. While their claims to 'science' no doubt have something to do with it, it is just as true that it is the popular approbation of such discourses that has legitimated their claims to scientificity, especially in the face of their continued failure (most visible in the current crisis).[19]

The rise of neo-classical theory was closely tied to the collapse of what is sometimes called the corporatist compromise of the advanced industrial world after World War II (although its roots go back to the early twentieth century). This involved a commitment to sharing the risks and rewards of capitalist economies between workers and capitalists. This translated into a commitment to a growing and increasingly secure middle class as its income was pegged to the general growth of the economy. Since the 1980s, the working and middle classes have increasingly become the objects, simultaneously, of a discourse of concern, and economic and political attack. As their economic position has been steadily eroded, despite the continuous growth of the economy, economic disparity and inequality has risen sharply. Equally significant has been the shift of risk and responsibility from the government and corporations onto individuals and families of the working and middle classes.

The second development, which I have already alluded to, was the appearance, sometime in the 1980s, of a series of discourses of the 'new economy.' These discourses were politically and culturally crucial and highly visible. This notion has taken many different forms, based in any number of economic developments (sometimes the rise of finance, or of technologies, or of globalization, or entrepreneurialism, or . . .). Each time it is taken to signal the 'natural' and inevitable fact that the economy is somehow (often in ways left unexplicated) different than anything we have seen before, and therefore not susceptible to the crises and failures of previous incarnations of capitalism. Of course, each time a new crisis or failure disproves the claim, the discourse quickly disappears, until the crisis is over and then, it is re-invented with no memory of its previous incarnations.

Conjuncturalism and multiple timelines

I have argued that cultural studies is a practice of radical contextuality, meaning not only that its conceptual tools and political projects are themselves derived 'in conversation with' the context but that its object of study is a context, or more accurately, a conjuncture. The first part of its contextuality is the result of its commitment to study relations and relationalities and to what is sometimes described as anti-anti-essentialism, which asserts that what something is, is only its relations. The second part, its conjuncturalism, is a political choice, based on the assumption that there are certain kinds of political struggle and possibility that are best approached at a certain level of analysis understood as the attempt to establish a temporary balance or settlement in the field of forces. I realize that many people think that 'conjuncture' is simply the cultural studies' term for context, but in so far as context usually identifies a delimited time-space, a form of geo-periodization, it is a more empiricist and naturalized category than the conjuncture, which operates in a different register.

Conjuncturalism is a description of change, articulation and contradiction; it describes a mobile multiplicity the unity of which is always temporary and fractured. A conjuncture is constituted by, at and as the articulation of multiple, overlapping, competing, reinforcing, etc. lines of force and transformation, destabilization and (re-)stabilization, with differing temporalities and spatialities, producing a potentially but never actually chaotic assemblage or articulations of contradictions and contestations. Thus it is always a kind of totality, always temporary, complex and fragile, that one takes hold of, constituted as what David Scott (2004, p. 7) calls 'a problem space:' 'to think of different historical conjunctures as constituting different conceptual-ideological problem-spaces, and to think of these problem-spaces less as generators of new propositions than as generators of new questions and new demands.' To mis-analyze a conjuncture, to misidentify its problem-space is to fail to understand what's going on and likely, to fail to formulate political strategies that can get us from here to some other imagined/better place.

The first step toward a conjunctural analysis of the current crisis might be to acknowledge that the limited narrative I have recounted earlier, limited not only to the economic domain, but also by a specific geo-historical periodization, is simply not up to the task of providing even the grounds of a conjunctural analysis. The rise of neo-classical policies and of finance capitalism cannot be understood as if they came into being independently of many other changes, many other, sometimes intimately related, vectors of change that were shaping the American and to varying degrees, the global context. Moreover, such limited narratives completely ignore how deeply contested these 'economic' changes were; they in fact miss how generally contested everything about these decades were.

They forget that the 'crisis' can be located in other temporalities that extend back to the 1950s and 1960s, to the Vietnam War and the growing US trade deficit and national debt (which at the very least made it more difficult for the United States to meet growing consumer expectations and demands). This eventually pushed Nixon to devalue the dollar and to suspend the gold standard, which in turn eventually led to the collapse of the Bretton Woods financial accords (but not the other institutions), creating the new financial economy of floating exchange rates. [Not coincidentally, in 1972, the Chicago Mercantile market begins selling currency futures (Michaels 1988).]

Now we are beginning to link the contemporary 'economic' crisis to even more tumultuous times, and even broader notions of the crises of our times. We are back to the 1950s and 1960s, to the Cold War (and the ideological, cultural and economic struggles for political domination) and to anti-colonial nationalist struggles for independence. We are back to the emergence of new forms of communitarianism and identity-based political formations (such as the civil rights movement, the feminist and gay rights movements), the anti-war movement and the counterculture. We are back to the beginnings of new patterns of social and economic immigration (both within and across national boundaries). And we are in the midst of technological (including the explosion of media and information technologies) and cultural changes so profound and so immediately lived that culture itself increasingly became a central site of struggle and self-identification. The culture wars began long before the 1980s!

We are beginning to see the possibility that the contemporary crisis is only a part of the ongoing story of the multiple and fragmented struggles with, within and against a way of living (constructed by, within and against complex structures of power) constituting what I call a way of being modern that found its fullest expression in the post-war Western capitalist democracies. I have called this 'liberal modernity.' The irony and paradox of contemporary life is that as soon as liberal modernity appeared to be fully realizing itself, it came under attack from all sides.[20]

It was in this context of struggles that not only the contemporary configurations of progressive and left-wing politics was given shape, but also that the various new conservatisms (including neo-conservatism, libertarian conservatism, religious-fundamentalist conservatism, and a variety of other political conservatisms) arose. This is obviously an extraordinarily complicated tale, and books have been written that only begin to scratch the surface of the complexity of the articulations involved. The 1960s were a crucial decade in shaping such contradictions and conflicts, and those very conflicts helped to give shape and power to the new coalitions of conservatives in the late 1970s and 1980s.

Just as the Cold War shaped the conditions of possibility for the Democratic Party's domination of a period of post-war liberal modernity, the global crisis of the 1970s and the events leading up to the end of the Cold War (symbolized by the fall of the Berlin Wall in 1989) shaped the ground – political, cultural and economic – on which a series of coalitions among various conservatisms and neo-classical economics, having won control of the Republican Party, attempted to deconstruct liberal modernity even as they attempted to achieve a new temporary position of leadership and balance in the field of forces. It may well be the case that we can locate the rise of finance capital and the success of neo-classical economics in relation to the rise of the new right as a contemporary alliance politics, but this relation was never a necessary one, never guaranteed. It was an articulation, as the politics of finance capital was moved – it took real work – from Rockefeller's soft Keynesian Republicanism to contemporary neo-classical and libertarian conservatism. We should constantly remind ourselves that the political is not automatically given by economic changes!

During the many months of the 'economic' crisis, as the crisis worsened, I heard many progressives fantasize (but mistaking their fantasies for realities) that this was the end of 'neo-liberalism,'[21] the end of neo-classical domination, even the end of capitalism. I find such prognoses unlikely, especially when they take the next step to claim that we are witnessing the beginning of a new era and a new paradigm. Such diagnoses often conflate temporary hegemonic victories, through which a particular 'ruling block' comes to define the leading position, the terms of the temporary balance in the field of forces, with total domination and victory. I do not think 'neo-liberalism' was ever victorious in anything other than a partial, fragile and temporary way (which does not deny the devastating consequences of its policies and its ability to transform an actually existing lived relation – the market – and by highlighting its empowering effectivities to make it into a popular ideology). Still, it may be more reasonable to assume that the balance of forces is once again shifting (we do not yet know how seriously, for what duration or even towards what sort of position). It may be more accurate to say that, at least thus far, those who championed the market as a model of social relations have been unable to offer a solution to the current crisis (in both economic and broader terms). Thus, the story I am telling suggests that we are still living in the conjunctural struggles against liberal modernity and for . . . various contradictory and complicitous visions of an other modernity, a struggle over the coming modernity.

Modernities and the struggle over value

At this point I want to turn from offering a narrative that constructs the conjuncture to an analytic that enables me to locate the economic crisis within the conjuncture. I want to return to the derivative, not as the essence of but as an effective way into understanding the specificity of the contemporary (financial, economic, social) crisis conjuncturally. My analysis starts with the derivative as a key articulatory point of the 'economic' crisis, in the first instance and of broader conjunctural crises or contradictions in the second instance. But in both instances, the derivative both depends on and helps construct the larger conjuncture, and enables the conjunctural analysis.

A conjunctural analysis demands that one move out, as it were, from the singular event as a point of articulation or crystallization,[22] moving out to configure a larger structure of relationships, contradictions and contestations. There are in fact at least two different models of the practice of conjuncturalism and which one uses depends on the problem space and the politics one is confronting. (It is not a purely epistemological choice!) The first adds the determinations, looking at the relationships across the cultural, social, political and economic domains. It is Althusser's overdetermination (and structure in dominance) and Williams' relations among all the elements. It is a move, predicated on Polanyi's argument that modernity disembeds a (naturally?) embedded economy, an argument I have taken up elsewhere to talk about the need to analyze the different forms of embedded disembeddedness (Grossberg 2010). But this practice of conjuncturalism can be seen as still reproducing a certain territorializing logic constitutive of euro-modernity by which social reality is organized into discrete domains (e.g. the production of economics, politics and culture as relatively autonomous domains) in space-time.

But given my assumption that we are dealing with a problem space constituted as a struggle over multiple modernities, it seems best to avoid a practice that re-inscribes at least one significant logic of the very modernity that is being challenged. In epistemological terms, we need to find a way to de-colonize the practices of conjunctural analysis. And so, I turn to the second practice, which analyzes the conjuncture as a set of transversal or dimensional vectors, forces that are reconfiguring the conjuncture and defining the lines of struggle and emergence.

I want then to relocate the derivative precisely as a point of articulation of a number of different vectors or lines of force that are reconstituting the problem space of an emergent conjuncture. I am not suggesting that we are at the end of one conjuncture and the beginning of another; that is not the best way of thinking the temporality of conjunctures. My argument proposes that the derivative and its crisis can be seen as an articulation of, as articulated to at least two vectors of change that are constituting the contemporary conjuncture as a problem-space(s), defined by the struggle over/for an other modernity. Once again, I can only give the briefest sense of how this work might proceed.

I approach the task with a set of tools, three concepts/temporalities, each rather controversial, as my ground. First, I want to think the crisis in relation to the collapse of Bretton Woods and the problem of the universal equivalent. Second, I want to return to Smith's paradox of value (concerning the relation between use and exchange value) and the transformation problem (concerning the relation of exchange value and price). In particular, I want to take up Stuart Hall's (2003) and Moishe Postone's (1993) radically contextual reading of Marx's labor theory of value. Finally, I want to return to one of the most important but often ignored debates in twentieth century economics, which helped to constitute the distribution of 'the left' and 'the right' in the economic field: the problem of calculation. I want to suggest that these three conceptual contestations, each with its own timeline, are articulated together – and one of those sites at which they are articulated is the contemporary functioning and failure of the derivative as a transformative economic instrument. And precisely as a point of articulation, the functioning (or disfunctioning) of the derivative is constituted on and helps to constitute some of the vectors that are defining the struggles over modernity in the contemporary conjuncture.

The universal equivalent

I have already suggested that most existing and traditional theories of value have assumed that the only way to measure and compare different concrete values (and even more, different forms of concrete value) is to have a third term, a standard to serve as a measure through which equivalence can be defined and established. In economic terms, it is generally assumed that economic systems (especially as they expand to include multiple commodities or forms of capital) require a universal standard. However, as Marx (1992, p. 161) warned, 'the commodity that figures as universal equivalent is ... excluded from the ... universal relative form of value. If the ... commodity serving as universal equivalent, were, at the same time, to share in the relative form of value, it would have to serve as it own equivalent.' As Spivak (2006, p. 156) explains, 'the commodity which becomes the universal equivalent must be excluded from the commodity function.' It cannot itself become an object to be traded for variable prices in a market; otherwise it would 'operate on two registers at once, both measuring and carrying value' (p. 157).

Simmel (1991, p. 24) provides us another way of thinking about this: 'the question of what something is worth is increasingly displaced by the question of how much it is worth.' Thus, Simmel distinguishes two questions: the production or fact of worthiness, and the comparative measure, translation or commensuration of that worthiness. I might suggest that Marx's paradox of the universal equivalent can be reread into Simmel's terms: the same element cannot provide both the substance (worthiness) and measure of value.

Any financial system – and given the complexity of money in any economy, any monetarized economy – depends on the notion of a universal equivalent through which different forms of embodied (concrete) value can be commensurated. For the classical economists (and hence for Marx), under conditions of industrial capitalism, this was gold, although it is certainly the case – as various countries have gone off and on the gold standard, that money itself – within the space of a national domestic economy, serves as the universal equivalent or in my terms, as the fundamental commensurating machine. The key to my argument is that the contemporary explosion and use of derivatives is at least in part a response to, first, the move from gold to money as the universal equivalent on a global scale and second, the denial of the universal equivalent. On this argument, the current credit crisis can be seen, perhaps, as the failure of the derivative, which itself must be located within a larger configuration of the contemporary impossibility of a universal commensuration.

It is not coincidental that derivatives emerged – in their present form (which is partly defined by the quantitative explosion and transformation of their use) – after the collapse of Bretton Woods although they certainly did exist and were used earlier. When Nixon floated the dollar, he took away any notion of a stable universal equivalent for international transactions. The derivative then offers itself as a new universal equivalent, a new kind of universal equivalent, in which the logic of commensuration is internal to rather than external of the machinery of comparative measure.

In that sense, the collapse/failure of the derivatives market has itself to be related to crises of value in specific capital formations, such as commodity markets, which have had to confront the new hyper-differentiation of markets. One could perhaps argue, for example, that what is frequently dismissed as branding and niche-marketing signals a radical restructuring of value beyond our capacity to measure it. The result is, apparently, a situation of the increasing sense of the unpredictability of value itself.

The contextuality of the labor theory of value

One of the ironic failures of both cultural studies and Marxist theory, since both share a commitment to radical contextuality or, in the latter's terms, historical specificity, is that they have failed to treat political economy itself – and in particular, the labor theory of value, as a contingent and contextually grounded theory.

After all, Marx (1973, p. 705) himself did project that 'As soon as labour in the direct form has ceased to be the great well-spring of wealth, labour-time ceases and must cease to be its measure, and hence, exchange value [must cease to be the measure] of use value.' He even located such a transformation in the very nature of value more concretely:

> But to the degree that large industry develops, the creation of real wealth comes to depend less on labour time and the amount of labour employed than on the power of the agencies set in motion during labour time, whose 'powerful effectiveness' is itself . . . out of all proportion to the direct labour time spend on their production, but depends rather on the general state of science and on the progress of technology . . . Real wealth manifests itself, rather . . . in the monstrous disproportion between the labour time applied and its product, as well as in the qualitative imbalance between labour, reduced to a pure abstraction, and the power of the production process it superintends.' (Marx 1973, pp. 704–705)

Interesting, this transformation of the process of value production is not presented in terms of a dialectic of either absolute or relative exploitation. At the same time, it remains unclear whether Marx is presenting this as some kind of transcendence or re-articulation of the labor theory of value. It also raises interesting and important questions about some of the constitutive distinctions that are often assumed in Marxist analyses – productive versus unproductive labor, real versus fictitious capital – and which are increasingly problematic in the contemporary world.

The most original and important effort to date to present a radically contextualist reading of Marx's theory of value is offered by Moishe Postone. Although I have no reason to think Postone would be glad to be affiliated with cultural studies, this is exactly what I want to do, to suggest that cultural studies must embrace a radically contextual theory of value and hence, a radically contextual reading of Marx's labor theory of value. On the other side of the relation, it seems to me that Stuart Hall (2003, p. 116) has already suggested that cultural studies must follow this route, by arguing that the very notion of abstract labor, on which Marx's labor theory of value depends, must itself be taken as a historically specific category: 'there is no "production-in-general": only distinct forms of production, specific to time and conditions. One of these distinct forms is, rather confusingly, "general production": production based on a type of labour, which is not specific to a particular branch of production, but which has been "generalized": abstract labour.' He thus poses the question, key to Marx, of 'the form under which value becomes exchange value ... which are peculiar to specific historical conditions (the forms and conditions of commodity-production)' (p. 116).

Postone (1993, p. 25) argues that understanding Marx's theory of value requires separating wealth from its specific form based on a particular determinate form of social relation (i.e. of mediation) – namely, value based on the expenditure of abstract labor time. Consequently, we must understand value, as Marx used it, to be 'a historically specific and transitory category of social wealth intrinsically related to a historically specific mode of production.'

Postone finds it ironic that traditional Marxism sees capitalism as a transformation of the mode of distribution –the exchange of labor power for wages – while assuming a given mode of production – industrial production – based on value as the source of wealth.[23] Consequently, the Marxist critique has generally been assumed to be a critique of social relations from the standpoint of labor. But, he queries, what if Marx's theory is 'a historically specific critical theory of modern capitalist society – one that rests upon a critique of labor, of the form of mediation and of the mode of producing in that society' (p. 43). In that case, Marx's critique of capitalism is a critique of a particular form of mediation, of the social character of labor as a historically determinate social relationship. Thus, for Postone, it is not so much a question of the distribution of wealth as of the form of wealth itself.

Marx's analysis and privilege of the commodity in his theory is based on its double structure: it is 'simultaneously a use value for the other and a means of exchange for the producer' (Postone 1993, p. 148). Labor itself is similarly doubled, as concrete and abstract labor, which can then be seen, according to Postone, to be historically specific categories of a 'determinate form of social interdependence.' It is in the commodity that the two forms of labor are embodied and bound together. As a result, 'labor itself constitutes a social mediation in lieu of overt social relations' (p. 151), or in other worlds, labor appears to mediate itself, to provide its own grounding and as a result, value – as understood in Marx – can be seen to be a general and socially total form of mediation. Since labor as this total and self-grounded mediation necessarily objectifies itself in commodities, the social relations that are the essential character of capitalist society can only exist in objectified form. Further, this duality (of labor, of the commodity) is externalized once more in the relationship between the commodity and money, a doubling through which the commodity, a thing to be used (up) is socially mediated by money, which appears (again) as a universal mediation in and of itself, a total and self-grounded mediation in the form of a social relationship. Value is a self-distributing form of wealth, which appears not to be mediated by other forms of social relations (such as forms of material wealth). Thus Postone concludes (1993, p. 167), 'value is an objectification not of labor per se but of a historically specific function of labor. Labor does not play such a role in other social formations, or does so only marginally.'

Or in other words, the commodity for Marx is a historically specific kind of commensurating apparatus.

To put it in the simplest terms for a moment, Postone argues that Marx's labor theory of value is specific to a particular mode of production – industrial capitalism, and that Marx himself foresaw the coming of another configuration of capitalism in which the specific organization of value, the specific deployment of labor, and the specific form of wealth that preoccupied the first volume of *Capital* would no longer serve as the basis for a viable analysis. As a result, he argues, even more controversially, that Marx's critique of capitalism was not a critique of commodified social relations from the perspective of labor (since the duality of labor is intimately connected to form of the commodity as well as of wealth itself).

I do not mean to suggest that labor as the source of value, and the commodity as its doubled embodiment, is now irrelevant to questions of economic value. After all, at the very least, however one conceptualizes economies within a conjuncture, they are more complex and multiple than many descriptions have assumed. I do mean to suggest that it is being displaced or challenged, to some extent, by other logics and sources of value. I am not sure what an analysis of the conjuncture will conclude about such struggles, logics and sources. Contemporary theorizations of immaterial labor, while perhaps contributing to a more contextual understanding of the nature and production of value in the current conjuncture, seem at best partial (often sounding as if mental labor has not been crucial in previous configurations of capitalism) and strikingly more theoretical than empirical. My point lies elsewhere: it is simply that the uncertainly of the role of labor in the production of value – expressed and made visible in at least some of the discourses and practices of the neo-classical and financial redirections of the global capitalist economy – is contributing to a sense of uncertainty and crisis as well as a series of struggles, around conceptions and practices of value.[24]

The problem of calculation

It may seem odd for me to try to rescue at least a part of the argument of the Austrian theorists (of course, they thought of themselves as liberals), but I want to suggest that we have allowed Milton Friedman (and his political allies) too much power to define the argument between Keynes and the Austrian economists.[25] This has become all the more obvious in the current crises and in that context, I want to do a bit of rescuing of the Austrian school. In general, and especially in the current context, the argument is often glossed as a dispute between fiscal and monetary policy as the two mutually exclusive poles of economic policy and imagination. But there is another, in fact more important dimension to their difference, which goes back to the 'socialist calculation debate' over the role of the price mechanism and the possibility of planning.

The simple version of the Keynes/neo-classical dispute is that the latter believed that all uncertainty could be reduced to measureable risk while the former did not, but this seems to me to oversimplify the Austrian liberals, Hayek (1944/1994) and von Mises (1966), not only by oversimplifying their position but also by glossing over its messiness. Von Mises for example did believe that society is impossible without the (individual psychological) process that he called calculation. But what is often missed is that calculation precedes measurement! In fact, calculation is the prerequisite of any rational action. And in fact, he concludes, one must address the problem of calculation before any theory of market economy is possible precisely because calculation is what constructs the difference and relationship between means and ends. (The neo-classicist fetishism of mathematical modeling suggests that they might have overlooked this point.)

Just as importantly, von Mises (1966, p. 212) argues, 'The main task of economic calculation is not to deal with the problems of unchanging or only slightly changing market situations and prices, but to deal with change.' And he later explains (1966, p. 392), 'A price . . . does not indicate a relationship to something unchanging, but merely the instantaneous position in a kaleidoscopically changing assemblage. In this collection of things considered valuable by the value judgments of acting men each particle's place is interrelated with those of all other particles. What is called a price is always a relationship within an integrated system, which is the composite effect of human relations.'[26]

There is another important element of Austrian theory, and of the debate with Keynes, that I want to mention. Von Mises argues that calculation is always about the future: one is calculating future prices and, in such calculations, knowledge of the past or even the present (prices) is not necessary. For Keynes, similarly, economic calculation is about the future, but precisely because it involves imagining the future under conditions of uncertainty, it is only possible on the basis of the assumption that the future will look like the past (and the present) and therefore, past and present prices correctly sum up future prospects.

The derivative, commensuration and modernity

I want to reconnect to the derivative in order to suggest that, following Bryan and Rafferty (2006), the derivative, in its contemporary form, can be seen as the articulation of a response to each of these three conceptual and temporal problematics.[27] First, it proposes a mechanism of commensuration, of establishing equivalences and relations, among disparate and different elements, without appealing to the existence of a third standard term. Second, against LiPuma and Lee (and others), the derivative is not simply another expression of the commodity form, a binary structure holding together abstract and concrete risk, but the re-invention or at least the re-imagination of another form of economic exchange, one that refuses the need for such a binary structure grounded in a stable abstract term, in favor of an infinitely changing process of calculation, in precisely the sense that von Mises proposed it (although of course the derivatives attempted to mathematize/quantify what von Mises believed had to precede the mathematical, and that might have been its downfall).

This argument has to be located in a broader analysis of the conjuncture. As I have said, I believe that the problem-space of the contemporary conjuncture – especially when viewed from the United States – can be described as a struggle over the possibility of multiple – or other – modernities, other ways of being modern. I have to say immediately that I do not mean to talk about alternative articulations or localizations of the limited set made possible by European or North Atlantic modernity. I am not talking about difference, negativity and hybridity but about the possibility of positivities, otherness, and radical alterity. I want to follow the World Social Forum, sort of, to say other modernities are possible, other ways of being modern are open to us, so when de Sousa Santos says (2002, p. 13), 'we are facing modern problems for which there are no modern solutions,'[28] I want to say: 'we are facing (euro-)modern problems for which the dominant existing modernities have no solution.[29]

In fact, I see the derivative and its current dissemination and crisis as an expression of at least two constitutive moments or vectors as it were, in the struggle over the 'coming' modernity. It poses both the problem and a temporary solution, however inadequate or imaginary they may be, to these vectors of struggle and transformation.

The first of these vectors I simply want to acknowledge here since I have written about it extensively elsewhere (Grossberg 2005): a crisis of or struggle over temporality itself, in particular of the relation of the present and the future. This struggle is articulated into struggles over kids, an increasingly apocalyptic sense of time (by both the right and the left, even around the current economic crisis), the tyranny of short-termism, and a diminishing sense of our responsibility to and for the future (even the incorporation of the future into the present). It is not merely that derivatives offer a new temporality/spatiality but that in their universality as machines of calculation, they offer a new ontology (diagram) that may be taken to enable negotiations across the multiplicity of spatio-temporalities.

My description of the second vector depends directly upon a refusal of the euro-modernist ontology, which as I have suggested, sees the 'economy' as at least partially disembedded, as a domain or a distributed set of practices. (It owes a very real debt to conversations with Dick Bryan and John Clarke.) Rather than Polanyi's dual movement of disembedding and re-embedding, I want to propose seeing 'the economic' as a process that defines a dimension of every practice: as von Mises would have it, the economic is precisely constituted as a logic or calculus of value, a practice of commensuration. That is to say, every practice is located within relations of commensuration. Moreover, every society must have commensurating apparatuses or logics, in fact, a complex ecology of them.[30]

In order to explain this, let me return to Simmel's (1991) distinction between something's worth (value) and how much it is worth (comparative value or commensuration). In the contemporary conjuncture, too often, the diagnosis is made, almost in advance of any empirical work, that all value is being reduced to exchange value and even worse, to money itself. This is not a sufficient characterization if only because such a vision of the present has been ascribed for well over 100 years. Thus, Simmel (1991, p. 23), writing originally in 1896, suggested that 'the continuously required estimation according to monetary value eventually causes this to seem the only valid one; more and more people speed past the specific value of things, which cannot be expressed in terms of money.' And again, 'Indeed objects themselves are devalued of their higher significance through their equivalence with this means of exchange' (p. 24). The point is that Simmel thinks both of these moments – what something is worth and how much it is worth – are necessary: 'Where things are conceived of in their direct relationships to one another – thus not reduced to the common denominator of money – then much more rounding off and comparison of one unit to another occurs' (p. 28). Money for Simmel, is not even the expression of value but what I want to call a machine of commensuration: money 'has its entire meaning only as a transition ... it is only the bridge to definitive values, and one cannot live on a bridge' (p. 25).

So we need to separate the question of value from the question of the existence of value as an economic matter. A general theory of value might start with the assumption that all human activity produces value; value constitutes the effectivity of the social – of all social practices. Value can be defined as the actualization of potentiality as potentiality, or the presencing of the virtual as virtual. That is, value is the making present of the actual as an opening onto the virtual, as always actualizing more than the actual. Value is the production of a surplus (i.e. that is not the actual)[31] so that value is the production of the real as always greater than, in excess of, the actual.

We can then distinguish the question of the production and nature of value from its commensuration, where the latter describes a possible dimension of every practice or event. I want to postulate the existence (or lack thereof) of multiple different commensurating machines, with different 'powers.' This idea is perhaps similar to Strathern's (1999, p. 166) notion of compensation: 'Compensation travels by its own means of evaluation. A transaction which transforms human energies into other values.' As Kirsch (2001, p. 157) describes it, 'Strathern ... suggests that compensation is like a "universal translator" which, under certain circumstances, can convert anything into wealth.'

Such commensurating machines are, I propose, akin to Deleuze and Guattari's apparatuses of capture, but of a particular sort.[32] They put into relation (1) a measure of value, establishing a ground of equivalence that allows for comparison and (2) a medium of value, establishing a ground of difference that allows for evaluation ('exchange'). Actually I am tempted to suggest that an apparatus of capture is a particular sort – a capitalist sort – of commensurating machine.

Within euro-modernities, it is almost universally assumed that commensuration is only possible either (1) by comparing the two terms to be commensurated to a third – stable – term that serves as a standard. This is Marx's universal equivalent, or the consequent of Smith's invisible hand, or (2) by appealing to the translation or reduction or homogenization of both terms into another – third – set of terms, what Espeland and Stevens (1998, p. 314) call a 'common metric.' Povinelli (2001, p. 320) gets at this dialectical or reductionist notion of commensuration, although I do not agree with her equation of commensuration with (linguistic) translation: 'the concept of incommensurability is closely related to linguistic indeterminacy . . . if indeterminacy refers to the possibility of describing a phenomenon in two or more equally true ways, then incommensurability refers to a state in which two phenomena (or worlds) cannot be compared by a third without producing serious distortion.'[33]

Both views see commensuration as a practice of standardization, although Espeland and Stevens do recognize that commensuration is 'a fundamental feature of social life' (1998, p. 315). Moreover, they celebrate the fact that 'Commensuration is fundamentally relative. It creates relations between attributes or dimensions where value is revealed in the comparison . . . Commensuration is radically inclusive . . . The capacity to create relationships between virtually anything is extraordinary' (p. 317). And now we are back, close to the derivative and to von Mises.

I would make three modifications here. First, commensuration is the articulation of a particular kind of relationality, always on top of already existing relations, an articulation of an articulation. Second, commensuration is not the production of value but the adequation of values; it is the condition of possibility of appropriation. And third, commensuration is not (necessarily) a matter of meaning, understanding or translation, although euro-modernity has often defined it as a hermeneutic problem. It is more material – a matter of weighing, of measuring without necessarily being enumerated or quantified. In fact, I am tempted to say that commensurability is always of the untranslatable, which is what calls commensuration into existence. Commensuration, moreover, can take many forms; there are many logics/apparatuses of commensuration. It can offer forms of equalization, standardization, reduction, relativism, or it can refuse both relativism and all forms of absolutism. It is not a matter of coordination but the possibility that enables coordination, like Foucault's relation of a non-relation, like Deleuze's refrain. Commensuration is not a particular kind of equivalence or mediation, but specific apparatuses construct specific notions of equivalence or mediation, including the possibility of mediation without negation or dialectics.

My claim, then, is rather simple: derivatives are invented as an attempt to respond to a crisis of commensuration brought about by the collapse or impossibility of any standard of commensuration. They appear to offer the possibility of calculating infinite and infinitely changing relations of adequation.[34] In that sense, and given the contemporary context, they are extremely interesting, and the financial crisis brought about in part by the failure of such a logic of commensuration poses serious challenges to us. Their failure, especially if it is the failure of such a logic, throws us back into the conjuncture in all its complexities.

The crises of commensuration in the contemporary conjuncture

Let me bring this argument into the contemporary conjuncture: the contemporary conjuncture, as a struggle over modernity, is expressed in/constituted by, articulated with a widely dispersed and somewhat disaggregated series of 'crises of commensuration,' across virtually every vector and terrain, albeit constructed by and along different temporalities or timelines. In fact, one of the most powerful contemporary vectors of struggle and change in the contemporary conjuncture is a series of crises of values that point to the collapse at worst, the uncertainty at best, of most if not all of our commensurating machines. We seem to be living in the midst of, or at least facing the threat, of the impossibility of valuation and commensuration; across all dimensions of human activity, from religion and politics to knowledge and economics, there is at least the appearance of a growing inability to find any common ground or logic upon which one can constitute, measure, compare and possibly adjudicate (or compromise) differences.

These multiple crises are calling the very possibility of commensuration into question. Sometimes they mark the failure or collapse of, or the struggle against, some existing commensuration machine (such as the universal equivalent, or the critique of euro-centric value systems or hierarchies of privilege). Sometimes, a crisis of commensuration appears at the site where we are publicly called upon to meet demands of commensuration for which we have no apparatus, such as when we have to confront the challenge of ontological pluralism and radical alterity.[35]

But it is important not to think that the multiple crises are simply expressions of a single, real, crisis, which has yet to be located or is fundamentally, somehow, economic (in the territorialized euro-modern sense, thus returning us to economic reductionism). At the same time, I do not think that the multiple appearances of crises of commensuration are simply random. They are not all 'the same' as it were (e.g. all 'epistemological,' or translation). Instead, one has to look at how they are produced and articulated contextually. For such crises are always local, and so, across the conjuncture, the crisis (crises) – in this case of commensuration – is never complete or total.

In European modernity, there are two dominant kinds of commensurating machines, each with the possibility of a multiplicity of apparatuses or logics, located primarily within the two most 'disembedded' domains – economics and culture – as competing loci of the elliptical spaces of value, often presenting themselves as competing modes of being-in-the-world. This explains, to a large extent, why these two realms or logics are so often structured in direct opposition to and competition with one another.

For example, to oversimplify an already oversimplified example, consider the value produced in the affective practices of domestic life. These values have been commensurated through different apparatuses, including socio-economic machines (in which such value is 'exchanged' for security, livelihood, etc.) and religious-cultural machines. In the contemporary conjuncture, the calculations of such commensurations have been called into question, increasingly, by developments such as the growing visibility and condemnation of domestic violence, the increasing need for women to enter the workforce, the rise of domestic labor, etc.

The crises of commensuration constitute the context within which the derivative – think back to von Mises – and its failure have to be located. Rather than beginning with the assumption that all values have been reduced to exchange or monetary value, or that this is another example of the failure of deregulated (free-market capitalism), I want to propose another view of the crisis. It is not the only possible view, but it may be a useful view in our attempt to get a better understanding of the conjuncture. I suggest that the starting point of the crisis lies in the apparent claim that all values' can be commensurated through economic machines, that 'economics' is, as it were, the necessary medium of translation. Thus capitalism's power lies in its ability to articulate the relations among values without necessarily privileging its own so that, for example, it is still possible that the notion of wealth (as the accumulation of value) remains ambiguous. Or perhaps the commensurating machines that conservative/free-market economic theory and policy have tried to put into place are failing because, to speak somewhat metaphorically, the commensurating machines began to claim to produce value itself, because they claim to be the only commensurating machine or because the commensurating machines deny their own mediating position as commensurating.

We can see crises of commensuration in politics, and in culture. In politics, it is producing the extraordinary celebration and power of partisanship – or better, of particular forms of partisanship – and extremism against moderation and compromise. It is visible in the increasingly common equation of moral and political calculation, which means that one can never accept defeat (even in electoral terms, there must always be a conspiracy or something external to blame). It is the failure of strategic thinking! In culture (as euro-modernity constructs it), I might point to the widespread inability to escape the relativism that seems to have emerged from the critique of various foundationalisms,[36] which in a circuitous way, and from a variety of positions, has helped to fuel the rejection of the value of education and knowledge. However, the ironic return of scientism – the belief that science is the only and ultimate explanation of all reality – is also a moment of fundamentalism.

As the dominant commensurating apparatuses come under attack, as they are deconstructed, there seems to be a tendency for them to increasingly become what Deleuze and Guattari (1977) might describe as 'paranoiac machines,' in which they claim to or act as if they produce values. It is as if mediation denies its own position as mediation. And as a result, such commensurating machines then claim to be the only possible source of value. I think the name for such value practice is fundamentalism – whether religious, political, economic or financial. The rise of fundamentalism is the other side of this dismantling of the possibility of commensuration; it is what I might call a negative economy of value as the production and appropriation of value without the possibility of commensuration. In fundamentalism, some particular set of relations/values appears not only absolute but also as the absolute negation of any other. This goes beyond the negativity of difference in euro-modernity because fundamentalism refuses to allow its negativity to be coded into a system of hierarchy. Fundamentalism is non-hierarchical, refusing the reality or possibility of the other, and thus demanding the extermination of the other. But the rise of fundamentalism, as a particular affective form of the refusal of calculation, as a particular absolute partisan investment, cannot be laid at the door of any single cause, group or political position. One of the great 'mysteries' of the contemporary world is the extraordinary rise of everyday violence, even of the most horrific kinds. Even 'genocide' itself seems to have become more ordinary, a reconstitutions of relations among neighbors, according to principles and intensities of fundamentalism.

Our response to the current 'economic' crisis does not have to be framed in economistic terms, for even, as Donald Mackenzie (cited in Pryke 2007, p. 576) does, in economic terms: 'might it be possible even in high modernity to perform a different economic world.' The challenge is to find or invent other commensurating machines that are capable of adjudicating otherness via (and not in spite of) their difference, that refuse to universalize themselves, and just as importantly, that reject a measure of the future defined by growth and expansion.[37] But it is also to find or invent spaces in which practices need not be articulated by or into relations of commensuration. It is to imagine other ways of being modern, ways that not only allow the possibility of other worlds but their right to co-exist alongside our own. Only by reconstituting our imagination of the possible, of the value of the real, can we hope to find a way from here to somewhere else. As the Zapatistas have said: 'we will walk the same path of history but we will not repeat it; we are from before, yes, but we are new.'[38]

Acknowledgements

The author is grateful to many people who have helped him with this paper, including John Clarke, Mark Hayward, Carey Richter, Dana DeSoto, John Pickles, Arturo Escobar, David Ruccio and Dick Bryan. Dick Bryan provided the key insight that allowed this paper to move forward: namely, that commensuration as the economic was constitutive of every practice. Eric Pineault introduced the author to the importance of Simmel's work.

Notes

1 See, e.g. the recently launched *Journal of Cultural Economy*.

2 See my chapter, 'Rescuing economies from economists,' in Grossberg (2010).

3 Polanyi (1944/2001) postulates a 'natural state' in which economic relations (markets?) are intertwined with and inseparable from other social relations. The rise of capitalism (or is it modernity?) results in the sustained effort to disembed the market from such interconnectivities, and to create an autonomous sphere of the market: the economy. The economy continues to be defined as a set of social relations albeit social relations that are no longer bound together with non-economic relations. Of course, Polanyi suggests that this disembedding is never entirely successful, and that modern economies are characterized by a dual movement of embedding and disembedding. I wonder if it is possible to argue that the transformation of the financial markets by entirely mathematical instruments (derivatives) can be seen as a more radical effort at disembedding, one in which economic events are no longer assumed to involve social relationships at all. I would also like to point out that the notion of a disembedded economy, a freestanding economy as it were, is an ontological notion, and therefore not the equivalent of the epistemological claims characterized by cultural studies as economic reductionism.

4 I have heard a number of cultural scholars suggest that, given the crisis, we do not have the luxury of the time it would take for us to understand the economy. So having not done the work before, we can now justify not doing it now. Yet sometimes the same people claim that their critiques of capitalism predicted (or in even more inflated terms, contributed to) the

current crisis. Such claims are completely unfounded, except in the most banal terms. Since it is unlikely that our interventions will have a strong impact in the short term, we need to think in the long term, in which better stories do make better politics. We need to find better ways of doing economics as it were.

5 At the moment I am writing this, my favorite example comes from the normally staid pages of *The Economist*, which dipped into its reservoir of images to come up with 'The Night of the Living Dead' ('A ghoulish prospect', February 28, 2009, p. 73). A more sober use of the catastrophic rhetoric is Nocera (2009, p. 1). On the other side, Robert Shiller (2009) seems to recognize the danger of such language as a self-fulfilling prophecy: This inflationary rhetoric is visible in the disproportionate number of photographs from the depression that the mainstream press has used.

6 I am grateful to David Ruccio for adding precision to this quick summary.

7 The figures come from Bryan and Rafferty (2007).

8 This makes the current financial crisis different from previous crises. Even the *New York Times* seemed to recognize this in a column comparing the current crisis with that of 1906–1907. See Strouse (2009).

9 Even as I write, *Wired* has an essay arguing: 'The financial world doesn't need new regulations. It needs radical transparency. Make companies report results in easy to understand, easy to crunch numbers – and let investors do the rest' (Roth 2009, p. 81).

10 It turns out that much of this work was done by physicists and mathematicians rather than economists, who had at best a rather cynical view of the possibilities of a science of economics. For popular descriptions, see Overbye (2009) and Salmon (2009).

11 There are serious arguments about whether such affective relations are internal to the market or not. These are connected to debates, e.g. over whether the rule of law is a condition of possibility of the market or whether the market produces the rule of law. One must acknowledge, if only in terms of common sense, that there is something odd when the very financial institutions of credit seem to refuse to participate in the very markets that define their mode of operation and their reason for being.

12 See also chapter 30 of *Capital*, volume 3 (Marx n.d.).

13 Banking capital works according to the ratio of original money to the reserve ratio (or money multiplier), thereby producing further money far in excess of its original amount. Marx contrasts the circuit of money capital (M-C-M') to the circuit of commodity capital (C-M-C'). The second of these circuits, the object of discussion in the first volume of *Capital*, has a different view of money – when Marx introduces the importance of credit to initiating and capitalizing the circuit of commodity production, and when he discusses the universal equivalent (Marx 1992, chapters 3 and 4). However, I would argue that credit is insufficiently theorized in the first volume and that it is only in the third volume of *Capital* that credit and finance capital itself comes under careful scrutiny.

14 The concept of the beauty contest is introduced in Keynes (1936, chapter 12).

15 So we need to talk about money. Money is generally argued to have four functions, and exist in four forms. Its functions are as a medium of exchange, a standard of deferred payment, a unit or account (a measure or standard of relative wealth) and a store of value. Its four types are commodity money where money is the commodity it is made of, representative money which function as tokens or certificates that can be exchanged for particular commodities, credit money that define a claim or obligation, and fiat money whose values is determined by legal statute.

16 As David Ruccio reminded me, without losing sight of the general.

17 Each of these must be recognized as the product of complex forces and struggles. For example, to take one very controversial claim, the housing bubble was certainly not caused by the Community Reinvestment Act of 1977, which ordered Fannie Mae and Freddie Mac to invest in lower income housing – a push from the liberal center and the left – but however, we would be remiss not to see the ways that the discourses of this Act were able to be deployed in ways that may not have been intended to produce results that were never desired.

18 While I know that many on the left dismiss such ideas, it should be noted that much 'democratic theory' seems to assume, similarly, that if only we had a perfect political market, then people would all reach the best conclusion, even the right conclusion – usually identified as the one I hold.

19 It is interesting that none of the hostility against the financial regime seems to be aimed against the economists who not only provided the arguments, but in many cases, sought the influence on public policy. (A similar observation might be made about the political scientists who have 'scientifically' legitimated disastrous foreign and domestic policies.)

20 Contexts and conjunctures have complex relations. Potentially, any context may encompass more than one problem-space, more than one conjuncture, and both contexts and conjunctures have to be seen as multiple, overlapping and embedded.

21 For a critique of the category of neo-liberalism, see Grossberg (2010) and Clarke (2010, in this issue).

22 This is not the same as a symptom, which can be read in Hegelian terms, because it suggests a hidden cause. A symptom is always a symptom of something else.

23 Industrial capitalism can be understood more accurately as that mode of production in which not only the appropriation of surplus value (or the surplus value) is a function of capital but so is the creation of the surplus a function of capital. It is usually distinguished from commercial capitalism, and finance capitalism.

24 David Ruccio has suggested to me that I am underplaying part of the context of Marx's theory: 'it's not only a critique of the capitalism of his day; it's also a critique of the discourse of the classical political economy, which was based on a labor theory of value' (personal communication, June 2009).

I realize that one could read Postone's argument – and my use of it – as historicist, and I am willing to accept that up to a point. I would argue that the sort of radical contextualism I am advocating does not entail a commitment to either developmentalism (Hegel) or relativism (as in much of contemporary post-structuralist and anthropological theorizing). Instead, while contextualism does argue that theory and politics develop out of and in response to particular contexts, it does not deny the utility of certain generalizations, nor does it hold to a form of objectivist referentiality. Again, theories are measured by their ability to respond to the present and the possibilities of the future.

25 I also think it is worth re-reading Hayek (1944/1994) since his argument for radically open, competitive markets can be seen to operate against the conservative argument for deregulation. Hayek understood that it required work, government work, to create markets and to sustain them as competitive.

26 I must acknowledge my debt to Salerno (1990). One can see on this model of economic calculation why the logic of calculus, as the study of change in relations among functions, in which integration and differentiation are inverse logics, makes sense.

27 There is an interesting question to be considered, but not here: the relation of the derivative to and as money.

28 The full quotation is: 'The conditions that brought about the crisis of modernity have not yet become the conditions to overcome the crisis beyond modernity. Hence the complexity of our transitional period portrayed by oppositional postmodern theory: we are facing modern problems for which there are no modern solutions . . . What is necessary is to start from the disjuncture between the modernity of the problems and the postmodernity of the possible solutions, and to turn such disjunction into the urge to ground theories and practices capable of reinventing social emancipation out of the wrecked emancipatory promises of modernity' (Santos 2002, p. 13).

29 The obvious question that I must face is, what do I mean by modernity or by ways of being modern? Am I essentializing it? Or deconstructing to such an extreme that it knows no boundaries? My response is, I hope not. Rather, I have offered a kind of Foucauldean diagram, following a turn to a kind of Deleuzean ontology of multiple realities as a way of de-colonizing thought itself. I suggest that euro-modernity is only one expression of the diagram, and perhaps not even the first one, although it certainly has both claimed that temporal position and attempted to universalize itself as the only modernity. That diagram can be schematized along three dimensions: first, modernity involves a stratification of time-space that involves the possibility of articulating the event (the absolute moment of the now) and the temporality of change, as well as the spaces of experience and institutions. In Europe, this produces a diagram that articulates the present with everyday life and history with the state. Second, modernity entails a coding of

difference (in euro-modernity, through negativity and dialectics) and a territorialization of forces and determinations (in euro-modernity, into bounded domains). See Grossberg (2010).

30 I am aware that this could easily slide into a new universalizing conception of the economic (cf. theories of scarcity or rational choice) but I think it can be avoided: first, by recognizing that it neither creates a domain of economic practices nor a logic of economics; second, and more importantly, by acknowledging that commensuration does not in any way define the essence of a practice, and every practice can be articulated by any number of vectors of which commensuration is only one. In other words, not every practice is, at any or every moment, articulated into relations of commensuration. The attempts to universalize a particular logic of commensuration or to fetishize the fact of commensuration itself, are the result of forms of euro-modern power.

31 I am using Deleuze and Guattari's (1987) concepts here: the real includes both the actual and the virtual, the latter being distinguished from the merely possible, which is not in fact real.

32 I would connect this to Deleuze and Guattari's (1987) machines of capture as the actualization of the surplus.

33 My argument here can and should be connected to two other lines of thought: first, a reading of the Frankfurt School's argument that the crisis of modernity was the reduction of everything to a common standard of the commodity, and to Adorno's (1990) efforts to think beyond the crisis through a 'negative dialectics.' And second, it is similar in some ways to Lyotard's (1988) arguments about post-modernity and language-games, although I think his position too easily leads to relativism since he abandoned the link, in Wittgenstein, between language-games and forms of life.

34 I remember reading a book, *Mr. Tompkins in Paperback*, by George Gamow, which attempted to tell you what it would be like to live in a relativistic universe. That is, we know relativity is true, but our experience is still Newtonian. I might use this to suggest that we continue to live in a world described by geometry and trigonometry, even through we know that change is the fundamental 'fact' of existence. In fact, we live in a world of calculus – the mathematics of change – although we do not always experience it that way.

35 Mario Blaser (2009), an anthropologist who works primarily with indigeneous peoples of Paraguay, tells of the following event what took place in British Columbia: Greenpeace sees a whale stranded in a small inlet and want to 'save' it by leading it back out to the ocean. The local indigenous people see that the spirit of their beloved tribal leader and chief has returned to watch over them. They are sure that if their chief is taken from them again (for example, in Greenpeace's misperception of the whale), they would surely suffer. How does one adjudicate such a difference? How does one commensurate the systems of value/reality?

36 Obviously, here, I am referring to the full range of theories that challenged epistemological foundationalism in all its forms (including logical positivism

and empiricism) and positivist forms of ontological realism, including the emergence of science studies, the so-called linguistic turn, the various forms of social constructionism, possible worlds theory, etc.

37 Growth has become, apparently, the sole measure of economic success. Giving that up will also entail, I think, reigning in the assumption that economies flourish through the celebration of consumerism. Of course, in the end, the choice may not belong to the peoples of the North Atlantic modern worlds, given the changing balance of national, political and economic forces defined by the geo-political shift towards the emerging global claims of China, India, etc.

38 'The Fourth Key,' discourse from the March of the Color of the Earth in Cuautla, Morelos, March 7, 2001.

References

Adorno, T. (1990) *Negative Dialectics*, London, Routledge.

Blaser, M. (2009) 'Political ontology: cultural studies without culture?', *Cultural Studies*, vol. 23, nos. 5–6, pp. 873–896.

Bryan, D. & Rafferty, R. (2006) *Capitalism with Derivatives*, New York, Palgrave Macmillan.

Bryan, D. & Rafferty, R. (2007) 'Financial derivatives and the theory of money', *Economy & Society*, vol. 36, no. 1, pp. 134–158.

Clarke, J. (2010) 'After neo-liberalism? Markets, states and the reinvention of public welfare', *Cultural Studies*, vol. 24, no. 3, pp. 375–394.

Deleuze, G. & Guattari, F. (1977) *Anti-Oedipus*, New York, Viking.

Deleuze, G. & Guattari, F. (1987) *A Thousand Plateaus*, Minneapolis, MN, University of Minnesota Press.

Espeland, W. N. & Stevens, M. L. (1998) 'Commensuration as a social process', *American Review of Sociology*, vol. 24, pp. 313–343.

Foucault, M. (2008) *The Birth of Biopolitics*, New York, Palgrave Macmillan.

Grossberg, L. (2005) *Caught In the Crossfire: Kids, Politics and America's Future*, Boulder, CO, Paradigm.

Grossberg, L. (2010) *Cultural Studies in the future Tense*, Durham, NC, Duke University Press.

Hall, S. (2003) 'Marx's notes on method: a "reading" of the "1857 Introduction to the Grundrisse"', *Cultural Studies*, vol. 17, no. 2, pp. 113–149.

Hardt, M. & Negri, A. (in press) *Commonwealth*, Cambridge, MA, Harvard University Press.

Hayek, F. A. (1994) *The Road to Serfdom*, Chicago, IL, University of Chicago Press. (Originally published 1944.)

Henwood, D. (1977) *Wall Street*, London, Verso.

Keynes, J. M. (1936) *General Theory of Employment Interest and Money*, New York, Harcourt, Brace & Co.

Kirsch, S. (2001) 'Property effects: social networks and compensation claims in Melanesia', *Social Anthropology*, vol. 9, no. 2, pp. 147–163.

LiPuma, E. & Lee, B. (2004) *Financial Derivatives and the Globalization of Risk*, Durham, NC, Duke University Press.

Lyotard, J.-F. (1988) *The Differend*, Minneapolis, MN, University of Minnesota Press.

Mackenzie, D. (2008) *An Engine, Not a Camera*, Cambridge, MA, MIT Press.

Martin, R. (2007) *An Empire of Indifference*, Durham, NC, Duke University Press.

Marx, K. (1973) *Grundrisse*, New York, Vintage.

Marx, K. (1992) *Capital, Volume 1*, London, Penguin.

Marx, K. (n.d.) *Capital, Volume 3*, chapter 27. Available at: http://www.marxists.org/archive/marx/works/1894-c3/ch27.htm

Michaels, W. B. (1988) *The Gold Standard and the Logic of Naturalism*, Berkeley, CA, University of California Press.

Michie, J. (2009) 'End our reliance on the City casino', *The Guardian*, 18 March. Available at: http://www.guardian.co.uk/commentisfree/2009/mar/18/economics-financial-crisis

Nocera, J. (2009) 'Flying blind', *New York Times Book Review*, 15 February.

Overbye, D. (2009) 'They tried to outsmart Wall Street', *New York Times*, 10 March, p. D1.

Polanyi, K. (2001) *The Great Transformation*, Boston, MA, Beacon. (Originally published 1944.)

Postone, M. (1993) *Time, Labor, and Social Domination*, Cambridge, Cambridge University Press.

Povinelli, E. (2001) 'Radical worlds: the anthropology of incommensurability and inconceivability', *American Review of Anthropology*, vol. 30, pp. 319–334.

Pryke, M. (2007) 'Geomoney: an option on frost, going long on clouds', *Geoforum*, vol. 38, pp. 576–588.

Pryke, M. & Allen, J. (2002) 'Monetized time-space: derivatives – money's "new imaginary"?', *Economy and Society*, vol. 29, no. 2, pp. 264–284.

Roth, D. (2009) 'The road map for recovery', *Wired*, March.

Salerno, J. T. (1990) 'Ludvig von Mises as social rationalist', *The Review of Austrian Economics*, vol. 4, pp. 26–54.

Salmon, F. (2009) 'A formula for disaster', *Wired*, March.

Santos, B. de S. (2002) *Toward a New Legal Common Sense*, London, Butterworths.

Scott, D. (2004) *Conscripts of Modernity*, Durham, NC, Duke University Press.

Shiller, R. (2009) 'Expect the worst and you may get it', *New York Times*, 22 February.

Simmel, G. (1991) 'Money in modern culture', *Theory Culture & Society*, vol. 8, pp. 17–31.

Spivak, G. (2006) 'Scattered speculations on the question of value', in *In Other Words*, New York, Routledge, pp. 154–175.

Strathern, M. (1999) 'What is intellectual property after?', in *Actor Network Theory and After*, eds J. Law & J. Hassard, Oxford, Blackwells.

Strouse, J. (2009) 'When the economy really did "fall off a cliff"', *New York Times*, 23 March, p. A19.

von Mises, L. (1966) *Human Action*, Chicago, IL, Henry Regnery.

Jayson Harsin

THE LOST HISTORIES OF AMERICAN ECONOMIC RIGHTS

This article examines the concept and the discontinuous historical usage of the term 'economic rights' in American political discourse from the perspective of democratic political freedom. It views the idea and ideology of 'economic rights' as a discursive marker pointing to historically contingent relations between government, national economy and individual freedom. It focuses on the only two American presidential articulations of an Economic Bill of Rights and their conjunctures: one by Franklin Roosevelt and another by Ronald Reagan. These two articulations represent two opposing political traditions of economic rights in the United States: the neo-liberal laissez-faire *free market tradition and the liberal welfare-state tradition. Both of these liberal traditions are haunted by an older democratic-republican discourse of economic rights, from which they continue to draw normative and affective energy without ever confronting its guiding premises. Contemporary popular discourses about the economic crisis demonstrate the continuation of deeply entrenched though historically outdated understandings of the promise and possibilities of individual freedom and autonomy within the folds of a society completely transformed by capitalist modernity. Present considerations of this history reveal possible resources for political struggles.*

Economic freedom is also an important corollary of human rights. The time has come to recognize that the basic economic rights to own, use, and exchange property, to create and produce, free of state control, are a fundamental part of human freedom and essential components to a decent and humane world for all peoples. (Ronald Reagan, December 8, 1988)

The Founding Fathers of our country knew that without economic freedom there can be no political freedom . . . . Over the past 40 years, however, the growth of government has left our citizens with less control over their economic lives. What America needs now is an Economic Bill of Rights that guarantees four fundamental freedoms: . . . to work . . . to

> enjoy the fruits of one's labor ... and to own and control one's property; ... to participate in a free market. (Ronald Reagan, July 3, 1987)

In the following paper I want to argue that the concept of 'economic rights' is useful to a critical analysis of the present conjuncture and to political struggle within it. I approach the term as it has been defined through use in American political life and as a concept I derive from comparisons with its usage in other contexts, (but not as a concept derived exclusively from global human rights discourse). In the first part of the paper, I demonstrate what I mean by 'economic rights' as it was first coined in US presidential discourse by Franklin D. Roosevelt (FDR), and as it was later redefined by Ronald Reagan. In the second part of the paper, I turn to older considerations of the same categories, moving toward a conjunctural analysis of the New Deal and Reagan Revolution. I will end by looking at the present economic crisis from the perspective historical economic rights articulations.

Based on a history[1] of conjunctural changes in American economic rights discourse, I argue that economic rights have been increasingly detached from political rights; or, put differently, the rapport between imaginaries of economic freedom and political freedom have been carefully disarticulated in classic liberal 'separate spheres' fashion. My considerations of economic rights here are mediated by considerations chiefly of theories of democratic citizenship. Conceptions of the economic have always been central to conceptions of democracy (Ober 2000). However, thinking economic rights historically and conjuncturally casts doubts on procedural emphases for strengthening inclusive democracy (Young 1995, Habermas 1998), as well as democratizing institutions that would ideally allow more people to have a say in institutional decision-making.

My goal here is to briefly explore two antithetical American popular conceptualizations of 'economic rights,' both within their historically contingent conjunctures and as part of a larger genealogy of economic rights discourse in the United States. Both versions had policy aspirations and I examine these two major discourses (and their popular variants from social Darwinism to anarchism) in order to show how economic rights is a historically empty signifier that marks the rewritable articulations between national economy, government and freedom. This treatment of economic rights thus disposes of any essential, timeless, or natural definition of economic rights, and instead pursues the historical use of the term and idea in order to analyze what that use may illuminate about American politics and culture in the present.

Despite the substantive contingency of the concept, an initial historical overview locates economic rights in the United States in the context of a particular democratic constitutional regime, a regime which becomes progressively liberal in its orientation as it moves away from the democratic-republican moorings of the Revolutionary and founding period of US history. At its core, the discourse of economic rights consists of a simple proposition issuing from its ancient Greco-Roman ancestry, namely that the citizen cannot be politically free and independent if he/she is economically dependent or beholden to others. This proposition is shared by all the antagonists in the genealogical drama of economic rights: Jefferson versus Hamilton; Jackson versus Clay/Webster; FDR/Johnson versus Hoover/Reagan. But it is interpreted differently by different sets of antagonists. However, for purposes of space, I will limit myself to the two major popular conceptualizations that materialized in FDR and Reagan.

In the United States today, we are living in a historical a priori, as Foucault called it, of economic rights (a particular articulation of individual freedom, government, and economics) bequeathed by Reagan, and one could argue that the current economic crisis suggests we are at a crucial juncture that could shift the relations between government, economy, and freedom once again.

Competing conceptions of economic rights

On September 23, 1932, in a campaign speech to the Commonwealth Club of San Francisco, FDR made a bold call for a supplement to the US Constitutional Bill of Rights with 'an economic declaration of rights, an economic constitutional order,' or as he would refer to it in 1944, an 'economic bill of rights'(EBR) (Roosevelt 1932/1938, 1944). In doing so, he was proposing a set of social policies and a course of political action to resist and contain what he described as a threat to the individual freedom of Americans. The American preoccupation with individual freedom, how to nurture it and how to protect it against real and imagined dangers has a long history going as far back as the debate between Alexander Hamilton and Thomas Jefferson over the proper relation between individual freedom, power of government, and the national economy. In a strategic narrative, FDR explained the enduring historical dilemma thus:

> Woodrow Wilson, elected in 1912, saw the situation more clearly [than his predecessors]. Where Jefferson had feared the encroachment of political power on the lives of individuals, Wilson knew that the new power was financial. He saw, in the highly centralized economic system, the despot of the twentieth century, on whom great masses of individuals relied for their safety and their livelihood, and whose irresponsibility and greed (if it were not controlled) would reduce them to starvation and penury . . . (Roosevelt 1932/1938, p. 339)

This particular 're-appraisal of values,' as FDR called it, provided the cultural-political vision for the 'revolution in government' known as the New Deal. It was a cultural-political vision in that he saw the solution to the problem of despotic financial power not just in a change in governmental policies, but also in the way a culture viewed freedom and the changing threats to it. If there was no cultural change, it was unlikely that any political party in power would be capable of providing acceptable solutions to a national citizenry whose consent was required. By 1947, with FDR's economic rights discourse vying for dominance in American politics, it appeared that a major cultural shift was in fact underway.

Forty years later, after a host of other issue cycles, institutional purges, and legal shifts had marginalized many of FDR's ideas, Ronald Reagan, a confessed admirer of FDR, gave a series of public addresses that also called for an economic bill of rights. Like FDR, Reagan declared that his EBR would 'complement and strengthen Jefferson's political Bill of Rights.'[2] However, Reagan's attempt to complement and strengthen Jefferson's commitment to freedom was built around an entirely different articulation of both the threat to individual freedom and the proposed solution to eliminate it. Distanced from the sufferings and struggles of both the industrialization of the United States during the early twentieth century and the racial and economic issues of late civil rights movement of mid-century, Reagan's EBR transported the nation back to the early nineteenth century. In Reagan's narrative imagination, big business would not be regulated to protect the sacred rights of the individual, as FDR proposed. On the contrary, it was the federal government itself that needed to be regulated, for it was the new threat to individual freedom.

Furthermore, Reagan's conception of freedom centered on an individual's freedom to enter a 'free market' unfettered by a potentially tyrannical government, and keep his/her earnings; government taxation was tantamount to theft in his rhetorical inversion of Proudhon's infamous dictum 'Property is theft.' According to Reagan:

> The Bill of Rights was adopted by our forefathers to protect the people from the threat posed by government to our basic political liberties. Now, over 200 years later, the chief danger of big government is the threat to our economic liberties, to our basic right to earn our own keep and keep what we earn. Here the problem is a bloated federal government that overtaxes, overspends, overborrows, and overregulates. (Reagan 1987b)

The difference between solutions proposed by FDR and Reagan reflect not only a difference in perception regarding the threat to individual liberty. Both of these charismatic politicians may also be viewed as popular political theorists who offered different and conflicting understandings of the way the aforementioned trio of government, economy, and individual freedom should relate to one another.

For FDR in 1932, the government exists to protect individual freedom from historically shifting threats to it, threats which he saw emerging the project of corporate capitalism to subject all other arenas of life (politics, work, leisure) to its quest for profit. An individual had little choice in life if some force, meaning the federal government, as powerful as the corporations could not step in and regulate the latter in the name of freedom for the beleaguered individual. However, central to Reagan's neo-*laissez-faire* political imaginary was an implicit theory of the autonomous individual. This theory, in terms of the individual's relation to political and economic government, was exactly the opposite of the vision articulated by FDR. Reagan's discourse completely jettisoned the question of corporate threat, imagining instead an ideal typical individual who, if free of state intrusion, could 'go just as far and reach just as high as . . . your individual talents and energies will take you' (Reagan 1987a). Reagan's government would supposedly refrain from meddling in an individual's economic life (thanks to a legal apparatus that treated corporations as individual citizens), refrain from excessive taxation and protecting the market from regulations.

How in some 40 odd years did this re-conceptualization of the government–economy–individual freedom triangle take effect, so that by the time of Reagan there was no need to even entertain the concerns that had motivated the political discourse of the Progressive era to propose a variety of visions for government regulation of the market and redistribution in the name of individual freedom? If for several years citizenship and individual freedom were publicly presented as bound to economic regulations and interventionist government, what sort of work accomplished their detachment? While Reagan's economic rights discourse was part of a larger political imaginary that instituted a major reversal in American political discourse and policy practices, the arguments and tropes that constituted his vision inhabited an American economic rights discourse several centuries old. His implied theories of individual agency, government, and their relationship to economic life, though a departure from FDR's, contained echoes of popular discursive precedents across the last centuries, from William Graham Sumner, Andrew Carnegie, and Russell Conwell, to as far back as Cotton Mather. To understand these transformations and adaptations, I now want to briefly sketch the transition between two anchoring conjunctures of this history: the New Deal and the Reagan Revolution.

The FDR and Reagan conjunctures

The emergent conjuncture FDR responded to and helped shape had its roots in the post-Civil War development of national identity, growing federal intervention in the market, and a revolution in cultural subjectivity that itself derived especially from pervasive technological and economic changes and the popular discourses that accompanied them.

After the 1860s, the country began to move toward its current widely recognized identity that privileges federal over state identity: the United States, not these United States. This phenomenon was related to a judicial revolution sparked by the Fourteenth Amendment, but also emerged in tandem with revolutions in communication and transportation (not to mention the migratory push of economic dislocations in an increasingly industrial economy), which brought people from different regions into more frequent contact and helped them to think beyond the local or regional affiliations. The rise of nationalism and the United States entry into nineteenth and early twentieth century imperialism with the Spanish-American War also encouraged new attachments to the federal government and promoted attachment to the 'nation form.'

Secondly, despite the enduring discursive frame of a *laissez-faire* and minimalist government, government in the latter half of the nineteenth century 'subsidized railroad construction, maintained high protective tariffs and a tight money supply, used its power to crush strikes, and in other ways supported the nation's most powerful economic interests' (Diner 1998, p. 14). A contradiction between *laissez-faire* and justificatory social Darwinist discourses and the reality of state intervention to promote national economic development is closely bound up with a third feature of the emergent conjuncture: the changing economic reality.

Finally, the period between the Civil War and World War I was also marked by the diminishing presence of the democratic-republican[3] white-male proprietor (farmer or shopkeeper). Historian Steven Diner notes that the period is characterized by an increasing malaise in the citizenry about the most obvious effect of the growing industrial capitalism – namely, that people exercised less and less control over their everyday lives (Diner 1998, p. 4). As James Livingston (1994) has provocatively argued, the rise of corporate capitalism and the demise of landed republican proprietorship created a new cultural subjectivity. Democratic-republican (what Livingston calls 'modern') subjectivity was symbolized by the male freeholder and assumed to be rational and autonomous. A moral personality (the issue of character) came to be assumed only by reverting to the figure of the freeholder or by embracing historical time and its new social conditions. The latter emphasized the 'proletarianization of males,' and thus the emergence of a 'social self.' In a strange paradox, people were less in control of their place in the economy, yet that insecurity produced, according to Livingston, a strange new sort of social self, an interdependent subjectivity.

FDR's EBR was produced through an adroit negotiation of this historical conjuncture. The Progressive intellectuals and politicians had previously raised the issue of individual freedom or self-government threatened by new economic powers. Indeed, the issue remained at the forefront of intellectual thought and public discourse through the 1920s, demonstrated by the trail of

John Dewey's writings which try to theorize the relationship between new economic forms of power and their effect on social unity and politics. The issue began to recede from public discourse partly due to the ideological u-turn induced by the red scare of 1919, but largely due to the economic prosperity of the 1920s overseen by Republican presidents who, like Herbert Hoover, identified US national identity with individualism and *laissez-faire*, small federal government. Hoover's 1922 conservative classic, *American Individualism*, defined the United States in terms of its difference from the discredited European states which he described as apparently all too willing to sacrifice individual freedom to the paternalism and the vainglorious nature of the nation-state. The worst economic depression the country had ever known provided the conditions for a re-visioning of this popular individualist ideology of the 1920s. In this context emerged a politician and his advisors who could clearly recognize the conditions and carry out a long-term project of re-organizing social knowledge.

But how was FDR's response conjuncturally possible? First, he and his strategists picked up the Progressive reconceptualization of individual freedom with its stated economic and political enemies. As commentators since Hofstadter (1955) have noted, the public discourse of proto-economic rights in the Progessive era occurred in conditions of relative prosperity. This suggests that the public and intellectual discourse recognized something even more serious than the need for protection against the vagaries of the economic cycle – the control of economic modernity. As FDR would describe in his Commonwealth Club Address, the era was anxiously aware that the old agrarian myth of economic and political independence (self-government) was indeed a myth by 1932. Thus, FDR was picking up the American critique of capitalist modernity in a new conjuncture that forced the center leftwards. He was not just contemplating policy options in an ongoing intellectual debate about modernity in a time of relative prosperity. In 1933 the civilian unemployment rate is estimated to have been as high as 25 percent or 15 million people, and for non-farm employees it was closer to 38 percent (Fearon 1987, p. 138). There was a palpable anxiety about *not just being but becoming poor* under the conditions of this conjuncture. FDR's (by which I mean his communication team's) adroit reinterpretation of American history that saw government's function and size (as well as its relation to individual freedom) as historically contingent, his divisions of government, freedom, and rights into economic and political forms, and his re-articulation of government inactivity with the encouragement of communism and fascism – all remain important examples of effective strategic conjunctural negotiation (and fertile ground for strategies in the present).

Yet FDR's call for the political and possibly constitutional acknowledgment of economic rights was met with hostility by a part of the American population. And, if American collective memory would not soon forget the trauma of the Great Depression and the frames FDR offered to confront it, economic rights nonetheless failed to make a permanent home in American public discourse and law. The shift in public discourse away from FDR's discourse of economic rights must be seen as conjunctural and contingent, extra-disursive and discursive.

From the post-war conjuncture to the Reagan revolution[4]

Throughout the 1950s and 1960s, FDR's economic rights discourse and specifically his statement on the EBR continued to inform American political discourse and to exert influence on US socio-economic policy agendas, including Democratic Party platforms. However, during this time, cultural shifts were beginning to create a conjuncture very unlike the one that had originally facilitated FDR's discourse. It is important to identify some of them in order to understand the larger cultural situation that in many ways encouraged Reagan's great u-turn in economic rights discourse and policy.

The Reagan conjuncture is characterized most of all by a distrust of an interventionist/activist federal government. Five major cultural currents developed in the decades preceding Reagan and contributed to this widespread distrust, permitting Reagan's own, and very different, discourse of economic rights to flourish. These include: (1) the Cold War vilification of extending socio-economic rights such as health care; (2) a massive turn inward by the citizen-subject, linked to the rise of consumer culture, widespread prosperity in the 1950s, and the 'therapeutic self'; (3) a political cultural shift in which poverty and social programs became racialized; (4) a two-pronged dissatisfaction with the federal government issuing from the New Left generally and against the Vietnam War in particular; (5) an economic crisis in the 1970s marked by soaring inflation and unemployment rates.

First, the Cold War attacked much of the social knowledge that underpinned the New Deal such as socio-economic interdependence of citizens and the need for a vigilant government to regulate corporations. New forms of social belonging based partly on an overarching ideology of consumerism and Cold War fear eclipsed the concerns of an economic human rights discourse launched by FDR and taken up in the United Nation's Declaration of Human Rights. The social knowledge that drove the narratives of the New Deal was baited as the fast track to Bolshevism in the 1950s (Poen 1979). Such developments made calls for economic rights seem untimely, if not altogether unnecessary. That was until Lyndon Johnson alerted the country to a problem that had unsurprisingly gone unnoticed in the prior 15 years of public discourse – the richest country in the world had a poverty problem. Yet, a strange cultural calculus was underway, one that would conspire with already-existing post-war trends to reverse the momentum towards the realization (in law, public discourse, and material conditions) of FDR's economic rights.

In close relation to Cold War anti-communist ideologies articulated to policies on regulation and redistribution is the economic shifts in the booming 1950s, themselves closely related to federal policies such as the GI Bill, new cultural technologies like television, and new subjectivities that re-imagined social life, the self and individual freedom. Rising like a phoenix from the ashes of pre-war depression and labor-management strife, American corporate capitalism began a new project during the 1950s, what Liz Cohen (2003) has called 'A Consumer's Republic.' It was a project of recoding freedom which renewed the early twentieth century project of consumer capitalism, adapting it to the new social conditions of corporate dependence, in the process helping to erase the memory of the contradictions posed by the agrarian myth and democratic-republican political economy. Unions began their long decline in membership, and corporate welfare (through the provision of pensions and health insurance) partially offset the demands for a full-bodied American welfare state.

The expansion of consumer capitalism initiated a turn away from participatory democracy and socio-economic solutions to public problems, instead favoring an increasingly self-directed therapeutic model for social cures. One paradox of the conjuncture was that consumerism increased but economic independence decreased. As evident in the long, slow demise of the family farm and the small-scale entrepreneur, the threat to the economic independence of the citizen was potentially bigger and more obtrusive than ever (Decker 1997, p. 102). Ideological struggles were waged over the framing of these socio-economic changes. David Riesman's *The Lonely Crowd* appeared in 1950, announcing that the producer-oriented personality had been replaced by a consumer-oriented personality. The quintessence of this change in economic citizen-subject, Riesman lamented, was perfectly demonstrated by the popular Dale Carnegie's self-improvement manual *How to Win Friends and Influence People* (1936). Three major books appeared in 1956 complementing Riesman's claims. William Whyte's *The Organization Man*, C. Wright Mills' *The Power Elite*, and Robert L. Heilbroner's *The Quest For Wealth* '[e]ach pondered what Heilbroner called "the dehumanization of the personality" in corporate society' (Decker 1997, p. 103). Individual freedom was suffering in this period, these authors suggested (as had Dewey in the early 1930s in his 'Individualism, Old and New' essays), due to State-corporate organization of society. FDR's endorsement of the large planning State that inevitably transferred the locus of individual freedom from production to leisure/private life no doubt contributed to the shift in these conditions. His proposal of an EBR did nothing to reduce the advancement of the corporatization of American culture.

Despite these critics' assaults on the giant organization, the source of individual freedom had been transferred in American public and popular discourse from production to consumption. In a sweeping discussion of post-war America, historian Liz Cohen (2003) saw that shift in conceptions of freedom and citizenship entrenched in late twentieth century American consumer culture (and continuing to this day). According to Cohen, the new citizen-consumer has roots in the Great Depression, where he/she was put to into the service of saving capitalism and, with government, of safeguarding rights of consumers for the 'general good.' However, this more deliberate citizen-consumer (deliberately buying goods from businesses displaying the National Recovery Administration's blue eagle sticker and the slogan 'we do our part'),[5] invested in the culture of consumption, gave way after World War II to the 'purchaser citizen.' For the latter ideal typical consumer, 'satisfying personal wants actually served the national interest, since economic recovery after a decade and a half of depression and war depended on a dynamic mass consumption economy' (Cohen 2003, pp. 8–9). The purchaser citizen judges government policies based on how well they serve individual consumption. A good sign of how the consumer republic had taken over the political imaginary in the 1950s was the 1959 debate between Richard Nixon and Nikita Khrushchev, where:

> the two leaders did not discuss missiles, bombs, or even modes of government. Rather, they argued over the relative merits of American and Soviet washing machines, televisions, and electric ranges. According to the American vice-president, the essence of the good life provided by democracy was contained within the walls of the suburban home. (May 1999, p. 158)

But the impact of consumerism on citizenship/political culture also corresponded to a post-war consensus between business and labor. In 1956, 33 percent of the private sector labor force was unionized; by 1998, that number had dropped to 0.1 percent. Real weekly earnings of American workers increased steadily until they hit a peak in 1972–1973. By 1956 there were more Americans in white-collar service jobs than in manufacturing (Farber & Western 2001). The American labor movement had been a formidable advocate for economic rights from the late nineteenth century to World War II. But the prosperity of the 1950s in a Keynesian and military industrial complex economy defused the urgency of demands for economic rights in the 1930s that had percolated upward to FDR's presidential discourse. In addition, the Cold War ideological link of communism with labor power helped produce the Taft–Hartley Act of 1947, which outlawed sympathy strikes and obligated unions to prove their anti-communist credentials (by having leaders sign affidavits). Thus, a major voice in the American discourse of liberal welfare economic rights was muffled. Interestingly, when the American economy began to change in the 1970s and gaps between rich and poor began increasing each successive year, the dominant response was not a return to a Rooseveltean government-planned economy or redistributive solution. Quite the opposite.

Since scholars like Cohen see the post-war conjuncture as a process of shifting citizenship imaginaries from participatory democracy to participatory consumerism, it is important to understand their roots in FDR's own economic rights discourse. In this set of relations, the issue of race became articulated to economic rights, and FDR's own economic rights discourse provided its discursive condition of possibility. By the late 1950s, ever-present racial problems boiled in the contradictions of post-war social policy. Policies that aimed to provide economic security for returning servicemen, such as the GI Bill of Rights, were sabotaged in implementation through widespread race and class discrimination. Returning African-American war veterans could not take advantage of the GI Bill's educational opportunities if they were turned away from colleges across the color line. Likewise, many African-American war veterans were unable to qualify for loans from private banks or building and loan associations with discriminatory lending practices. In addition, these government agencies respected and reinforced 'red-lining' practices to keep African-Americans out of white neighborhoods (Cohen 2003, pp. 169–170). Thus, both the educational and home ownership opportunities afforded by the GI Bill were limited in scope and differentially applied. The policy failed to relieve a serious housing crisis among African-Americans that included 'doubling up' in small spaces such as trailers, and continued in the supposed boom times of the 1950s.

The GI Bill of Rights was only the beginning of the post-war racialization of economic rights. While demands for regulation of the economy and its huge concentrations of capital in the name of individual freedom were supplanted by the celebration of 1950s consumerist freedom, a racialized material reality that contradicted the official ideology of openness and prosperity had developed differentially in tandem. The irony of FDR's economic rights proposals in this context is that even those initiatives he did see passed into law, such as the GI Bill of Rights and the Social Security Act of 1935, were denied in practice to large numbers of African-Americans due to discriminatory implementation.

FDR's 1944 proposal of an EBR specifically stipulated that these rights should belong to all Americans regardless of race or creed; economic rights would be granted to all Americans and thus protect citizens in a race-blind fashion. For this reason, FDR did not address head-on the issue of racism in American culture and history with specific legislation. Such a move, historians have acknowledged, allowed him to maintain the fragile Democratic coalition of southern Democrats, labor, and urban ethnics (Dawley 1991, pp. 391–392). Yet, the strengths and weaknesses of New Deal economic rights laws (primarily the Social Security Act of 1935), when compared with the inclusiveness of FDR's proposed EBR, became evident when confronted by the material realities of the post-war period.

These factors, prior to the 1960s, kept large numbers of African-Americans from receiving the benefits of the Social Security Act, part of FDR's EBR. African-Americans' need for these benefits, however, was enormous. In fact, African-Americans faced an economic situation that was not nearly as open to upward mobility for deskilled laborers in industry as it had been for past generations of ethnic immigrants into American urban areas. In short, FDR signed into law a two-tiered system that was differentiated not by race but by participation in the labor market. Children, the people who have to raise them, and people who cannott get a job are those excluded from the labor market. They have access to a secondary tier of benefits, one that does not secure economic rights. Thus, women, children, and those to whom the market is not kind (disproportionately, African-Americans) are excluded from the economic rights legacy that FDR left in law, even if his 1944 EBR was more expansive.

The New Deal's Social Security Act began to show its limitations to reformers in the 1960s on race and gender grounds. Its gender limitations stemmed from the idea that 'kicking women out of the labor force was the solution to unemployment,' a widespread masculine idea during the 1930s (Bernstein 1985). Labor interests and maternalist groups who helped shape the Social Security Act figured women exclusively as mothers, unpaid domestic workers, and an income subsidy that kept mothers out of the workforce, the domain of men, was completely consonant with these groups' aims. Women who were making claims on the state were also seen as 'deserving,' because of 'respectable' reasons such as the death of or desertion by a spouse. They were also, for the most part, white (Goldberg *et al.* 2001).

Race combined with the gender exclusion of these New Deal economic rights policies in powerful ways that came to overwhelm economic rights discourse from the 1960s to the present. In practice, it was premised on the exclusion of African-Americans from the budding welfare state, and assumed that contributory old-age insurance and unemployment insurance would eventually include all Americans and leave only a very small number of destitute or non-employable on public assistance. But once African-Americans gained political rights and African-American urban poverty gained notice in the 1960s, the public assistance rolls swelled with formerly excluded poor African-Americans. In addition, reformers could not predict that the Vietnam War and America's shifting international position in the 1970s would make increasingly impossible the assumption that federal funding could be available for middle-class and anti-poverty programs (Skocpol 1988, p. 306).

This racialized material situation (unameliorated African-American poverty as structure for reproduced African-American poverty) combined with other cultural factors I have mentioned (the turn 'inward,' the cult of consumption, the decline of labor power in the Cold War) to encourage news and public opinion formation figuring public assistance in racial terms, without seeing the racist structural origins of much poverty. The civil rights movement had turned more economically-demanding (see King's [1967] call for a Poor People's Bill of Rights) and shared the cultural spotlight on race in the 1960s with the militant black power movement. Whites, especially the majority not living in close proximity with African-Americans, continued to imagine them (and continue to do so today) in ways that did not correspond to their lived reality. This is especially true of public opinion about poverty, work ethic, and African-Americans.[6] Majorities of white Americans wrongly believe that there are more African-Americans than whites living in poverty, for example (Gilens 1999).

In addition, African-American welfare recipients in the 1960s swelled. The increase was due partly to huge de-industrialization that left thousands of African-American men unemployed in the northern cities to which they had fled by the millions in the 1940s and 1950s. It was also due to the work of the civil rights movement to secure for African-Americans the government assistance for which they were eligible and had been deprived. But this rise in African-American welfare recipients was met with new social welfare practices and discourses that shifted the locus of the problem of poverty from society and economic structure (solutions to which were redistribution, education, housing, regulation) to the individual or the family. The shift in discourses of poverty and social welfare produced a therapeutic, non-economic solution to it. The poverty subject becomes medicalized, labeled as suffering from a psychopathology identified as 'dependency.' This idea of dependency was popularized in the 'culture of poverty'/cycle of poverty thesis (Goldberg *et al.* 2001, p. 76, Schram 2000, p. 60). The rise of conservative think tanks in the 1960s and 1970s, including the Heritage Foundation, the American Enterprise Institute, and the Cato Institute, helped circulate these conceptions of the source of and solution to poverty through countless pamphlets, press releases and public appearances (Hood 1995). Reagan would draw heavily on this shift in institutional knowledge and discourse about poverty.

The issues of race, federal assistance, and white resentment combined in a distrust of the federal government. A racially embedded, white southern distrust toward the federal government was reawakened during the civil rights movement. President Eisenhower's enforcement of the Brown ruling (1954) by ordering federal troops into Little Rock, Arkansas in 1957 re-tapped the Southern distrust. By 1963, civil rights demonstrations exploded across the nation, and President Kennedy televisually announced that the nation was facing a 'moral crisis' (Foner 1998, p. 280). The Civil Rights Act of 1964 was more reason for racist southerners to distrust the federal government. Thus George Wallace in 1964 developed what Richard Nixon would follow as the 'Southern Strategy,' whereby Southern whites would be coaxed from the Democratic Party on the issue of race (coded in appeals to Federalism, separation of powers, and 'law and order') and Southern racists like Wallace who 'delivered' votes to the Republicans would gain some issue power in the Party's agenda (p. 315). A chief Nixon White House aide made a diary entry in 1969 which admitted the new racialized Republican strategy to vilify the Federal Welfare policy (in Gilens 1999, p. 126).

Not just limited to the South, the racially motivated resentment of government policies continued with race riots and housing and busing rulings, including the 1963 California passage of Proposition 14, which repealed a 'fair housing law' banning racial discrimination in the sale of real estate. Reagan used the issue as a major part of his platform that won him the 1966 California gubernatorial election, defending the right of homeowners in a 'free society' to 'discriminate against Negroes' if they chose' (Gilens 1999, p. 126). Here was a good example of the growing shift of economy–government–freedom discursive relations. In addition, working class whites in Boston, New York's Canarsie, and other neighborhoods responded vociferously to court rulings that required busing to achieve integration. The net result was a growing white cultural discontent with government, channeled mainly at the federal level.

As mentioned earlier, FDR's economic rights were not grounded in participatory democracy, and this fact of political alienation exchanged for consumer freedom played a role in new social movements. In so far as the New Left and other social movements were reactions against centralized power, they may also be seen as the return of the politically repressed in FDR's material EBR policies. The New Left cried out for equality and participatory democracy, just as they did so in opposition to 'corporate liberalism' and the centralization of economy and government. Thus the New Left's 'parallel organizations' sought to go around the government and other established institutions, if not to overturn them, with their 'freedom schools, free universities, free cities . . . and self-controlled communities' (Zinn 1971, p. 47). But the New Left and countercultural effects on individualism were paving the way for an altogether new political landscape in the 1970s. At the same time, the post-war political culture had been attracting more and more adherents to the neo-*laissez-faire*, libertarian wing of the Republican Party, the Goldwater–Reagan wing. This wing was kept at bay within its own party until the mid-1970s (taken as a lesson from Goldwater's defeat in 1964). Yet by the 1980s, the GOP's formerly contained anti-statism could now trumpet its creed without serious party opposition.

All of these political and cultural developments must also be put in the context of a struggle between Keynesian and Hayekean economic imaginaries within an elite institutional sphere of debate. The inflation of the 1970s led major economists and politicians to slowly reject Keynesian policies of spending and ownership of the 'commanding heights of the economy.' Spearheaded transatlantically by Ronald Reagan and Margaret Thatcher, privatization of state-owned industry and deregulation of markets became the new mantra for prosperity. This complex economic debate was won at elite and global institutional levels and passed down to public discourse and policy often without significant public scrutiny, certainly while producing and managing populist dissatisfaction, often articulated to race, immigration, and government. In the convergence of these conjunctural factors, the Reagan–Goldwater wing of the Republican Party seized the day, astutely reading and taking advantage of the discursive and policy possibilities in a conjuncture changed by the aforementioned confluence of factors. More recently, this economic rights imaginary has sought to penetrate the farthest reaches of the globe (Hertz 2003, Yergin & Stanislaw 2002) and has done so under the interference of a global war on terror.

Discourses of the present crisis and the history of economic rights

All of which brings us to the present moment. An empirical documentation of the discursive production of the crisis and its possible solutions is an important first step in figuring out what resources are most useful from the history of American economic rights. Mediation of the crisis is vital to its contingent political imaginary. People ask questions such as, 'Does this crisis affect just me?' (How broad is the scope?) Diagnostic and Prescriptive frames (Snow & Benford 1988, p. 200) of the crisis will offer causes and solutions. News media have a bad reputation for compressing debate and simplifying issues. How might a more radically democratic concept of economic rights find voice today? Can new media play a key role in challenging the impediments of old media? How did they appear in this public discourse of economic crisis?

While economic conditions have changed in the present conjuncture and the discourse of economic rights is being reconstituted, this is taking place in ways that fail to re-think the foundational premises in the liberal social welfare and *laissez-faire* articulations of economy–government–individual freedom triad. It is perhaps obvious to note that Reagan and FDR, along with their primary economic theorists, Friedman/Hayek and Keynes, have had an increased presence in American public discourse about the economic crisis and the deliberations over policy directions for the United States and world.[7] The major economic theorists behind both men's economic visions,[8] Keynes and Friedman, also show spikes.[9] They all four appear as something like popular economic spiritual leaders. Keynes in particular has enjoyed a resurgent popularity, playing the genius who fell into neglect and whom we should re-enlist for understanding and resolving the crisis. Unfortunately, most of the frames are simple and amount to little more than a popular plea for an increased government role in primary and occasionally regulating the economy, without a serious structural reconsideration of government–economy–freedom.

In 'Paradigm Lost' (*Boston Globe* 21 December 2008), Drake Bennett writes, 'Classical economics was devastated by the Great Depression, and in the years afterward gave way to the ideas of the British economist John Maynard Keynes: that individually rational economic decisions could add up to collectively disastrous consequences, that the "stickiness" of prices and wages could lead to long-term unemployment and stagnation, and that the government, as a result, has to step in to kick-start the economy.' In the *New Republic*, John B. Judis (2009) devoted an entire feature article to Keynes, 'A Man For All Seasons,' discussing favorably Keynes' contributions to solving the Great Depression and prophesying post-war economic cycles. He ends by urging the Obama administration (and thus a consenting public) to 'venture into some areas that Keynes contemplated but previous administrations have avoided,' while noting that Obama will have to consider areas that Keynes could not anticipate, such as government subsidizing some industries over others (for example, due to global warming and finite oil supplies). Likewise, Keynes was invoked by Forbes.com, where a headline read: 'What Would Keynes Do?' (Bartlett 2008). The lead paragraph reads: 'Every day that goes by makes clearer the parallels between the current financial crisis and the one that led to the Great Depression.' The aspects of Keynes' thought are also, importantly, selectively distilled.

In the same Forbes.com article, Bruce Bartlett (2008), former Treasury Department economist, praises Keynes' insight that the government must step in under certain conditions, mainly when money is supplied faster than people spend it – when '[b]anks, businesses, and households are hoarding cash.' Bartlett wants to stimulate growth and consumption. He mentions that government investment in green public works programs would be one way to help out, but he argues that it would take too much time to help immediately. For him, the government must start buying 'tangibles,' from labor to raw materials.

After the Bush government's nationalization of Fannie Mae and Freddie Mac (to say nothing of Republicans' support of the auto bailout), a new window of opportunity appears for enduring political struggles, not the least of which is economic rights, an umbrella concept that shelters a myriad of social welfare or even radically democratic policy vistas. Those policy vistas stand little chance of being seriously considered without the circulation of strategic discourse, followed by the production of public opinion (whether measured by opinion polls or YouTube videos, blogs, letters to political representatives, or people organized into rallies). But the struggle is not then big versus small government in this context, but rather how the role of government gets articulated to concepts and histories of democracy, freedom, and economy.

Economists as 'liberal' as Paul Krugman (2008) and Bruce Bartlett (2008) insist that the government has an important interventionist role to play in the economy. But that role is mostly limited to 'public spending' to prime spending and growth in the market economy. Few widely circulating voices (non-'radical'-branded, non-academics) go so far as to use this crisis to rethink the market consumer economy that worships growth, and creates vast disparities in wealth, standard of living, and thus freedoms. They certainly have not used the crisis yet to re-think the relationship of freedom–economy–democracy. Benjamin Barber's recent somewhat tepid reconsideration of hegemonic discourses of the 'good life' as neo-liberal consumerist is about as close as I have seen in public discourse, albeit appearing in the political niche publication *The Nation*. Barber (2009) questions the economy of consumer growth and the cultural values that drive it. 'The issue,' he writes circumspectly, 'is not the death of capitalism but what kind of capitalism – standing in which relationship to culture, to democracy, to life.'

Barber calls for what I understand as a cultural revolution. The current crisis, Barber contends, cannot be solved by consumer stimulus and more multiplex malls. He suggests cutting consumer spending from 70 percent of gross domestic product (GDP) (currently) to 50 percent over the next 10 years, 'bringing it roughly where Germany's GDP is today. The Germans have a commensurate standard of living and considerably greater equality. Imagine all the things we could do without having to shop: play and pray, create and relate, read and walk, listen and procreate – make art, make friends, make homes, make love.' While his particular statement will surely strike some negatively as a bit hippy-ish, he seems correct to note that a shift from consumerist values of the good life to something else will require a 'fundamental cultural change,' which will no doubt work in unpredictable but necessary relations with the political and economic domains.

The lost histories of economic rights (American and others, including those of Ancient Greece) are histories of the present that provide tools for thinking the present conjuncture in radically different democratic ways. It provides the opportunity to rethink at once a naturalized economic hegemony and an out-of-control technocratized caricature of democracy, and to popularize an alternative. Political rights were abstracted from everyday conditions of economic, gender, and race exploitation (which in reality were inseparable). From these conditions arose struggles for social, economic and civil rights as ways of attacking the hegemony of liberal modernity. Looking at the current crisis from the genealogical economic rights perspective shows some interesting changes and overlooked possibilities. There are several cultural-political-economic shifts across the genealogy and from FDR to Reagan and the present. For now, I will introduce four and their implications for current interventions.

(1) *The change in articulations of religion to economic rights and political imaginaries generally*. There is obviously no necessary correspondence between Christianity (I emphasize it since it is the dominant religion in the United States) and unconstrained capitalism. In the colonial period, there was preacher Cotton Mather and others preaching that the Devil was recognized in the discourse of equality, always tempting the vulnerable

with fantasies of shirking work and rising above the station God had assigned them. However, there was preacher George Davis Herron (1890/1990) who was part of the widespread social gospel movement at the end of the nineteenth century. Similarly, labor activism and socialism were also articulated to Christianity at the end of the nineteenth and beginning of the twentieth century. According to historian Herbert Gutman, the socialist lawyer and later presidential Eugene Debs 'bristled with Christian indignation at human suffering and cannot be understood outside that framework' (1977, p. 98). Like other social institutions, Left Christianity and its articulations of religion to economy and politics have suffered greatly since the Cold War. More recently, the American Christian Right has managed to articulate its social issues to the free market (http://www.publiceye.org/magazine/v21n1/meagher_tax_revolt.html). American religious practices and discourses of the past were often articulated to what I have called the democratic-republican tradition of economic rights.

(2) *The change in the articulations of race to economic security as freedom*. This relationship has often been replaced by articulations of race to cultural recognition/representation (which I am not arguing is unimportant; just replete with effects on material wellbeing when disarticulated from the economic). Economic rights became racialized partly as a result of FDR's failure to address existing racial divisions of labor and the way many white Americans viewed benefits, and his Social Security Act's legal distinction between welfare and social security – another concession to southern leaders – that 'laid the basis for the eventual politicization of this division along racially charged lines' (Skocpol 1988, p. 302). At the same time, from Reagan to the present widely circulating race cards that have articulated social welfare/economic rights to theft, as in Reagan's trope of the 'Cadillac-driving welfare queen' using multiple names to collect multiple checks (Gilens 1999). Compare this to Martin Luther King's late plans for a poor people's movement, part of which emphasized the historical relationship of race to poverty in the United States (King 1967).

(3) *The change in articulation of political freedom/rights as dependent on economic security*. Before FDR, Woodrow Wilson made the 'new freedom' a pillar of his presidential platform. The 'administration of a great business . . . is not a private affair,' he proclaimed; 'it is a public affair' (Wilson 1913, p. 288). Furthermore, in his 1912 campaign he declared, 'I feel confident that if Jefferson were living in our day he would see what we see: that the individual is caught in a great confused nexus of all sorts of complicated circumstances, and that to let him alone is to leave him helpless as against the obstacles with which he has to contend; and that, therefore, law in our day must come to the assistance of the individual . . . Freedom to-day is something more than being let alone. The program of a government of

freedom must in these days be positive, not negative merely' (Wilson 1913). Are there not resources in this discourse? There are plenty other such statements, from icons of American public life. One can claim, with appeals to these icons, that democracy's political rights require positive economic rights based on corporate regulation and redistribution, not on liberal grounds that everyone deserves them *tout court*. The argument from democracy is harder to refute in the context of foreign military projects in its name.

(4) *The Ecological Factor*. Greenhouse Effect, Global Warming, and Climate Change discourses have been picking up speed in the United States since the 1980s. Obviously there was no opportunity to consider what consumer capitalism was doing *environmentally* to the United States or the world in 1932 when FDR proposed his economic rights. In that sense, the crisis of global warming is something to which the economic crisis can be articulated. This is clear in Barber's response earlier, as well as the conservative Bruce Bartlett's (the best the latter can do is admit that Green economic changes would be nice but would take too long, so money should be pumped into consumer spending immediately). The opportunity is here to re-think the very values and effects of the practices underlying the economy. Popular economic discourses are struggling to articulate with and disarticulate from environmental demands.

When George Bush and his legacy (however damaged they are by the Iraq War, the economic crisis, and the loss to Obama) call for the spread of free elections, free markets, and democracy in Iraq, articulating it to the War on Terror, as Bush did so many times since 2003, one must interject, 'What do you mean by democracy? The Founders of the United States, like leaders of previous democratic experiments, emphasized that one could not be politically free without a high degree of economic security. Unconstrained markets threaten an individual's economic and thus political security and freedom' (see Foner 1998, Goldwin & Schambra 1982, McCoy 1980, Nedelsky 1990, Wood 1969/1993). If American society does not overall have a vibrant interest in civic life (especially outside of presidential elections), it is not necessarily problematic for democracy and economic rights. The fact is that everyone continues to trumpet the sacral term 'democracy' as support for policy claims, especially deregulation. Why surrender democracy and freedom when there are icons in the American political tradition that clearly did not equate democracy with 'free' unconstrained markets and growth?

If the current form of post-Fordist American consumer economy was partly materialized through widely circulated discourses about the consubstantiation of freedom with un-regulated 'free' markets, via institutions such as the workplace (reading propaganda littering break rooms, mandatory films) (see Fones-Wolf 1994), schools, films (thanks to blacklists, for example), and opinion leaders, in addition to government purging of 'radical' opponents – then indeed a consideration of repressed forms of economic rights and democracy will require more than a few editorials in newspapers, presentations at professional conferences, or an article or two in professional journals. It will require multiple energies, articulations, and struggles, for which history provides resources.

> My position hasn't changed much. I think a political strategy which doesn't take account of cultural questions is living in the past. This does not imply that they should take priority over all the other kinds of struggle: the problem is precisely that they're seen as separate sectors – the 'economic wing', the political wing and the 'cultural wing.' Only when they are not seen as sectors can the effect of the important cultural arguments come through: that there is none of these sectors that does not immediately involve the others; that a lot of the major economic and industrial disputes are about cultural institutions. Whenever there's a move to concentrate on just one sector, it's often understandable in the context of the time, but it's always theoretically wrong. (Raymond Williams, *Screen Education*, summer 1979)

Notes

1 The method is historical and discourse-analytical. The archive consists of a synthesis of wide-ranging American histories, primary-source pamphlets, speeches, presidential press conferences and memoranda, and newspaper and magazine articles.

2 Of course, Jefferson was the author of the Declaration of Independence, not the US Constitution (Jefferson 1782/2005).

3 I choose to employ 'democratic-republican' as its ideas about economic rights are similar to those espoused by the political party founded by Thomas Jefferson and James Madison, though scholars often refer to it as 'republicanism' or 'civic republicanism.'

4 For a more detailed argument about the prelude to the Reagan conjuncture see Harsin (2005, chapter 6).

5 Former general and flamboyant head of the NRA Hugh Johnson devised these ways for citizens to recognize businesses that had voluntarily supported a new code devised to rescue the country and redeem US economic practice. The code's hallmarks were support of a 35–40 cent minimum wage; the abolition of child labor; and a 40 hour work week (Cohen 2003, pp. 8–10).

6 On the public opinion issue see Gilens (1999) and Neubeck and Cazenave (2001).

7 A search of 'major newspapers and wires' on Lexis-Nexis in early March 2009 for FDR in the prior six months revealed over 2,000 results, over 1,000 more than a year before. A search of Ronald Reagan in the prior six

months found Reagan a strong public presence, with over 3,000 citations, roughly the same number as the year before (of course closer analysis is needed to determine whether he was cited critically or favorably). The increase for Reagan was much clearer in magazines, where he rose over 100 percent, while FDR also rose in both categories by over 100 percent (accessed March 7, 2009).

8 I mean roughly speaking. It is true that both FDR and Reagan moved between various economic policies which could be viewed as inconsistent, certainly in FDR's case, but the policy facts still stand with de-regulation and regulation, taxation, social security, labor law, and securities, etc.

9 Again, the preferred Republican theorist (Friedman) had more initial attention, while Keynes has been cited slightly more in the six months since Bush publicly declared a crisis (332 > 317). Results were similar for searches of television network and cable news shows and popular talk show transcripts; likewise for blogs.

References

Barber, B. (2009) 'A revolution in spirit', *The Nation*, 22 February. Available at: http://www.thenation.com/doc/20090209/barber (accessed 7 March 2009).

Bartlett, B. (2008) 'What would Keynes do?', *Forbes*, 5 December. Available at: http://www.forbes.com/2008/12/04/depression-deflation-velocity-oped-cx_bb_1205bartlett.html (accessed 7 March 2009).

Bennett, D. (2008) 'Paradigm lost', *Boston Globe*, 21 December.

Bernstein, I. (1985) *A Caring Society: The New Deal, the Worker, and the Great Depression*, Boston, MA, Houghton Mifflin.

Carnegie, D. (1981) *How to Win Friends & Influence People*, NY, Pocket Books.

Cohen, L. (2003) *A Consumer's Republic*, New York, Alfred A. Knopf.

Dawley, A. (1991) *Struggles for Justice: Social Responsibility and the Liberal State*, Cambridge, Harvard University Press.

Decker, J. L. (1997) *Made in America: Self-styled Success from Horatio Alger to Oprah Winfrey*, Minneapolis, MN, University of Minnesota.

Dewey, J. (1984) *Individualism, Old and New. The later works, 1925–1953*, Vol. 5, 1929–1930. Carbondale: Southern Illinois University Press.

Diner, S. J. (1998) *A Very Different Age: Americans of the Progressive Era*, New York, Hill and Wang.

Farber, H. S. & Western, B. (2001) 'Accounting for the decline of unions in the private sector, 1973–1998', *Journal of Labor Research*, vol. 22, no. 3, pp. 459.

Fearon, P. (1987) *War, Prosperity, and Depression: the U.S. Economy, 1917–45*, Lawrence, KS, University of Kansas Press.

Foner, E. (1998) *The Story of American Freedom*, New York, New Press.

Fones-Wolf, E. (1994) *Selling Free Enterprise*, Urbana, IL, University of Illinois Press.

Gilens, M. (1999) *Why Americans Hate Welfare*, Chicago, IL, University of Chicago Press.

Goldberg, G. S. & Collins, S. D. (2001) *Washington's New Poor Law: Welfare 'Reform' and the Roads not Taken, 1935 to the Present*, New York, Apex Press.

Goldwin, R. A. & Schambra, W. A. (eds) (1982) *How Capitalist is the Constitution?* Washington, DC, American Enterprise Institute.

Gutman, H. (1977) *Work, Culture, and Society in Industrializing America*, New York, Vintage.

Habermas, J. (1998) *Between Facts and Norms: Contributions to a Discourse Theory of Law and Democracy*, Cambridge, MIT Press.

Harsin, J. P. (2005) *Two Episodes in the American Discourse of Economic Rights: Franklin Delano Roosevelt and Ronald Reagan*, Unpublished PhD Dissertation, Northwestern University, Evanston, IL.

Heilbroner, R. L. (1956) *The Quest for Wealth: A Study of Acquisitive Man*, New York, Simon and Schuster.

Herron, G. D. (1990) 'The message of Jesus to men of wealth'. Available at: http://douglassarchives.org/herr_a14.htm (accessed 22 June 2000). (Originally published 1890.)

Hertz, N. (2003) *The silent take-over: Global capitalism and the death of democracy*, New York, HarperCollins.

Hofstadter, R. (1955) *The Age of Reform: From Bryan to FDR*, New York, Alfred A. Knopf.

Hood, J. (1995) 'Send in the tanks – think tanks – NR's guide to the new majority', 11 December. Available at: http://www.findarticles.com/p/articles/mi_m1282/is_n23_v47/ai_17863078

Jefferson, T. (2005) *Notes on the State of Virginia*. Available at: http://www.samford.edu/~drbains/relg304/jeff-notes.html/ (accessed 22 May 2006). (Originally published 1782.)

Judis, J. B. (2009) 'A man for all seasons', *New Republic*, January 21.

King, M. L. Jr (1967) 'Where do we go from here?' Available at: http://www.indiana.edu/~ivieweb/mlkwhere.html (accessed 11 May 2009).

Krugman, P. (2008) 'What to Do', *New York Review of Books*, vol. 55, no. 20. Available at: http://www.nybooks.com/articles/22151 (accessed 7 March 2009).

Livingston, J. (1994) *Pragmatism and the Political Economy of Cultural Revolution, 1850–1940*, Chapel Hill, NC, University of North Carolina Press.

May, E. T. (1999) *Homeward Bound*, New York, Basic Books.

McCoy, D. (1980) *The Elusive Republic: Political Economy in Jeffersonian America*, New York, Norton.

Nedelsky, J. (1990) *Private Property and the Limits of American Constitutionalism*, Chicago, IL, University of Chicago Press.

Neubeck, K. J. & Cazenave, N. A. (2001) *Welfare Racism: Playing the Race Card against America's Poor*, New York, Routledge.

Ober, J. (2000) 'Quasi rights: participatory citizenship and negative liberties in democratic Athens', *Social Philosophy and Policy*, vol. 17, no. 1, pp. 27–61.

Poen, M. (1979) *Harry S. Truman versus the Medical Lobby*, Columbia, MO, University of Missouri Press.

Reagan, R. (1987) 'Address to the nation on the Venice economic summit, arms control, and the deficit', 15 June. Available at: http://originalsources.com/ (accessed 9 July 2003).

Reagan, R. (1987) 'Remarks announcing America's economic bill of rights', in *Public Papers of the Presidents*, 3 July, Washington, DC: US Government Printing Office, CD-Rom (accessed 1 March 2000).

Reisman, D. (1950) *The Lonely Crowd*, New Haven, CT, Yale University Press, Studies in National Policy.

Roosevelt, F. D. (1938) 'Campaign address on progressive government', in *The Public Papers and Addresses of Franklin D. Roosevelt, volume 1. The Genesis of the New Deal, 1928–1932*, ed. S. I. Rosenman, New York, Random House. (Originally published 1932.)

Roosevelt, F. D. (1944) 'State of the Union address', 11 January. Available at: http://www.presidency.ucsb.edu/ (accessed 1 August 2003).

Schram, S. F. (2000) *After Welfare: The Culture of Postindustrial Social Policy*, New York, New York University Press.

Skocpol, T. (1988) The limits of the New Deal system and the roots of contemporary welfare dilemmas. In *The Politics of Social Policy in the United States*, eds. M. Weir *et al.*, Princeton, NJ, Princeton University Press, pp. 293–312.

Snow, D. A. & Benford, R. (1988) 'Ideology, frame resonance, and participant mobilization', *International Social Movement Research*, vol. 1, pp. 197–217.

Whyte, Jr., W. H. (1956) *The Organization Man*, NY, Simon and Schuster.

Wilson, W. (1913) *The New Freedom*, New York, Doubleday. Available at: http://www.gutenberg.org/etext/14811 (accessed 20 April 2003).

Wood, G. (1993) *Creation of the American Republic*, New York, Norton. (Originally published 1969.)

Yergin, D. & Stanislaw, J. (2002) *The Commanding Heights. The Battle for the World Economy*, New York, Touchstone Book.

Young, I. M. (1995) 'Communication and the other: beyond deliberative democracy', in *Democracy and Difference*, ed. S. Benhabib, Princeton NJ, Princeton University Press.

Zinn, H. (1971) 'Marxism and the New Left', in *Politics of the New Left*, ed. M. Stolz, Beverly Hills, CA, Glencoe Press.

Darrin Hicks & Mathew Dunn

SPIRITS IN THE NIGHT

Reasonableness and the etho-politics of securities law

As the faith in a rational and efficient market collapses there has been a frantic search to account for the irrational motives underwriting economic behavior. A new popular discourse of economics grounded in behaviorism, models of social contagion, and the sociobiology of affect has emerged. We focus on one particularly influential instantiation of this new discourse, George Akerlof and Robert Schiller's work on Animal Spirits, which marries behavioral and neuro-economics to Keynes' insights on the role of affect on economic fluctuation. Animal Sprits, *we contend, is an attempt to define the parameters of and establish the strategies for the etho-political governance of the economy. To trace the historical emergence of this mode of etho-politics, we examine the contestation over what constitutes reasonable ethical demands on finance capital as they were formulated during the debates surrounding the passage of the 1933 Securities Act. We conclude that through re-examining this debate about the vulnerability of investors and the limits of the ethical demands this vulnerability warrants, we can recover reasonableness as a critical ideal to contest the terms of etho-politics, so as to alter what economists and policy-makers consider radical and necessary.*

The affective labor performed in the securities industry is critical to its success. Experienced investors demand that their brokers do more than provide accurate information and demonstrate facility in reading market trends. They desire a longstanding, personal relationship with them. Because they understand that such a relationship is a prerequisite for making sound financial judgments, particularly the broker's ability to deliver individualized risk assessments grounded in a detailed knowledge of their client's life-projects. The broker–client relationship is premised on care and commitment, relational goods constituted in and through communicative work. And it is the promise of such a caring and committed relationship that animates the advertising strategies of large brokerage houses and commercial banks. This commitment is the foundation of investors trust and confidence in the market, affective orientations needed to facilitate taking on greater risks in pursuit of greater profits.

Of course for the millions invested in mutual funds this so-called 'committed relationship' is nothing more than an empty promise. The vast majority of investors must rely on short infrequent consultations with relatively inexperienced and low-paid representatives from large investment firms, or more likely on forms of mediated contact such as quarterly reports, financial journalism and company websites. These virtual forms of human contact employ the language of care in their emotional marketing strategies but they cannot provide sufficient advice to make the financial decisions necessary to secure the 'value' of one's life. Left to choose a mutual fund, a choice often made on a marketing strategy like a celebrity endorsement, such as TIAA-CREF's immensely popular 'Lance Armstrong Livestrong Fund,' and told to ignore their quarterly statements for the next 20 years, they close their eyes and hope for the best.

This invitation to blind trust was often justified by pointing to the fact that mutual funds expose their contributors, most of whom have no experience in or knowledge of the market, to less risk than traditional forms of investment. Because of their greater vulnerability, mutual fund managers owe contributors a fiduciary duty; a duty to guide all investment decisions by the needs of contributors and what ensures their long-term security. This means avoiding investments in corporations with toxic asset-filled and overleveraged balance sheets. Or using the power of the fund's massive stock holdings as leverage to demand the directors of these public corporations to act in the interest of their owners (which is, by the way, the fund, and by extension, its contributors). Yet, despite owning almost 70 percent of the publicly traded shares, pension and mutual fund managers rarely exercise any meaningful supervision of 'board governance and structure, executive compensation, director elections, stock options proxy proposals or dividend policies' (Morgenson 2009, p. 2). They do not scour the balance sheets or balk at the compensation schemes that encouraged managers to manipulate short-term earnings at the expense of the corporation's long-term health. Fund managers in the search for larger returns have completely failed to perform their fiduciary duty. What they did, instead, was to assume that as long as the huge payouts on their bets in the market were rolling in, they should not ask questions. They blindly trusted that the future would be the same as the present. In short, they did exactly what the contributors did; they closed their eyes and hoped for the best.

The result has been a massive loss in confidence and the evisceration of trust. While every economist understands that confidence and trust play a critical role in the market, many of them do not have the conceptual tools to understand these affects and, thus, do not know how to restore them. Macro-economists have been deeply humbled by the present. Unable to predict or explain the present, they are now acknowledging that their belief in a rational and efficient market has not only been falsified, but is perhaps, as Jeremy Grantham (2009) has persuasively argued, the 'ultimate cause of the crisis.'

As the orthodoxy collapses, there has been a frantic search to account for the 'irrational' motives underwriting economic behavior. A new popular discourse of economics grounded in behaviorism has emerged, the best known works of this genre being Steven Levitt and Stephen Drubner's (2006) *Freakonomics*, Dan Ariely's (2008) *Predictably Irrational*, and Leonard Mlodinow's (2009) *The Drunkard's Walk*. This discourse has been married to the more technical, but increasingly popular, neuroscientific account of economic motives, set out by Andrew Lo (2009). Lo used magnetic resonance imaging to show that making money stimulates the same reward circuitry as cocaine. He argues that the last decade of prosperity anesthetized financiers' brains, lulling them into a state of complacency that caused them to take unwarranted risks.

Our interest lies in how these discourses inspire new forms of economic governance; a project exemplified by George Akerlof and Robert Schiller's (2009) book *Animal Spirits*. Akerlof and Schiller marry behavioral and neuroeconomics to Keynes' insights on monetary policy. *Animal Sprits* refer to the attitudes that shape economic behavior, most notably confidence, fear, bad faith corruption, and a sensitivity to unfairness. These spirits circulate through 'stories' we tell ourselves and others about our economic fortunes (and here they make the familiar argument that modern forms of mediation have sped up this circulation to the point these stories become self-fulfilling prophecies), 'possessing' agents and causing system wide fluctuations we experience as boom and bust cycles. For Akerlof and Schiller animal spirits are purely irrational remainders that, while not directly addressable, may be modified by rational policies. The presence of animal spirits, they argue, necessitates the steady hand of government to stimulate the economy as means of boosting confidence. Specifically by setting firm targets for aggregate demand and credit the uncertainty fueling market volatility settles, hopefully restoring confidence and, more importantly making clear the need for an appropriately large stimulus. In short, they take an unconventional route to justify a conventional response: classic Keynesian monetary policy.

We find ourselves, surprisingly, agreeing with Richard Posner (2009), that Akerlof and Schiller's inability to invent any novel policy proposals is explained by their bifurcation of reason and emotion, the rational and irrational; a split that Keynes did not make himself. Roberto Marchionatti (1999) shows that animal spirits for Keynes refer to the forces that lead investors to decide to invest in the face of volatility and uncertainty. Animal spirits are not motivated by a set of irrational urges, but the weight we give to particular types of evidence about how others will react to our presence in a shared environment.

What separates animal spirits from traditional models of economic rationality is that we do not weigh this evidence in terms of our calculations of probability. The conditions of uncertainty and volatility Keynes is concerned with explaining occur in relation to events where 'there is no scientific basis on which to form any calculable probability whatever' (quoted in Marchionatti 1999, p. 421). Rather, when we make a judgment that we will profit from engaging others in a particular environment we do so based on a reading of what he calls the 'atmosphere.' Here he is speaking to the sense that we have of the economic, political and social environment and whether we should engage in cooperative activity or disengage, a sense that we draw from in deciding to enter a room, a discussion, or an investment climate.

Teresa Brennan's (2004) *The Transmission of Affect* and Allan Lind's 'Fairness Heuristic Theory' (2001) also address the ability to 'read' the 'atmosphere' in just this way. Minimally, this skill involves the ability to be highly attuned to how others' feelings affect their judgment and to sense fluctuations in their intensity. Keynes suggested that the clearest embodiment of this skill was the successful entrepreneur (a very good stock analyst would also have this skill). His work on animal spirits was his attempt to explicate this ability, this form of knowledge and wisdom, in terms of how it conditions economic judgment. He did so, Marchionatti suggests, through the term 'reasonability.' Taking this term seriously, we suggest, opens up the possibility of accounting for how one may govern the economy through intervening in the 'atmosphere,' by directing our sense of what is reasonable or not. We argue that the 1933 Securities Act was just such an effort. Before we detail how, we briefly examine the least sexy, but most powerful term of etho-political governance: reasonableness.

Reasonableness has become '*the* normative standard for thinking and practice in a context that is both plural and democratic' (Rasmussen 2004, p. 525). It is at the heart of American jurisprudence. We could not think or practice criminal law, torts, contracts, corporate law, and the regulation of communication media without the concept. It is a ubiquitous feature of political argument. An analysis of the invocations of reasonableness in the *New York Times* editorial page from 1860 to 2004 (appearing in 22,314 editorials) reveals that reasonableness has several distinct meanings, modifies a large, but stable, class of referents, and works through a set of image schemata that demonstrate how reason is profoundly conditioned by our bodily experience (Hicks *et al.* 2005, Hicks 2006).

Here we address the referents the term conditions; the most common of these being demands, feelings, and amounts. What we want to draw attention to is that we describe each according to its intensity. That is, they are each described as unreasonable when they are either too intense, or less commonly, when they are too restrained. Moreover, reasonableness tends to modify each of these referents as they are in relation to others. One of the most common, and most important, uses of reasonableness is as a term that 'governs' how much we ought to feel for, charge, or demand from others. For example, Jack Bratich's (2003) work on conspiracy addresses the intensity of thought. Bratich notes that a defining feature of liberal governance is an internalized skepticism that guards us against excess conviction, keeping us from becoming too dogmatic or overly zealous. When this skepticism becomes excessive, however, liberal subjects quickly label it as conspiracy thinking, a paranoid style, as unreasonable. Reasonableness here works to 'moderate' thought, to keep it in 'balance,' and to render certain intensities of it as dangerous. This is true of feelings, amounts, and demands as well. It is certainly the case with 'animal spirits.' This is why reasonableness is such an important part of what Nikolas Rose has called etho-politics, the governing of choice through the activation and direction of feelings, sentiments, and values (Rose 2000).

Reasonableness, in this guise, often works as a means of legitimation. Often, but not always. For the remainder of the paper, we will explore a contest over the meaning of the term as it applies to the ethical demands we make on financial agents. The debate over the inclusion of reasonableness as fiduciary duty in the Securities Act of 1933 has been forgotten. This is because it was stricken at the last moment, but only after a year of intense contestation in Congress and the press. Defining reasonableness in terms of fiduciary obligation would have changed the character of the US finance capitalism; at least this was the claim of the business lobby that fought so hard against it. Franklin D. Roosevelt and his aide, Adolf Berle, used reasonableness as an etho-political intervention into the animal sprits that drove the post-depression economy. Here, we tell the story of the fight over the securities act in order demonstrate that reasonableness does not have to be a term of liberal legitimation. Roberto Unger's (1987) account of negative capability inspires this project, a genealogy that traces the historical path of losing ideas to show that the formative contexts that define our practical and passionate attachments are more malleable than we think. We aim to recover reasonableness as a critical ideal to contest the terms of liberal governance, so to alter what we consider radical and necessary. We begin with Franklin D. Roosevelt's etho-political vision of economic governance, detail the fight over the securities act, then move to a discussion of what constitutes a reasonable ethical demand on financial agents, and end with a parable about the dangers of the present narrative of crisis and reform.

Franklin D. Roosevelt's etho-politics

With weeks remaining in the 1932 presidential campaign, Roosevelt announced to the Commonwealth Club the 'day of enlightened administration had come.' (Roosevelt 1932) Bemoaning an increasing concentration of corporate power, Roosevelt warned, 'We are steering a steady course towards an economic oligarchy, if we are not there already' (Roosevelt 1932). His cure was not corporate dissimulation. Instead, Roosevelt insisted on 'modifying and controlling our economic units' to satisfy two basic rights: the right to earn a living wage, and the right to the safety of our savings and property (Roosevelt 1932). These conclusions directly contradicted the prevailing view that economic security had nothing to do with political freedom: 'Our government formal and informal, political and economic owes to everyone an avenue to possess himself of a portion of that plenty sufficient for his needs, through his own work' (Roosevelt 1932).

In his speech, Roosevelt distinguishes between two targets and methods of governance: the formal and informal, the political and the economic. This distinction serves two purposes. Rhetorically, as Jayson Harsin points out, it is a strategy that highlights the penetration of economic power into political life, threatening the rights of citizens to life and property, as the depression made clear (Harsin, this issue). Accountability and democratic control are therefore the correctives. The second distinction contrasts different modes of governance: formal and informal. Law and legislation constitute formal governance. But Roosevelt describes informal governance in expressly etho-political terms.

> I am very clear that they ['the great financial and industrial combinations'] must fearlessly and competently assume the responsibility which goes with power . . . [I]nstead of acting each for himself they must act together to achieve the common end. They must, where necessary, sacrifice this or that private advantage; and in reciprocal self-denial must seek a general advantage. It is here that formal government – political government, if you choose, comes in. Whenever in the pursuit of this objective the lone wolf, the unethical competitor, the reckless promoter, the Ishmael or Insull whose hand is against every man's, declines in achieving an end recognized as for being for the public welfare, and threatens to drag the industry back to a state of anarchy the government may properly be asked to apply restraint. (Roosevelt 1932)

This is a clear threat. The state will regulate if self-regulating 'enlightened businessmen' fail. Most importantly, Roosevelt is describing the ethical demands of power: responsibility, collaboration, the duty of self-abnegation, reciprocity, and a profound shift from self to public interest. These are the normative terms of 'informal' governance. They include the virtues and skills, norms and techniques, used to govern the ethical conduct of economic actors. Since it is not limited to 'formal' channels of governance, the state should be ready to hand with 'such assistance and balance as government can give' (Roosevelt 1932).

Taking a myriad of forms, such as 'public–private partnerships,' and 'ethics review boards,' these techniques of 'assistance and balance' later proved essential for inventing techniques, programs and policies for governing the economy 'at a distance' (Rose & Miller 2008, p. 39). If the economy is understood in ethical terms resulting from the economic impacts on family and community life, it can be articulated to a host of social and community ills. The corporation can be held responsible for its effects on these ills and corporations can be recruited to address these ills through direct mediation or philanthropic programs. These etho-political interventions may embody a hybrid form of formal and informal, juridical and ethical, modes of governance. We contend that the Securities Act is such an intervention. To understand how, we must examine the source of Roosevelt's model of etho-politics.

While disagreements concerning the extent of Roosevelt's written contribution to the Commonwealth Club address remain, all agree Adolf Berle, Professor of Law at Columbia University and member of Roosevelt's 'brain-trust,' wrote the sections on corporate concentration and the role of extant legal doctrine (Houck 2004, p. 265, Harsin 2005). Both the statement of the problem and the proposed solution set out in the speech came directly from his book, written with economist Gardiner Means, *The Modern Corporation and Private Property* (Berle & Means 1932), which *Time* magazine called the 'economic bible of the New Deal' (Tsuk 2005, p. 196). The book lays out how ownership and control slowly separated as stockholders traded their legal position of private ownership for the role of recipient of capital returns. Passive ownership replaced active control. Corporate managers, they maintained, who ran the day-today operations of the firm actually controlled the ownership.

Berle and Means framed this problem, quite literally, in terms of 'animal spirits.'

> It has often been said that the owner of a horse is responsible. If the horse lives he must feed it. If the horse dies he must bury it. No such responsibility attaches to a share of stock. The owner is practically powerless through his own efforts to affect the underlying property. The spiritual values that formerly went with ownership have been separated from it ... the responsibility and the substance which have been an integral part of ownership in the past are being transferred to a separate group in whose hands lies control. (Berle & Means 1932, p. 66)

This arrangement severed the interests between stockholders and managers and with it the relationship between self-interest and efficiency. Corporate managers owned so little of the company's stock no incentive remained to increase the corporation's value. Whereas stockholders preferred dividends from profits, managers preferred to reinvest profits, or worse, use profits to build opulent temples to work in, 'perks,' and to inflate salaries with bonuses. Moreover, powerful incentives to produce prompted shadow accounting methods meant to show greater profits, resulting in short-term gains in share price. Consequently, 'the managerial use of shareholder's property might be both self-interested and inefficient' (Tsuk 2005, p. 186).

Berle and Means drew a close parallel between passive ownership and workers who surrender their labor. In his review of the book for the *Nation,* titled 'Capitalist Confiscation,' Ernest Gruening concluded the 'American property "owner" has become simply a supplier of his savings to an economic super-state. He is hopeful of receiving a wage on that capital. What that wage shall be, or whether, indeed he shall receive any wage at all is matter determined wholly by others. He bids fair to be a capital wage slave!' (1933, p.117) The traditional logic of property and profits affording virtually unassailable rights to those property owners no longer has any real meaning when the sale of corporate securities dominates the economy.

The passive property owner's inability to exercise any meaningful control over her or his property, except to sell it at market rates, weakens her or his ethical right to demand compensation for mere ownership. That is, shareholders do not have an absolute right to the profits of capital. And while this allowed the corporation to seize 'the control' without any legitimate claim to ownership, the corporation simultaneously ceased to be a 'private business device' and, hence, ceased to be purely 'private property.' Therefore, publicly held business corporations were in essence public trusts. Corporate power, inasmuch as it depended on the 'existence and enforcement of the laws of contract and property by the state,' could be directed to promote the public interest, even when in tension with the interests of shareholders or the corporation itself (Tsuk 2005, p. 189). Berle and Means concluded *The Modern Corporation and Private Property* (1932) claiming corporate power should be exercised for the good of the community, maintaining corporate mangers and boards of directors were, in fact, fiduciaries for the community at large.

Here we come back to the Commonwealth Club address. Since Berle and Roosevelt maintained the untrammeled concentration of corporate power was legitimated through a self-serving interpretation of reasonableness at work in the so-called 'rule of reason' doctrine, redefining reasonableness to eliminate the rule was the solution. As Berle knew, and the Court's use of the 'rule of reason' doctrine made clear, reasonableness is not simply a legal formalism. It is the term used to define, justify, and contest the legitimacy of discretionary power. Reasonableness is the passage through which the ethical substance of the law enters and exits, and it uniquely addresses the juncture of formal and informal power, making it a ubiquitous, and indispensable, tool of liberal governance. The definition of reasonableness as fiduciary duty that Berle drafted in the Securities Act of 1933 would be the etho-political vehicle that he and Roosevelt would use to attempt to fundamentally reform the business culture of the United States. This fact was not lost on the financial community as the trenchant debate over the meaning of reasonableness at the heart of the Security Act made clear.

The fight over the Securities Act

The Roosevelt administration inherited a financial sector in ruins and Franklin D. Roosevelt turned his attention to restructuring the banking system and the securities market. In the 1920s there was a rush of inexperienced investors into a virtually unregulated market; hoping to cash in on the promises of the gilded age, the number of Americans owning stock increased five-fold with these new investors purchasing over $50 billion worth of securities (Means 1933, p. XX3). One-half of those securities had little or no value but issuers and underwriters, driven to increase the value of their securities, mislead and exploited their client's exuberance (Means 1933, p. XX3). Fraud was only part of the story; investment banks also fueled the speculative current. Complex corporate structures and pyramid schemes prevailed. Businesses over-expanded and over-borrowed. Bankers, were guilty of fiduciary neglect, frequently forgetting 'their duty of counselors; they allowed the potential profits to color their advice, and to lessen their precautionary investigations; they marketed securities with little of no consideration of the productive or wasteful consequences; they reaped a harvest on the popularity of management and fixed trusts' (Landis 1959–1960, p. 30). Out of the despair and anger of the subsequent depression, the Roosevelt administration proposed the Securities Act during its first 100 days.

The Securities Act of 1933 required issuers and brokers to disclose fully the character of securities sold. Roosevelt (1934) told Congress the Act was designed to 'give impetus to honest dealings in securities and thereby bring back public confidence.' Reinvigorating public confidence wholly depended, Roosevelt concluded, on restoring trust: 'What we seek is a return to a clearer understanding of the ancient truth that those who manage banks, corporations and other agencies handling or using other peoples' money are trustees acting for others.' In a conclusion echoing *The Modern Corporation and Private Property*, Roosevelt's administration meant to redefine the substance of corporate power as the value of trust to the community, and put it at the center of all the financial legislation at the heart of the New Deal.

The most important, and controversial, feature of the 1933 Act was its imposition of civil liability with stringent penalties for false and misleading information in the registration statement. Section 11 of the Act held everyone who prepared or signed the registration statement liable for any losses due to inaccuracy. In the case a misleading statement or material omission is discovered and the security has lost value due to the statement – for instance, if the registration statement does not report the profit reported was the result of the sale of a non-recurring asset or was really the projection of an anticipated profit (e.g. Enron), then investors can sue the seller to take back the security and refund them at the original selling price. The Act made all those who played a hand in representing the security liable to both the buyer and to each other. The uniqueness of the Securities Act was its focus on representation and the relational demands it placed upon those involved in it.

Wall Street immediately launched an attack on the Act and its framers, and those attacks were in large part carried out in the *New York Times*' editorial page. Antipathy to the Act originated in its reversal of the burden of proof. The Act stipulated it was defendant's burden to prove there were no false, omitted or misleading statements in the registration statement to recoup damages. This was because the vulnerable investors envisioned by the act typically did not see the registration statement. And even if they did, they did not have the requisite technical knowledge to read it critically. Framers of the Act understood the value of a security is inevitably determined by the reaction of professional analysts and the class of institutional investors who rely on the misleading information in the statement. The inquiry performed by these actors sets the market price and informs the judgment of brokers. Since any misstatement or omission in the registration statement tends to either overstate or understate the price of the security, the misrepresentation makes all purchasers victims of the misstatement (Turnquist 2000). To mitigate liability in those cases where the presence of a false statement was irrefutable, defendants had to demonstrate they exercised due diligence in ensuring the accuracy of the registration statement. Due diligence was established by proving defendants had after 'reasonable investigation, reasonable ground to believe and did believe, at the time such part of the registration statement became effective, that the statements therein were true and that there was no omission to state a material fact required to be stated therein or necessary to make the statements therein not misleading' (77a 1933).

The critical question is, of course, what constitutes reasonableness here; what is a 'reasonable investigation' and what are 'reasonable grounds to believe' that the registration statement is true?

The interpretation of the Act turns on the definition of reasonableness in section 11c. The original version of the Act stated that in 'determining what constitutes a reasonable investigation and reasonable ground for belief, the standard of reasonableness shall be that which is required of a person occupying a fiduciary relationship' (Means 1933, p.XX3). This is an especially high standard of loyalty and care as it requires the needs of the other to supercede their own. Despite considerable controversy in Congress, the weight of the President Roosevelt's support lead to the passage of the Act without a dissenting vote and it become law on May 27, 1933 (Landis 1959–1960).

This consensus was short-lived. Opponents of the Act argued it was unnecessary because, contrary to popular opinion, fraudulent securities played a minor role in the crash of 1929. The crash, they insisted, was the product of a 'world-wide depression, which has caused values and prices not alone of securities but of all commodities to fall precipitously' (Seligman 1934, p. 371). The Act was also portrayed as a dangerous economic threat and, as the Merchants Association of New York argued, 'unless action is taken before the adjournment of Congress, the country will be faced by increased unemployment and by bankruptcy of going concerns that are unable to finance themselves under the terms of the Act' (21 Changes 1934).

The Act's proponents claimed these predictions of economic stagnation were baseless fear-mongering. The Act had not been in force long enough to know its effects. Moreover the implicit conclusion 'long-term open-market lending will immediately boom after repeal of the Act' (Douglas 1934a, p. 521) ignored the real reasons for the anemic performance of the securities market, such as the decline in credit-worthiness, the unwillingness to finance debt at exorbitant prices, and the drying up of long-term savings (Flexner 1934, pp. 234–235). The lack of investment in railroads and municipal bonds, which were not subject to the Act, demonstrated, for proponents, that 'these factors – and not a legal confirmation of an ethical standard that men who use other people's money must be honest and competent – have dried up the securities market' (Flexner 1934, p. 234). What the Act's supporters suspected, and what we now know, is that the hiatus in private investment was partially the result of collusion by large banks to create the very financial effects they could point to as evidence against the act (Parrish 1970, p. 189).

The battle over the act proceeded largely in the affective terms of animal sprits, with each side making competing predictions about the Act's effect on trust and confidence. William O. Douglas, who would become the chair of the Securities and Exchange Commission (SEC) in 1936 and who would be appointed to the Supreme Court in 1939, claimed that this affective intensity was a sure sign that the Act's significance lay in its symbolic promise: 'It signifies that the money-changers are being driven from temples' (Douglas 1934b, p. 522).

The Act's whip was its fiduciary standard of reasonableness. A fiduciary relationship, which is founded in trust, care, and loyalty, imposes a duty upon the person with superior knowledge and skill to do all that is necessary and to act at all times in the best interest and for the benefit of the beneficiary. Just how far this fiduciary duty extended was unknown, but it was certain that this would be a jury question. That is, it would be juries, not judges, who would eventually determine if boards and brokers exercised reasonable care. The business lobby feared that not only did this leave the definition of reasonableness unfairly indeterminate, but that juries in small communities, naturally prejudiced against corporations and bankers, would tend to decide such questions in favor of the small investor.

It was precisely the fact that business would be accountable to the standards of honesty, care and competence defined by local communities which made the fiduciary standard of reasonableness such a promising, or threatening, etho-political tactic. As Nikolas Rose has shown, it is the language of community, in particular its articulation of affective and ethical bonds that constitute etho-politics (Rose 2000). If the corporation and all the individuals who profit from it exercise their powers for the benefit of the community, as Berle and Means claimed, then it would be the community who, in some part, decided what steps are necessary to fulfill this trust. While we will detail the etho-political features of fiduciary duty more fully in the following section, for now it is enough to note the duties of honesty, care and loyalty are first and foremost relational goods that are felt as affective bonds. That is, dishonesty, indifference and disloyalty hurt. When we understand a relationship we believed was premised on the promises of trust, care and loyalty is, in fact, not reciprocal, but that our trust was the means of our betrayal, we are understandably outraged. This outrage would, the business lobby feared, become all the evidence juries would need. This reconceptualization of reasonableness as ethical reciprocation was, Congressman Sam Rayburn argued, one of the motivations behind the act: 'The purpose of this bill is to place the owners of securities on a parity, as far as it possible, with the management of the corporations, and to place the buyer on the same plane, so far as information is concerned, with the seller' (Rayburn 1934, p. 151).

On April 15, 1934 the Merchants Association of New York drafted 21 amendments to the Act; with most of these presented as simple 'clarifying amendments.' The most important of these proposed changing the standard of reasonableness in section 11c from 'that required of a person occupying a fiduciary relationship' to 'that required of a reasonably prudent man in the management of his own property' (21 Changes 1934, p. N9).

Over the next six weeks the controversy over which meaning of reasonableness to endorse ignited, with the *Times* reporting on May 6 that the 'use of the term fiduciary brought violent protest' to the Senate floor' (Security Act Foes 1934, p. N9). On May 7 Senator Duncan Fletcher, Chair of the Banking and Currency Committee offered an amendment which redefined reasonableness in line with the Merchant Association's proposal from a fiduciary to a prudent man standard. But Fletcher's amendments did not last the week, as they were surreptitiously removed from the Bill's next printing. In his May 22 'In Washington,' Arthur Krock reported that the May 12 printing of the bill retained only the reliance amendment and reinserted the fiduciary standard of care, omitting Fletcher's amendment to section 11c. Krock, whose dislike of President Roosevelt and the New Deal was well known (Talese 1969, p. 43), claimed that 'the material changes between the May 7th and May 12th form of the bill had been made at the instance of J.M. Landis of the Federal Trade Commission and some of his fellow-thinkers, young Brain Trusters, who are the keepers of the president's mind and conscience in such matters' (Krock 1934, p. 22). The *Times* editorial page immediately denounced Senator Fletcher. In a May 23 editorial 'A Securities Act Mystery' the page recounted Senator Fletcher's attempt to deceive a 'a weary and confused Senate' by telling his colleagues that 'the amendment he was formally offering 'is the same as that, previously printed, except that I have made one slight change' (A Securities Act Mystery 1934, p. 18). Senator Fletcher's attempt to deceive, the editorial argued, 'excited in the Senate itself, a sense of indignation' (Securities Act Mystery 1934, p. 18). Fletcher's 'slight change,' the editorial argued, 'strengthens the suspicion of meddlesome intrigue outside the legislative body,' a conclusion that reinforced Krock's insinuation that President Roosevelt himself directed Landis to excise the amendment (Securities Act Mystery 1934, p. 18). The exposure of Fletcher's deception was an embarrassment for the Roosevelt administration. Berle would make one final plea to keep the fiduciary standard in the Act, but it was too late. The next day Fletcher's original amendments were reinserted in the printed version of the bill. The Amended Act was passed on June 2, 1934, with section 11c defining reasonableness as 'that required of a prudent man in the management of his own property.' This is the same definition in the Act today.

The ethical demands of finance

The prudential and fiduciary standards of reasonableness differ considerably in how each establishes the duties owed to investors and the scope of liability in representing securities to them. Under a fiduciary standard reasonableness entails an obligation to act in the interest of the other. Those brokers who sold securities with an eye only to their own profit, who encouraged clients to make risky investments based on unfounded speculation, thereby putting their financial wellbeing in jeopardy, would find themselves having to pay for those mistakes. In the amended legislation, however, the broker simply had to show that any prudent person, one who was aware of their needs and the resources they had to meet them, could have taken the claims in the security prospectus as reason to invest. Given that capital is always at risk, prudent judgment cannot be defined in terms of profit or sellers would always be liable for losses. Prudent judgment is characterized in the internal calculus of rational choice; a prudent actor is simply one who uses appropriate techniques to asses risk and to predict future market activity.

These two standards also operate from distinct orientations to power. The fiduciary standard is underwritten by a relational account of power while a prudential standard works through a projection of symmetry. In fiduciary relationships, reasonableness is determined by evaluating the use of power between the parties: Does the party with the authority that comes with knowledge, skill, and membership in a professional community treat the other, dependent party, with the discretion, and intelligence befitting a trustee? Is the vulnerable party, the one whose financial wellbeing is at stake, given adequate, accurate, and sensitive advice in a framework that teaches her or him how to assess the risks that come with a particular investment? Reasonableness does not presume equality; in fact, it assumes the parties are not equal in knowledge, skill, or power. Reasonableness becomes, in a fiduciary framework, a standard for measuring care in inherently unequal relationships. A standard demanding that investment advice display an understanding of the relative vulnerability of the investor and the expectation that the trustee works for the overall good of the investor, and by extension the public. The prudential standard, to the contrary, uses the projection of the brokers' self-interest onto the client as the guarantor of reasonableness. That is, the prudential standard hangs on the supposition that if professionals give investors the same information and advice on how to use their money that they use to invest their own and use the same means to calculate risk and predict the probability of profit for their clients as they would themselves, they have acted reasonably. The prudential standard works from the theoretical assumption that the two parties' needs and appetites for risk are identical, rendering actual differences in standing and vulnerability immaterial.

Vulnerability conditions what is a 'reasonable' ethical demand: for the fiduciary standard this is a complex evaluation; the prudential standard simply assumes that it does not exist. The ethical demands on fiduciaries include a demand of loyalty, to put the other's interest before one's own, and a demand to care, to be diligent in meeting the other's needs. The intensity of the ethical demands of loyalty and care, and its limits, are precisely what must be determined in and through the contestation over the meaning and applicability of reasonableness. And this renders reasonableness much more than an ideological tool of legitimation, even though when it is invoked as a defense of rationality and decorum it may function as such. Reasonableness, on the contrary, has the potential to serve as a critical ideal, one that stakeholders can use to articulate their exploitation and though which they can attempt to transform the cultures that make it possible (Cornell 1995).

Finally, each standard differs in its approach to governing in and through animal spirits. The fiduciary standard governs primarily through trust, using it as the basis for building confidence. The prudential standard works through building confidence, hoping to eliminate the need for trust. To see how, we must briefly trace the difference between trust and confidence, a distinction that is very usefully drawn by Earle and Seigrist (2006). Trust is the willingness to make oneself vulnerable to the other. Confidence is a belief, based on experience or evidence, that events will unfold as expected. The decision to trust is motivated by a judgment that the parties share values and display a commitment to treating each other with respect and care. Confidence is based on past performance or in the absence of performance data institutional regulations that constrain future performance. Trust and confidence both motivate social cooperation, but Earle's and Seigrist's essential finding is that judgments of trust dominate judgments of confidence. That is, we treat morality-relevant information as more important and it conditions judgments of performance. Hence, trust can preserve confidence even when performance is weak; we all know that when we trust others we judge their performance less harshly than we would otherwise. But confidence in a system or institution cannot restore trust once it has been lost. We may participate, but if we do we do so cautiously, always looking to increase our advantage, even if it comes at others' expense (Hicks *et al.* 2008).

Think of this in terms of economic judgments: if we are in a low-trust environment, say because of widespread fraud, deregulation, and the increasing use of opaque financial instruments, we will have little choice but to base our investment decisions on past performance, and remember each of the parties has an incentive to mask their actual performance and to project strength. Couple this with a rush of inexperienced investors into the market and with them a flood of relatively inexperienced advisors and brokers, and throw in the fiduciary neglect by experienced fund managers. And what you have is an economy increasingly held hostage to speculative bubbles and social contagions, driven by the vicious interpretative circles, that Schiller (2008) calls an information cascade. Moreover, the affective rush associated with short-term gains in an information cascade is contagious, leading others to invest far after the peak of the cycle. It is these people who find themselves insolvent once the value of their assets has fallen and they do not have the collateral to secure credit. The result is what we face now, a liquidity trap. The collapse of trust and confidence has made credit-worthy companies and households unwilling to borrow because of fear; they are hoarding cash rather than spending or lending it, causing a deflationary spiral that has intensified the effects of the recession.

How could we have avoided this scenario? Roosevelt's and Berle's answer was by addressing the animal spirits of confidence and trust simultaneously. The Securities Act addressed confidence by stipulating that securities transactions take place in a transparent environment where parties could expect full disclosure. The Act addressed trust through defining reasonableness as fiduciary duty and attaching it to severe civil liability. Roosevelt and Berle understood that trust dominates confidence. Their hope was that by constructing a high-trust environment investors would not become over-dependent on speculations about performance, instead investing in projects they thought secured our collective future. Moreover, if the corporation's obligation to serve the community could become embedded in the interpretative heart of the law – the understanding of what is reasonable – the power of animal spirits could be marshaled to redefine the business culture. If this etho-political intervention into the economy could take hold, especially if a host of informal etho-political programs supported it, the result might be regenerative. The vicious business cycles fueled by mistrust and false confidence would, they imagined, give way to virtuous circles of fiduciary trust and care, promoting an economic climate in which the initial capital and energy invested into corporate-community collaboratives would engender an even stronger commitment to future joint initiatives.

This remained a professor's dream, of course. The 13 months the financial lobby spent proclaiming that a shift to a fiduciary standard of reasonableness would halt economic recovery (an effort that was aided by the editorial pages of the *New York Times* and the *Washington Post*) and, more importantly, the collusion of the major investment banks to withdraw from the market so as to produce the evidence for these claims, proved too much. Faced with the threat Congress would not support the establishment of the SEC unless the fiduciary standard was stricken, Roosevelt gambled that if he conceded Berle's argument to Wall Street, the Securities Act would be good enough (Parrish 1970).

As we write, the Obama administration has just unveiled what it calls 'a sweeping overhaul of the financial regulatory system, a transformation on a scale not seen since the reforms that followed the great depression.' The 88 page document, even given the sheer numbers of its proposals, Joe Nocera says promises nothing 'even close to what Roosevelt accomplished during the great depression' (Nocera 2009, p. A1).

Now we must remind ourselves not to fall into a misplaced nostalgia for the 'good-old days' of New Deal. Anthony Marcus and Kirk Dombrowski are surely right to remind us the New Deal was designed to salvage capitalism, not to reform it (Marcus & Dombroski 2008). The New Deal, they remind us, birthed many cruel programs including the most ineffective national health system in the world, a Works Progress Administration (WPA) that undercut the price of labor-especially women's labor, a Housing Act that concentrated the poor, a Social Security Act which excluded African-Americans, and vast subsidies that drove up the price of food and promoted the growth of corporate farming (Marcus & Dombroski 2008, p. 171). None of this would have been prevented by the original Securities Act. But, we know that each of these policies is unreasonable. Our purpose has not been to add to the calls for a 'New' New Deal. Rather, it is to highlight the power of reasonableness as a term of etho-political governance, hopefully showing its potential as a site for revealing, contesting and transforming the cultural terms of that governance.

References

21 Changes. (1934) *New York Times*, 15 April, N9.

77a. (1933) *15 U.S.C.*, Truth in Securities Act.

Akerlof, G. A. & Schiller, R. J. (2009) *Animal Spirits: How Human Psychology Drives the Economy, and Why It Matters for Global Capitalism*, Princeton, NJ, Princeton University Press.

Ariely, D. (2008) *Predictably Irrational: The Hidden Forces that Shape our Decisions*, New York, Harper Collins.

Berle, A. A. & Means, G. C. (1932) *The Modern Corporation and Private Property*, New York, Macmillan.

Bratich, J. (2003) 'Making politics reasonable: conspiracism, subjectification, and governing through styles of thought', in *Foucault, Cultural Studies and Governmentality*, eds J. Z. Bratich, J. Packer & C. McCarthy, Albany, NY, State University of New York Press, pp. 67–100.

Brennan, T (2004) *The Transmission of Affect*, New York, Routledge.

Cook, J. & Young, B. (2007) *Fund Voting in 2006: An Analysis of 29 Large Fund Families' Voting Records*, Portland, ME, The Corporate Library (Executive Summary) Available at: http://www.complianceweek.com/s/documents/Compliance%20Week%202007/Resource%20Materials/Minow,%20Nell%20-%20The%20Corporate%20Library/FundVoting2006_ExecSumm.pdf (accessed 6 June 2009).

Cornell, D. (1995) *The Imaginary Domain: Abortion, Pornography and Sexual Harassment*, New York, Routledge.

Douglas, W. O. (1934a) 'Protecting the investor', *Yale Review*, March, pp. 521–533.

Douglas, W. O. (1934b) *Virtual Museum and Archive of SEC Securities History*, Securities and Exchange Commission Historical Society, 17 June.

Douglas, W. O. (1936) 'Termites of high finance', *Vital Speeches of the Day*, vol. 3, no. 3, pp. 86–92.

Earle, T. C. & Siegrist, M. (2006) 'Morality information, performance information, and the distinction between trust and confidence', *Journal of Applied Social Psychology*, vol. 36, no. 3, pp. 383–416.

Flexner, B. (1934) 'The fight on the Securities Act', *Altantic Monthly*, vol. 153, pp. 232–250.

Grantham, J. (2009) 'Rebalancing the books', *Financial Times*, 10 March. Available at: http://www.ft.com

Gruening, E. (1933) 'Capitalist confiscation, Editorial', *The Nation*, vol. 136, pp. 116–117 (The Nation Archive).

Harsin, J. P. (2005) *A tale of two citizenships: the economic rights discourse of Frandklin Delano Roosevelt and Ronald Reagan*, Unpublished Dissertation, Department of Communication Studies, Northwestern University, Evanston, IL.

Hicks, D. (2006) '(Un)Reasonable times: invocations of reasonableness in the *New York Times*', in *Proceedings of the Sixth International Conference of The International Association for the Study of Argument*, eds F. van Eemeren, A. Blair & C. Willard, Amsterdam, Kluwer, pp. 471–476.

Hicks, D., Margesson, R. & Warrenburg, K. (2005) 'Political reasonableness in contemporary argumentation theory: a content analysis of the *New York*

Times, 1860–2004', *Contemporary Argumentation and Debate*, vol. 26, pp. 1–12.

Hicks, D., Larson, C., Nelson, C., Olds, D. & Johnston, E. (2008) 'The influence of collaboration on program outcomes: the Colorado Nurse Family Partnership', *Evaluation Review*, vol. 32, no. 5, pp. 453–477.

Houck, D. W. (2004) 'FDR's Commonwealth Club address: redefining individualism, adjudicating greatness', *Rhetoric and Public Affairs*, vol. 7, no. 3, pp. 259–282.

Krock, A (1934) 'Securities Act is unlikely to be materially amended', *New York Times*, May 22, p. 22.

Landis, J. M. (1959–1960) 'Legislative history of the Securities Act of 1933', *George Washington Law Review*, vol. 28, pp. 29–49.

Levitt, S. & Drubner, S. (2006) *Freakonomics: A Rouge Economist Explores the Hidden Side of Everything*, New York, William Morrow.

Lind, E. A. (2001) 'Fairness heuristic theory: justice judgments are pivotal cognitions in organizational relations', in *Advances in Organizational Justice*, eds J. Greenberg & R. Cropanzano, Palo Alto, CA, Stanford University Press, pp. 56–88.

Lo, A. (2009) *Fear, Greed, and Crisis Management: A Neuroscientific Perspective*. Available at: http://freakonomics.blogs.nytimes.com/2009/01/09 (accessed 15 June 2009).

Marchionatti, R. (1999) 'On Keynes's animal spirits', *Kyklos*, vol. 52, no. 3, pp. 415–439.

Marcus, A. & Dombroski, K. (2008) 'Editorial: a new new deal', *Dialectical Anthropology*, vol. 32 vol. 3, pp. 169–174.

Means, G. C. (1933) 'Protecting the buyers of securities: a new approach: an analysis of risk which now beset the investor and the federal remedies proposed to meet the situation', *New York Times*, 9 April, p. XX3.

Mlodinow, L. (2009) *The Drunkard's Walk: How Randomness Rules our Lives*, New York, Vintage.

Morgenson, G. (2009) 'He doesn't let money managers off the hook', *New York Times(Business)*, 11 April.

Nocera, J. (2009) 'Only a hint of Roosevelt in financial overhaul', *New York Times(Business)*, 18 June, p.A1.

Parrish, M. E. (1970) *Securities Regulation and the New Deal*, New Haven, CT, Yale University Press.

Posner, R. (2009) 'Shorting reason', *The New Republic*, vol. 240, no. 6, pp. 30–33.

Rasmussen, D. M. (2004) 'Reasonability and the later Rawls: Editor's introduction', *Philosophy and Social Criticism*, vol. 30, pp. 523–524.

Rayburn, S. (1934) 'Should the federal Securities Act be amended: Con', *Congressional Digest*, vol. 13, no. 5, pp. 149–151.

Roosevelt, F. D. (Democratic Presidential Candidate) (1932) 'Speech to commonwealth club, September 23', in *Commonwealth Club*, Campaign speech, San Francisco, CA, American Rhetoric, 17 June.

Roosevelt, F. D. (1934) 'Message to Congress, March 29 1934', *Congressional Digest*, vol. 13, no. 5, pp. 131–132.

Rose, N. (2000) 'Community, citizenship and the third way', *American Behavioral Scientist*, vol. 43, pp. 1395–1411.

Rose, N. & Miller, P. (2008) *Governing the Present: Administering Economic, Social and Personal Life*, Cambridge, Polity.

Schiller, R. (2008) *The Subprime Solution: How Today's Global Financial Crisis Happened and What to Do about it*, Princeton, Princeton University Press.

'Securities Act Foes' (1934) *New York Times*, 6 May, p. N9.

'A Securities Act Mystery' (1934) *New York Times*, 22 May, p. 18.

Seligman, E. (1934) 'Amend the Securities Act, Editorial', *Altantic Monthly*, vol. 153, pp. 370–380.

Talese, G. (1969) 'The *New York Times*, part 1: inside a great newspaper', *Harpers*, pp. 54–78.

Tsuk, D. (2005) 'From pluralism to individualism: Berle and Means and 20th century American legal thought', trans. A. A. Berle & G. C. Means, *Law and Social Inquiry*, vol. 30, p. 179.

Turnquist, K. L. (2000) 'Note: pleading under section 11 of the Securities Act of 1933', *Michigan Law Review*, vol. 98, pp. 2395–2416.

Unger, R. M. (1987) *False Necessity: Anti-Necessitarian Social Theory in the Service of Radical Democracy*, Cambridge, Cambridge University Press.

John Clarke

AFTER NEO-LIBERALISM? Markets, states and the reinvention of public welfare[1]

This paper explores some aspects of the present crisis, including the problem of how to think about crises in the current conjuncture. It has four main parts: the first and second explore the changing imagery of markets as disenchantment sets in; the third considers what sort of crisis is taking place; and the fourth and final part of the paper considers how innovations and interventions directed at solving the crisis are being framed. It concludes that being 'after neo-liberalism' may not be the same as the disappearance of neo-liberalism.

The magic of the market

For the last 35 years, political, policy and popular narratives have centred on the magic of the market. Unlike cumbersome, intrusive, domineering states, markets were the flexible friends of humanity. Markets, we were told, made things work. They offered the most efficient and effective means of coordinating human action. They were dynamic and responsive, innovative and open. Thomas Frank captures something of this rise of market imagery:

> Wherever one looked in the nineties entrepreneurs were occupying the ideological space once filled by the noble sons of toil. It was businessmen who were sounding off against the arrogance of elites, railing against the privilege of old money, protesting false expertise and waging relentless, idealistic war against the principle of hierarchy wherever it could be found. They were market populists, adherents of a powerful new political mythology that had arisen from the ruins of the thirty-year backlash. Their fundamental faith was a simple one. The market and the people – both understood as grand principles of social life rather than particulars – were essentially one and the same. By its very nature the market was

> democratic, perfectly expressing the popular will through the machinery of supply and demand, poll and focus group, superstore and Internet. In fact, the market was more democratic than any of the formal institutions of democracy – elections, legislatures, government. The market was a community. The market was infinitely diverse, permitting without prejudice the articulation of any and all tastes and preferences. Most importantly of all, the market was militant about its democracy. It had no place for snobs, for hierarchies, for elitism, for pretense, and it would fight these things by its very nature. (Frank 2001, p. 29)

Frank's discussion of market populism points to the strange and compelling interplay between academic (neo-classical economics, especially), political and popular discourses in disseminating market imagery. And although Frank is primarily addressing the rise of market thinking in the US, there is certainly good reason to take seriously the transnational circuits through which market populism has circulated, not least the apparatuses of globalizing economic and social policy [World Bank, International Monetary Fund (IMF), World Trade Organization (WTO) and more].

Here I want to build on Frank's argument by pointing to several key features of this market-centric thinking and drawing out two of the vital elements of the magic of markets. The first feature is the unboundedness of markets: the potential of markets knew no limits because their dynamic character resembled a principle of perpetual motion. Nowhere could resist the arrival of market relations (a geo-political point underlined by the fall of communism and the transformation of former socialist societies to varieties of market economy). But unboundedness also referred to spheres of human activity. Some critics have pointed to the capacity of market logics to subsume, rather than just subordinate, 'non-economic' domains of social life:

> . . . the market's principles and mechanisms expand beyond their place in the economic sphere to convert other nonmarket spheres of life to their organizing logic. The sites of market "invasion" are primarily the state and civil society and their ideational and discursive regimes. This drive to invade and convert noncontractual sites entails marketization, contractualization, and privatization. Since market fundamentalism is a regime on the move, it is always involved in an effort to gain the balance of power by subjecting both polity and civil society to contractual powers and principles. (Somers 2008, p. 38, but see the discussion in Clarke 2007)

For market enthusiasts, there was no domain of social life that could not be improved by its engagement with market dynamics. While this was perhaps most visible in relation to state-related practices, such as social welfare or public service provision, it was claimed to extend to questions of sexual relationships, partner choice and household organization.

Markets could play these roles partly because their dynamics and logics were consistently identified as being 'pre-social'. Denise Riley (1985) uses this phrase to describe the relationship between biology and the social in theories of child development, such that biology always precedes the action of the social. In the context of the market, the basic dynamics of the market are represented as preceding the social by virtue of being natural forces – competition being the key referent that links biological, economic and psychological evolutionary theories (see, for example, Shermer 2009). Markets are thus associated with pre-social human conditions and dynamics – and, of course, not just human but natural: evolution through competition is the basic matrix. The pre-social characterization of markets also enables them to be represented as a-political, such that the market mechanism appears to precede politics. This double movement is most visible in the typical juxtaposition of market logics and 'social engineering' – the latter representing 'external interference' (usually by governments or states) into natural processes. Such interference is doomed to failure or worse since it will disturb the delicate dynamics and balances that only markets can combine.[2]

There are two other significant elements that contribute to the perceived magic of markets. The first is the promise of possibility: that tomorrow will be better. Market magic works on this promise – that disappointment or frustration can be overcome. This sense of deferred possibility links individuals and markets – individuals can have another chance to test their capacities; markets can always be perfected even if a particular example may not have functioned perfectly.[3] The other promise is that markets are expansive. They create more: more wealth, more goods, more results, more possibilities. This conception links the search for personal satisfaction, especially through consumption, to an urban landscape of growth and dynamism, and to the promise that freeing markets will reduce global poverty by creating more wealth (on the magic of the urban, see Pile 2005). Recently, the promise of the endless creation of new wealth has been counterposed to the 'social engineering' of redistributing actually existing wealth. Whether the crisis of global indebtedness will break or merely defer this promise remains to be seen.

But in these two promises – of possibility and of expansion – the magic of markets is bound up with a particular temporal logic. Market thinking is profoundly future oriented, but it is a future whose framing logics are relatively unchanging. The drive towards possibility and expansion is conditional on the basic mechanism of possibility and expansion – the market – remaining free to work its magic. The projections of the future in market thinking are thus both fantastic (wealth beyond your wildest dreams; or just the holiday of a lifetime) and banal: the future looks like the present, but larger.

Disenchantment: meeting markets with mood swings

Market populism has been associated with a language that is noticeably virile. Testimony is paid to the rational, efficient and effective qualities of market. These virtues exist in combination with the restless striving and boundless energy of markets; always dynamic, innovative and expansive. Market magic is also associated with power and potency – the ability to make things happen, to turn fantasies into realities, while nevertheless being 'hard headed' and geared to the 'bottom line'. We might trace this virile language a little further into the recurrent trope of 'market penetration' and recognize this as a profoundly masculinized discourse. These are masculine characteristics (from competition to penetration), even if, of course, they are contradictory ones. Hard-headed rationality sits alongside visionary entrepreneurialism; efficient allocation alongside fantasies of infinite (and infinitely expanding) wealth.[4]

But in 2008–2009 it seems that markets are not what they used to be. They are a shadow of their former virile selves, no longer relentlessly expanding but slipping into a period of decline, decay and, above all, depression. Depression is an interesting concept in relation to markets because it condenses two rather different, but significant sets of meanings. On the one hand, we encounter the hard evidentiary science of economics – in which depression refers to a specified trend in economic activity, measurable by a set of particular indicators.[5] Depressions – like the Great Depression of the 1930s – are profound and prolonged slumps in economic activity. On the other hand, depression is also a key term for describing mental states, emotional moods or clinical conditions. What intrigues me is the exchange between these two sites of depression – the economic and the emotional. There is something significant about the proliferation of terms describing mental states and emotional moods to talk about the state of markets. In these troubled and turbulent times, we have become accustomed to hearing about markets that are anxious, nervous, and unsettled. They are, it seems, prone to bouts of panic and hysteria in which they are infected by collective mood swings and a sort of viral irrationality. These mood swings of markets – moments of manic recovery offset by plummeting spirits – are leading us all into depression. There are several things that might be said about this shift, but here I want to concentrate on just two: engendering crisis and the question of faith.

By comparison with the virile, expansive and penetrative markets of the past, these currently enfeebled markets are being discursively feminized. Their irrationality and instability are couched in the language of emotional and affective conditions that have been – in Western cultures – coded as feminine (from the hysterical condition onwards). In contrast to the hard calculative logics that supposedly drove market expansiveness, the current markets are vulnerable entities. They are vulnerable to some characteristically feminine problems of gossip and loose talk that may precipitate a sudden decline in confidence. Lack of confidence can lead to a more generalized lack of faith, trust and confidence. These intangible conditions turn out to be at the core of our present troubles. For example, a recent BBC News viewpoint by Sir David Tang (Entrepreneur) merged both senses of depression into a compelling narrative about pessimism:

> *Pessimism is the most serious cause for the global economic tsunami*
>
> There is an ocean of people who are now feeling so depressed that not only have they become resigned to the fact that they are in deep trouble, but they have told everybody else that they are also in deep trouble.
>
> Pessimism has an uncanny knack of being self-fulfilling.
>
> No wonder almost every single quoted share in the world has gone down significantly, mostly by half, if not much more. [http://news.bbc.co.uk/go/pr/fr/-/2/hi/business/7785564.stm (accessed 31 January 2009)]

Meanwhile, a *Guardian* report on declining confidence managed to go further by weaving into its story the meteorological reference for depression in a distinctive variant of the pathetic fallacy. It also contained an interview in which the *mediation* of declining confidence was identified as a major contributor to, if not direct cause of, the present difficulties:

> Manchester's weather yesterday was a reflection of opinion on the streets about the economy: leaden clouds and persistent drizzle.
>
> 'I think there is a lack of belief in anything financial at the moment,' said Neil Baldwin, an investment banker. 'All the trouble with the banks, the way it has been reported by the BBC and Robert Peston in an almost gleeful way, has not helped.'
>
> 'When there is a downturn in the stockmarket the negative news is reported extensively but when it bounces back up it is not reported as much. There seems to be a constant desire for negative stories.'
>
> 'Do I have faith in the government? Not at all, they have not got a clue.'
>
> He said negativity in reporting stockmarket falls has eroded consumer confidence. As a result, people had reduced their consumption of items such as holidays, new cars and sofas. (Carter 2009)

This marks a further turn in the discourses circulating around the 'credit crunch' and its aftermath – a discourse of belief and faith, associated with questions of trust and confidence, but on what seems to be a grander scale. What emerges is large-scale disenchantment – the loss, or at least decline, of belief and faith in the key agents of contemporary economic and social life.

This was best express in a *Guardian* report (on the 14 January 2009) of an international survey, under the following heading:

> *Britain loses faith in economy*
> *Global poll shows UK least likely to trust politicians, banks or markets*

The story continued:

> British economic confidence has been shattered by the financial crisis, according to a unique international poll published today. It shows that people here are now less likely to trust banks, the stockmarket or the government's economic management than people in comparable nations . . .
>
> On most measures, British people emerged as among the most pessimistic of the 14,555 people questioned around the world. (Glover 2009)

The article moves between ideas of confidence, trust, belief and faith, but the mobilization of the concept of faith here is an interesting one, given the increasing salience of Faith as a governmental category in UK public and social policy (Faith schools, Faith communities, community cohesion and integration in a multi-Faith society and so on; see, for example, Dinham *et al.* 2009). Nevetheless, the loss of faith in the economy, markets, the banking system and government is a fairly spectacular national achievement. This scepticism about economic and political institutions is widespread internationally, according to the report, but concentrated in a particularly dense form in the UK.

What are we to make of this loss of faith? Is it just a temporary disenchantment – a moment in which the obvious failures of market and market related institutions and processes are simply and directly reflected in popular attitudes? Such a view would hold out the possibility of confidence being restored, faith renewed and magical enchantment restored. While not wanting to deny such possibilities, not least because forms of magical thinking often have ways of accommodating failure within their framing system, I want to take this moment of disenchantment to consider a rather different possibility. Is it possible that the discursive, political, policy and cultural dominance of market populism might have led both enthusiasts and critics to overstate its hold on the popular imaginary? Might people have been less in thrall to the magic of the market than we supposed?

There are two rather different points to be made here. The first is that descriptions of people's relationships to systems of thought (whether they are magical thinking, market populism or neo-liberal ideology) tend towards a rather binary view, with on/off settings. We might be better served by a more differentiated view of attachment and belief, being able to distinguish between enthusiasts or visionaries, their followers or acolytes, calculating converts, conditionally compliant audiences, keep your head down sceptics – as well as the heretical opposition. Identifying such positions might allow a more differentiated view of how people relate to particular discourses or ways of thinking – including market populism. But it tends to treat the field of belief as organized around a single pole and does not offer a sense of the multiple, overlapping, disjunctured discourses that formed what Gramsci (1971) thought of as common sense – that 'collection of traces without an inventory'. From such a starting point, we might view the spread of market populism as a *partial colonization* of common sense – building on, working with, and speaking through existing traces (after all market populism did not invent market thinking for the first time). Market populism – as the Frank quotation earlier makes clear – also involved harnessing or articulating other elements of Euro-Atlantic common sense to the logics of market populism: anti-elitism; questions of equity; desires for progress and pleasure and so on.

In this perspective, we might treat the present 'loss of faith' as the simultaneous dis-articulation of aspects of market populism and the revival of repressed or de-mobilized aspects of common sense, or, at least, those elements that circulated below the level of public discourse. Some involve other forms of anti-elitism (who trusts bankers, financiers and others who announce themselves as masters of the universe?); some concern other questions of equity and equality (the unequal distribution of risk, insecurity, vulnerability and misery); some address the corruptions and incompetence of 'politics' and 'politicians'; and some are about the lack of fit between market logics and other domains of social life.

Studies of popular conceptions of public services in the UK regularly point to a distinction between using public services and 'shopping' and a resistance to a consumer identity (e.g. Clarke *et al.* 2007, Needham 2007). People sometimes insist on aspects of privacy and intimacy against the intrusion of the market; they are sometimes cynical about the collapse of all value judgements to price; and they sometimes believe that 'economic' motives may not be trusted in matters of social or public interest. None of this is to argue that there is a state of 'original innocence' or proto-socialist ethics to offset against market populism, but it is to insist that thinking about the popular might try harder to escape the binary distinction between belief and non-belief, and that Gramsci's way of viewing common sense as a field of political struggle might be a productive way of doing so.

What sort of crisis is this?

This question was provoked by reading Michel Foucault's recently translated 1978–1979 lectures at the Collège de France (Foucault 2008). In them, he makes a passing, but characteristically provocative, distinction between a crisis of capitalism and a crisis of governmentality or liberalism:

> I would like to say that if it is true that a feature of the contemporary world, or of the modern world since the eighteenth century, really has been the constant presence of what may be called crises of capitalism, couldn't we also say that there have been crises of liberalism, which are not, of course, independent of crises of capitalism. The problem of the thirties I have just been referring to is indeed the proof of this. But crises of liberalism are not just the pure and simple or direct projection of these crises of capitalism in the political sphere. You can find crises of liberalism linked to crises of the capitalist economy. But you can also find them with a chronological gap with regard to these crises, and in any case the way in which these crises manifest themselves, are handled, call forth reactions, and prompt re-organizations is not directly deducible from the crises of capitalism. It is the crisis of the general apparatus (*dispositif*) of governmentality . . . (Foucault 2008, pp. 69–70)

The distinction is an interesting one and made me ponder how many types of crisis might be at stake in the present, as well as how they might be distinguished and related. As an obsessive crisis watcher, I began accumulating types of crisis (and I have no reason to assume that the list in table 1 is exhaustive)

As Foucault recognized, the temptation is to construct a model in which most of these are facets or aspects of a deeper, more fundamental crisis – a crisis of global capitalism, perhaps. I want to resist that temptation, not least because capitalism can be understood as *endemically* crisis prone. If crisis is endemic to the system dynamics of capitalism, then discovering a crisis of capitalism may not be a big step forward. But we also need to be attentive to the ways in which crisis may be simultaneously material and the focus of 'crisis talk': narratives, accounts and representations of the state of things that try to position people, politics and policies in favourable alignments. The appearance

TABLE 1 What sort of crisis have you got?

A financial crisis
An economic crisis
A crisis of confidence
A crisis of capitalism
A crisis of regulation
A crisis of governance
A crisis of government
A global crisis

of the word crisis in public or political discourse is never an innocent description: rather we are invited to perceive particular phenomena, causes, tendencies and potential routes to salvation.

In trying to keep this double aspect of crisis in view, the rest of this paper explores two things. The first arises from the question about how many crises might be *condensed* in this conjuncture – and what trying to think about their multiplicity might involve. The second aspect addresses the 'modes of thought' about the crisis and its resolution that currently dominate. Let me turn first to the political, institutional and discursive features of this crisis-ridden conjuncture. Thinking conjuncturally implies examining the multiple – and potentially heterogeneous – forces, tendencies and trajectories that are compressed or condensed into a particular moment. These tendencies have different weights, different effectivities, different histories and even different rhythms – but it is their combination or coming together that constitutes a conjuncture (see Clarke 2007, Grossberg 2006). In such a perspective, the search for the primary cause represents a mistaken analytical route – even if a prime mover was identifiable, it only gains its significance in its articulation with the other tendencies that together make up this specific conjuncture.

So, with this in mind, let me trace some of the tendencies that seem to be condensed in the present conjuncture of crisis. It is worth returning to disenchantment or the *crisis of market magic* (sometimes signalled, as we have seen, as a crisis of confidence, or a loss of faith or trust). It appears that key economic agents or actors in the global economic system have lost confidence (traders, shareholders, market makers, investors, as well as 'the markets' themselves in their strangely personified or anthropomorphized form). Nevertheless, there are many who believe that the magic might be restored by staying within, but renewing the faith. So, a few judicious sacrifices (senior executives, corporate bodies, even governments) might assuage anger and overcome doubt. Alternatively the refurbishment of some basic rituals and magical devices might revitalize confidence – the fetishes of transparency, openness, accountability and regulation have been waved with increasing vigour and the promise that both the magic and the (suitably controlled) virility of the market might be renewed. A third strategy has been the rather more materialist approach of 'throwing money at the problem'. After decades of being told that ' throwing money' at a variety of social or public problems is both wrong and counterproductive, there is a perverse pleasure in seeing the device being re-invented and on a scale that could not have been imagined previously (albeit not very successfully).

But such strategies may not overcome widespread disenchantment and the sentiments of popular dismay, outrage and scepticism that have flowed into the spaces vacated by magical thinking (or perhaps that were already there but suppressed by the discursive weight of market populism). If indeed, people have 'lost faith' in markets, economies (and governments), this is a significant feature of the conjuncture. The crisis of magic might be a fertile ground for the construction of new popular political imaginaries – though by no means a landscape necessarily to be occupied by progressive popular politics. I will return to these issues in the final section, but there are some other crisis tendencies that are worth some attention that cluster together around the sign of the 'post'. In particular, I am intrigued as to whether the conjuncture is marked by the interwoven crises of post-Fordism; post-national globalization and post-welfarist government.

In each of these formulations, the 'post' signified a movement beyond formations that had stabilized a certain sort of Northern capitalist system, in which Fordism, national territorial units, and welfarism provided what Jessop (2002) nicely terms a 'spatio-temporal fix', or following Gilroy (1993) we might call a particular formation of Atlantic modernity. Of course, the 'post' did not necessarily signify that these formations had gone away, just that their central places in this 'spatio-temporal fix' had been displaced or dislocated in the search for new formations that could secure economic, social and political integration on a global scale and with decreasing constraints on the desires of capital. Are we now encountering *a crisis of the 'posts'* – a failure to discover, stabilize and install a new 'spatio-temporal fix' that provides the conditions of economic, social and political integration? From the 'flexible accumulation strategies' of post-Fordism, the global North is increasingly haunted by fears about the condition of 'the real economy', while the export of mass manufacturing away from the Euro-Atlantic bloc is itself threatened by the volatility of global capital in crisis (e.g. reports of 20 million unemployed among China's 130 million migrant workers in China in January 2009 see: http://www.iht.com/articles/2009/02/06/business/06yuan.php?page=2).

Despite the rhetorical flourishes about globalization and the 'end of the nation' (or nation-state), nations were never wholly displaced as economic, cultural territorial or governmental entities, sites of action, or objects of attachment. They were certainly exposed to new politics of scale – with shifting configurations of forms of power, but 'post-national' did not denote a 'non-national' world. Nevertheless, as I will argue more fully in the next section, the current crisis has exposed the unfinished business of constructing a 'new world order'. Certainly nation-states have remained – albeit unevenly – the locus of a variety of politics, forms of power and types of public engagement (Newman & Clarke 2009).

These include the persistence of some varieties of collective welfare provision in the face of reform, retrenchment and reconfiguration. While Anglophone states have led the way in making welfare more conditional, more targeted and more oriented to market logics, other states have persisted with more universalist and more welfarist forms of provision.

This is not the place to explore the comparative dynamics of welfare systems, but it needs to be noted that they continue to involve high levels of public spending, that they have not all been subject to market logics (of either policy or system governance); and that such universalist public services still command strong popular support. As with post-national, we might treat post-welfarist as denoting a period of unresolved tendencies – but where welfarism remains a feature of institutional arrangements (more strongly in some places than others) and persists as a resource in popular discourse and popular memory that can be invoked in times of economic and social uncertainty.

These unresolved 'posts' suggest one way of addressing the question of whether we are 'after neo-liberalism'. They point to some of the potential failures of neo-liberalism as a political project that sought to liberate capital from the national and statist 'shackles' of Atlantic Fordism and make the world safe for accumulation. In such terms, it might be argued that the attempt to construct new systemic conditions (of post-national scales and spaces, of post-welfarist approaches to governing the social and of post-Fordist institutionalizations of capital) has – at best – engendered new contradictions, antagonisms and blockages.

However, the problem of even posing the question of 'after neo-liberalism', much less answering it, centres on whether there is any settled definition of neo-liberalism. As I have argued elsewhere (Clarke 2008), there are several, possibly overlapping but not coherent, conceptions of neo-liberalism. These range from a coherent class project on the part of capital to subjugate new spaces and sites to the process of accumulation (Harvey 2005) to a new political strategy of regulation to revive accumulation, creating the conditions for what Jessop (2002) has called the 'societalization' of a new regime of accumulation. But neo-liberalism is also used more broadly to refer to the processes of subjecting or subordinating social and political domains to the logic of the market and/or capital. Here there is a point of intersection – around logics of economization – between Marxist and Foucauldian derived ideas of neo-liberalism. Brown (2005), for example, treats neo-liberalism as destructive of democratic sites and logics by elevating the calculative logics of economic relations over political ones; while other Foucauldians stress the trajectory of an advanced liberal governmentality that summons agents to think of themselves as economic actors, as 'individuals' in their enterprising, self-directing, contracting, working and consuming selves (e.g. Rose 1999).

This intersection raises two significant points. First, both political economy and governmentality approaches point to significant changes in the place, scope and character of the 'economic'. Second, what the economic means in these two approaches is radically different – where the former designates a real and fundamental economy composed of specific forces, relations and practices, the latter treats the economic as a modality of governing. People and other forms of agency are invited or incited to them of themselves as economic actors, engaged in economic relationships and practices, internalizing economic logics or frameworks of calculation. I do not mean to deny that they have been made to blur, merge and mutually inform each other in much writing, but here I want to hang onto this difference because I think it illuminates different aspects of the current crisis. The distinction between the material economic and governing through economic subjects makes visible different dynamics of the last few decades – and might enable us to think about how they are entangled.

So the present crisis might be a crisis of neo-liberalism in the political economy sense – the interruption, or even collapse, of a regime of capital accumulation under the weight of its own social, spatial, political and economic contradictions. This crisis is global (in terms of the systemic regime and its dissemination of the consequences) and unevenly distributed – a reminder that globalization did not abolish space or territorial distinctions (regions, nations, etc) so much as rework and re-order them. Nevertheless, the instability and vulnerability of this regime suggests that new strategies may be needed to recreate value, restart accumulation and restore profitability. Will such strategies be 'post-neo-liberal'?

But we might also think of the current conjuncture as a crisis of neo-liberal governmentality in which the modes, sites and discourses of governing the present have become destabilized. Distance from, or scepticism about, economized subjectivity and government are widespread (and not merely the effect of the present). Alternative discourses are circulating more widely – about global governance, nationalization, ethical or moral capitalism, environmental alternatives and the relationship between faith and economic practices.[6] How is neo-liberal rule to be sustained when its articles of faith seem undermined, and its perceived material effects form a powerful and visceral contrast to its promises of autonomous, self-directing and enterprising agency?

Trying to hold onto such distinctions may seem a little arcane, but I think that trying to specify the meaning of neo-liberalism (and its logics and its limits, Clarke 2004a) might prevent some unproductive discussion about whether what emerges is the continuation of neo-liberalism, the reinvention of neo-liberalism or even the renewal of neo-liberalism under another name. At least we might take up Foucault's challenge to think about the distinction between a crisis of capitalism and a crisis of governmentality – and how they are articulated in the conjuncture.

Nostalgia, nationalism and new new deals

In a characteristic comment, Gramsci observed 'it may be ruled out that immediate economic crises of themselves produce fundamental historical events; they can simply create a terrain more favourable to the dissemination of certain modes of thought, and certain ways of posing and resolving questions . . . (1971, p. 184). In this final section, I want to explore some of the 'modes of thought' that have been circulating on the terrain of this crisis, particularly in the Anglo-American political and policy discourses that I am most familiar with. The first, and most striking, feature has been the 'nationalization' of the crisis (despite some embarrassment about the word nationalization itself). Although the scale, scope and even causes of the economic crisis are widely understood as 'global', the effects of, and responses to, it have been primarily defined in national terms: the conditions of the national economy, the fate of vital national industries, the loss of jobs in national economic sectors, the role of the national central bank, the failures and promises of national financial regulators and, above all, national governments expending national public resources on rescuing 'our' banks and other institutions.

Here is the inversion of the 'post national' world of corporate globalization: the nation – and in particular that much derided entity, the nation-state – becomes the means of salvation. The institutions of regional and global governance have played relatively small parts in the unfolding drama of this crisis by contrast with the national focus and the immense use of national public resources to try to stabilize the financial sector, shore up ailing industries and stem the loss of jobs. In all of this talk and action, the nationalization word has continued to be a source of distress for national political and governmental factors who take care to insist that, however large the public stake in a financial institution may be, this is 'not nationalization'. Indeed on March 8, Lord Mandelson (UK Secretary of State for Trade) insisted that bank nationalization was neither 'necessary nor desirable'.[7] Governments now find themselves negotiating a landscape structured around a revitalized national question: protectionism versus free trade; transnational capital versus national industries; state investment versus nationalization; global flows versus national regulation; global governance versus interstate collaboration.

The nationalization of crisis has also meant the 'statalization' of crisis as the state comes to be regarded as a powerful and resourceful political agent for managing the economic and political dynamics of the crisis. In the process, populations have been reinstated as national (with particular implications for migrant workers). This nationalization has been articulated in the slogan of 'British jobs for British workers' that has echoed its way around the British political scene – here voiced by striking workers, there mouthed by Prime Minister Brown and elsewhere emerging from the depths of the British National Party. Nationalism and globalization have been deeply intertwined for the past 20 years (Kalb 2005) alongside other framings of anti-globalization (Gilbert 2007). But in the present, the nationalization of the crisis and nationalism come together to form a potentially dangerous point of political articulation.

Perhaps the dominant discourse circulating is the expressed desire to get back to 'business as usual'. This is a difficult discourse to put to work given that it was business that got us here in the first place. But 'business as usual' tries to mark the crisis as the result of *abnormal* business, pathological practices and errors of judgement. Systemic failure, the pathology of finance capital, deep-rooted corruption? Not so, just a 'few bad apples' that can be detected and ejected to restore the sanctity and purity of the system. This time, it is true, the scale of bad apple-ness seems a little larger than usual and the demands of restoration are proving a difficult challenge. But the model is familiar: the system must be saved, even from itself.

Nevertheless, governments find themselves placed in the front line of managing this feat and having to negotiate some contradictory pressures as a result. In one corner we have the immediate demands for financial stabilization (for the international system and 'domestic' banks), combined with the demands from financial 'rescue' (or 'bail outs') from other enterprises, with the car industry in the vanguard.[8] Second, there are the demands to install new national, and possibly international, systems of regulation, surveillance, and scrutiny that will rein in the excesses of greed, gambling and risk-taking identified as causes of the present crisis. The search for regulation almost immediately meets its opposite – the insistence that only the freedom of the market can ensure that growth can be renewed and profits can be distributed.

Woven into the regulatory desires are the claims that a newly 'moral' or 'ethical' capitalism needs to be constructed. The 'casino capitalism' of the past needs to be tamed, restrained and made more people-friendly by injections of morality, ethical standards and a sense of social responsibility. So far, the politicians demanding such moralization – itself an uncanny echo of neo-conservative demands that the poor needed to be remoralized in the 1980s and 1990s – have been less than specific on the means by which such moral character might be induced.[9] But these calls for a moral capitalism represent a sort of muted political echo of popular scepticism and outrage about the crisis of the present – and the extent to which it combines broken promises (the 'property owning democracy' at the core of Anglo-American politics for the past three decades), political betrayal and corporate greed. Here, fleetingly perhaps, is one basis for a genuinely popular anti-capitalism – but the danger is that it might decompose into other directions (regressive nationalism, political authoritarianism, moral Puritanism – the elements that contributed to the 'other' strategy of the 1930s).

Finally, governments encounter profound demands for security – but not the securitization of the property market, nor the safety/security nexus of the modernized state in the struggles against the anti-social threats outside and within the nation. This is the return of an older discourse of security, sometimes known as 'social security': the collective provision by the state of resources that protect individuals, families and whole societies from the vagaries and vicissitudes of markets, whose profound and unpredictable dynamics once persuaded people that they could not be trusted to guarantee economic and social security or human welfare. Which brings us to the strange and deeply paradoxical return of welfarism – or at least some of the words associated with welfarism.

Both the US and UK governments (under Obama and Brown, respectively) have been deploying the language of the 'New Deal', promising to create a new new deal.[10] The specific national proposals are different, with the Obama plan having aspects of a public works programme more reminiscent of the original New Deal; while the UK programme still focuses on a mix of welfare-to-work and intensified conditionality (not to mention trying to engage private capital in providing services). The current and threatened depth of the crisis, however, makes both the language and the plans somewhat unstable. Brown, just prior to a visit to the United States, tried to register the scale of the crisis – and the reach of a renewed US-UK alliance – by promising a 'global new deal':

> I believe there is no challenge so great or so difficult that it cannot be overcome by America, Britain and the world working together. That is why President Obama and I will discuss this week a global new deal, whose impact can stretch from the villages of Africa to reforming the financial institutions of London and New York – and giving security to the hard-working families in every country. (*Sunday Times*, 1 March 2009, available at: http://www.timesonline.co.uk/tol/comment/columnists/guest_contributors/article5821821.ece)

I will only note that the global reach of this new deal is somewhat compromised by its characteristic New Labour framing: only 'hard working families' need apply. This points to a more general paradox of the possible new new deals: they are being invented on the cusp between neo-liberal anti-welfarism (or workfare, Peck 2001) and the possible need for post-neo-liberal strategies that can address questions of social security and social order. In the UK, the persistence of governmental concerns with tightening conditionality and getting people into work already looks odd in the context of rising unemployment, income insecurity and homelessness.[11] Such concerns have dominated New Labour's approach to 'welfare reform', but are being enlarged through the promised extension of psychotherapeutic counselling to the unemployed.[12]

If nothing else, though, this circulation of the imagery of the New Deal should give us pause for thought. What is being named and claimed through this idea? What sort of 'progressive imaginary' is being memorialized and revived? The New Deal was certainly a significant piece of state intervention into an economic and social crisis, all the more remarkable for overcoming (or at least temporarily suppressing) the objections of a US political class to collectivism in any form. But it may also be worth remembering that this was not a 'welfare state' in any developed sense – rather it was, as Edwin Amenta's study (2000) clearly demonstrates, a 'Work and Relief state', involving a variety of questions about compulsion, about inclusion and exclusion and about other areas of support or provision that we might now count as welfare. Not surprisingly in the United States, questions of racialized and gendered divisions were central to the functioning of the New Deal (and the Aid to Dependent Children programme that was later added, see, for example, Mink 1990, Quadagno 1996).[13] How will the new new deals address the complex 'landscapes of inequality' that neo-liberalism has reshaped globally, nationally, locally (Collins *et al.* 2008)? How will they contribute to the new landscapes of inequality that are being produced by the current crisis?

After neo-liberalism?

The answer to this question clearly depends, as I have suggested, on what one means by neo-liberalism. Certainly many of the features attributed to neo-liberalism are in crisis, or in suspension, or lack political, much less popular, credibility. The concentration of the search for solutions on previously denigrated and discredited terrain – the nation, the nation-state, public spending and public welfare – suggests that, at least, neo-liberal logics and orientations are not in good health. Declining faith in markets and financial institutions suggests that there are some limits to market populism's reach. But other aspects – the commitment to enterprise, a market-centric understanding of choice-as-freedom, and a scepticism about both the capacity and trustworthiness of government, politics and politicians (that neo-liberal protagonists did much to encourage) – seem only muted, rather than exhausted. Equally, its governmental logics – the quest for a narrowly defined efficiency, the drive to cheapen the cost of public services, the love affair with managerialism in its many forms – seem likely to become even more significant as the crisis of public indebtedness takes its place among the many crises that constitute the present conjuncture.

In this moment, it may be that answering the question of whether we are 'after neo-liberalism' also turns on the meaning of the words 'after'. Some time ago, I argued that neo-liberalism needed to be thought of as a globalizing and universalizing would-be hegemonic project (Clarke 2004a). It is, at least, no longer hegemonic – it fails to command popular and political assent; it cannot sustain its normalization and institutionalization as the dominant principle of common sense. That does not imply it has been replaced by some other organizing project or logic; nor that it has disappeared from political, governmental or popular thinking. On the contrary, many of its elements – not least the desires it names, articulates and promises to fulfil – remain in circulation. But they remain so as elements, fragments, or traces rather than a coherent and cohering project.

Finally, publics have to be negotiated and addressed, especially though not only, by national governments. They are spoken of – and spoken to – in the various circulating narratives of crisis (see the suggestive comments in Thompson 2009). States of anxiety, insecurity, outrage, scepticism and more have been mobilized, managed, negotiated, contained and directed – with few signs of success. As I indicated earlier, publics appear to be sceptical or faithless (although I suspect they always were – existing in conditions of what I have called passive dissent or Jeremy Gilbert has referred to more interestingly as 'disaffected consent'[14]). Despite these ambivalent alignments, perhaps the most striking feature of the discourses about public-ness is that publics have been summoned to perform the most abject role: they are the public whose future is almost entirely enfolded into the problem of public debt. These publics – and future publics – have been invited to pay the costs of corporate welfare (saving the system) while being told that the public services on which their welfare might depend needs to be retrenched again to balance the public books. But it is important that we recognize the ways in which these publics are also outraged, anxious and insecure – and that such collective emotions are directed at heterogeneous targets: bankers, governments, migrant workers, and 'the system'. Most worryingly, these publics are also deeply sceptical or cynical about politics – a problem for those who seek to construct political alternatives and political solutions.

Notes

1 This paper is based on a lecture at the Central European University on 2 March 2009, given while I was a visitor in the Department of Sociology and Social Anthropology. It also draws on a presentation to a workshop on *Culture (and Cultural Studies) After the Crunch*, organized by The Pavis Centre of the Open University and the Department of Sociology of the University of East London. I am deeply grateful to the many people who have offered comments and questions to help me think about these issues.

2 Of course, arguments persist in practice among market populists about what forms of state and government action are tolerable, ranging from the minimalist 'nightwatchman' state required to preserve the institutions of private property and the nation from predators to the more recent enthusiasm for a contracting state that can provide new sources of profit for predatory corporations.

3 There is some ambiguity about what it is that the market rewards – particularly between skill, enterprise and good fortune. References to casino capitalism tend to emphasize the 'chance' element – and the

mystery – of contemporary market-driven rewards. But this exists in an uncomfortable relation with any notion that markets should deliver just and proportionate outcomes. There is a persistent, if subordinate, belief that rewards should be 'earned' that has resurfaced in popular anger about disproportionate rewards in the financial services sector, and about rewards such as bonuses being paid for 'failure'.

4 Like others who have commented on this gendered language of markets, capital and capitalism, I think it is important to point to the ways in which such terms are shared by enthusiasts and critics alike (see Gibson-Graham 1996, Morris 2004, for example).

5 Although the definition (and the indicators) turn out to be contested: see, for example, Associated Press' sampling: 'Recession, depression, take your pick' at http://www.google.com/hostednews/ap/article/ALeqM5hySoApuU4iyBTZ6lZsCM5OrlWgrAD96M43380.

6 A different articulation of faith and the economic was provided in claims made by the Indonesian President at the World Islamic Economic Forum in Jakarta, March 2009, that Islamic banks were performing better in the crisis. http://news.bbc.co.uk/go/pr/fr/-/2/hi/asia-pacific/7918129.stm

7 In an interview on the Andrew Marr Show, reported at http://news.bbc.co.uk/2/hi/business/7931142.stm.

8 At this point, the car industry – with its extensive horizontal integration on a global scale – has become a series of 'national' car industries. Saab is cut adrift from General Motors to make its plea for protection to the Swedish Government, and so on. Bizarrely, the BBC (10 February 2009) reported that the 'Chinese car industry overtakes the US', although this referred to news that more cars were sold in China than in the United States. The Chinese car *industry* involves some significant international partnerships, including General Motors. http://news.bbc.co.uk/go/pr/fr/-/2/hi/business/7879372.

9 Lest we forget, the neo-conservatives answers to demoralization among the poor included the withdrawal of public support, the enforced learning of independence, the discovery that actions or choices were consequential for personal wellbeing – and, of course, that hard work and marriage were the foundations of a successful life and a successful society.

10 For policy aficionados, there is the critical point that the UK has already had new new deals (for young people, for the unemployed, for lone mothers, for disabled people and so on). So the present promise is (at least) a new new new deal. It is not recorded what Marx thought about history repeating itself more than once.

11 See, for example, Madeleine Bunting 'Workfare has arrived in Britain' The Guardian, 23 February 2009. http://www.guardian.co.uk/commentisfree/2009/feb/23/madeleine-bunting-welfare-reform.

12 *The Observer* reported ministers promising to train an extra 3600 counsellors (based in Cognitive Behaviour Therapy) and to open psychotherapy centres in every primary care trust in the National Health

Service (NHS): http://www.guardian.co.uk/politics/2009/mar/08/recession-therapy-nhs-mental-health.

13 Aid to Dependent Children subsequently became Aid for Families with Dependent Children (AFDC) which was the programme that President Clinton abolished through the Personal Responsibility and Work Opportunity Reconciliation Act in 1996 when claiming to 'end welfare as we know it' (Mink 2002).

14 'Disaffected consent' was a thought-provoking part of his contribution to an event on 'Culture (and Cultural Studies) after the Crunch' in London on 4 February 2009. Passive dissent appeared in the last chapter of Clarke (2004b).

References

Amenta, E. (2000) *Bold Relief*, Princenton, NJ, Princeton University Press.

Brown, W. (2005) *Edgework: Critical Essays on Knowledge and Politics*, Princeton, NJ, Princeton University Press.

Carter, H. (2009) 'The End of Boom and Bust is a Fallacy – The Economy Was Always Going to Crash', *The Guardian*, 14 January. Available at: http://www.guardian.co.uk/business/2009/jan/14/recession-public-confidence (accessed 12 April 2010).

Clarke, J. (2004a) 'Dissolving the public realm? The logics and limits of neo-liberalism', *Journal of Social Policy*, vol. 33, no. 1, pp. 27–48.

Clarke, J. (2004b) *Changing Welfare, Changing States: New Directions in Social Policy*, London, Sage.

Clarke, J. (2007) 'Subordinating the social? Problems of post-welfarist capitalism', *Cultural Studies*, vol. 21, no. 6, pp. 974–987.

Clarke, J. (2008) 'Living with/in and against neo-liberalism', *Focaal-European Journal of Anthropology*, vol. 51, pp. 135–147.

Clarke, J., Newman, J., Smith, N., Vidler, E. & Westmarland, L. (2007) *Creating Citizen-consumers: Changing Publics and Changing Public Services*, London, Sage.

Collins, J., di Leonardis, M. & Williams, B. (eds) (2008) *New Landscapes of Inequality*, Santa Fe, NM, School of Advanced Research Press.

Dinham. A., Furbey, R. & Lowndes, V. (eds) (2009) *Faith in the Public Realm: Controversies, Policies and Practices*, Bristol, The Policy Press.

Foucault, M. (2008) *The Birth of Bio-politics: Lectures at the Collège de France, 1978–1979*, Basingstoke, Palgrave Macmillan.

Frank, T. (2001) *One Market Under God: Extreme Capitalism, Market Populism and the End of Economic Democracy*, New York, Anchor Books.

Gibson-Graham, J. K. (1996) *The End of Capitalism (as we knew it)*, Malden, MA, Basil Blackwell Publishers.

Gilroy, P. (1993) *The Black Atlantic: Modernity and Double Consciousness*, Cambridge, MA, Harvard University Press.

Gilbert, J. (2007) *Anti-capitalism and Culture*, London, Sage.

Glover, J. (2009) 'Britain Loses Faith in Economy', *The Guardian*, 14 January. Available at: http://www.guardian.co.uk/business/2009/jan/14/british-economic-confidence-recession (accessed 12 April 2010).

Gramsci, A. (1971) *Selections from the Prison Notebooks*, ed. G. Nowell-Smith, London, Lawrence and Wishart.

Grossberg, L. (2006) 'Does cultural studies have futures? Should it? (or what's the matter with New York?): Cultural Studies: contexts and conjunctures', *Cultural Studies*, vol. 20, no. 1, pp. 1–32.

Harvey, D. (2005) *A Brief History of Neoliberalism*, Oxford, Oxford University Press.

Jessop, B. (2002) *The Future of the Capitalist State*, Cambridge, Polity.

Kalb, D. (2005) 'From flows to violence: politics and knowledge in the debates on globalization and empire', *Anthropological Theory*, vol. 5, no. 2, pp. 176–204.

Mink, G. (1990) 'The Lady and the Tramp: gender, race and the origins of the American welfare state', in *Women, the State and Welfare*, ed. L. Gordon, Madison, WI, University of Wisconsin Press, pp. 92–122.

Mink, G. (2002) *Welfare's End*, Ithaca, NY, Cornell University Press.

Morris, M. (2004) *Too Soon, Too Late: History in Popular Culture*, Bloomington, IN, Indiana University Press.

Needham, C. (2007) *The Reform of Public Services under New Labour: Narratives of Consumerism*, Basingstoke, Palgrave.

Newman, J. & Clarke, J. (2009) *Publics, Politics and Power: Remaking the Public in Public Services*, London, Sage.

Peck, J. (2001) *Workfare States*, New York, The Guilford Press.

Pile, S. (2005) *Real Cities: Modernity, Space and the Phantasmogorias of City Life*, London, Sage.

Quadagno, J. (1996) *The Color of Welfare*, Oxford, Oxford University Press.

Riley, D. (1985) *War in the Nursery: Theories of the Child and Mother*, London, Virago.

Rose, N (1999) *Powers of Freedom: Reframing Political Thought*, Cambridge, Cambridge University Press.

Shermer, M. (2009) *The Mind of the Market: How Biology and Psychology Shape our Economic Lives*, New York, Holt.

Somers, M. (2008) *Genealogies of Citizenship: Markets, Statelessness and the Right to Have Rights*, Cambridge, Cambridge University Press.

Thompson. G. (2009) 'How the financial crisis is being packaged for public consumption'. Available at: http://www.open.ac.uk/ccig/dialogues/blogs/how-the-financial-crisis-is-being-packaged-for-public-consumption (accessed 12 April 2010).

Steve Cross & Jo Littler

CELEBRITY AND *SCHADENFREUDE*

The cultural economy of fame in freefall

This paper explores the popularity of contemporary expressions of delight in celebrity downfall, or Schadenfreude *towards celebrity culture, and questions to what extent they can be understood as cultural critiques of economic inequality. For just as the economy has its own parables, so do 'cultural' expressions contain parables of normativity about economic life. We argue that* Schadenfreude's *relationship to 'equality' can be read in terms of social, cultural and economic blockages, and investigate some of the history to this feeling by exploring different arguments over the meaning and status of 'equality' in modern and post-modern societies. This survey of its contested meanings highlights the distinctions which have been made and elided between property and identity, the economic and the cultural, and the political and the private. These geneaologies are used to interpret* Schadenfreude, *and to highlight the tension between two different aspects of contemporary subjectivity: 'integrity' and marketability of the self. By drawing on these contested genealogies and theories of equality, we are also arguing that* Schadenfreude *toward celebrity in its most common contemporary form cannot be seen merely as a superstructural phenomenon of a neo-liberal base but rather as stitched into and as of a piece with this neo-liberal culture. We argue that whilst* Schadenfreude *is able to be articulated in different directions, it overwhelmingly works to express irritation at inequalities but not to change the wider rules of the current social system, and its political economy often actually entails it fuelling inequalities of wealth. In these terms,* Schadenfreude *can be perceived as being intimately related to autistic economic culture and as being able to be perpetuated by coasting on its own status as an autistic response.*

It is fair to say that academic work on celebrity has focused more on processes of identification and longing rather than disidentification and disgust. Celebrities have most often been interrogated as objects of *desire*; the star's specific attributes have been analysed in relation to specific social formations; and the popular contemporary rush towards the media spotlight has been discussed in terms of the ordinarily disempowered searching vicariously for the extraordinary validation that proximity to celebrity brings (Dyer 1986, 1998, Redmond & Holmes 2006, 2007, Littler 2003, Marshall 1997). Celebrity, in all these accounts, however methodologically and theoretically divergent they may be, is figured as offering a positive promise, even if that promise is not kept or remains unfulfilled. It is studied as a phenomenon that harnesses the potential of people to dream, that speaks of connections that can be magnified, that creates what we might call 'assemblages of emulation' rather than blind imitation.

A widespread popular hostility to celebrities undoubtedly exists. It emerges 'outside', or between the cracks, of 'professionally'-produced media culture (everyday banter, email jokes, bitchy blogs), but also within those not-so hallowed spaces themselves (snide comments in newspaper columns, 'revealing insights' in magazines devoted to celebrity lives). From all these various locations one particularly graphic motif is repeated again and again: the taking of pleasure in celebrity misfortune. Whether mocking Michael Jackson's fall from grace, breathlessly reporting Lindsay Lohan's losses or eagerly observing Britney's meltdowns, the act of gleefully watching or pushing celebrities from their pedestals has become a major cultural trope. The vastly increased speed of the adulation/abjection cycle is exemplified by the case of Susan Boyle, the *Britain's Got Talent 2009* contestant and favourite to win, who went from YouTube darling (100 million hits worldwide) to 'tragic SuBo' within three or four weeks.

To what extent might these expressions of pleasure in celebrity freefall – or *Schadenfreude* at celebrity downfalls – be viewed as intimately linked to contemporary economic formations? A number of commentators have pointed out that the phenomenon of celebrity is indicative of a society with profoundly unequal concentrations of power. For P. David Marshall, celebrity is a site of hegemonic struggle in capitalist democracies between 'overtly public individuals' and those constructed as an undifferentiated mass of 'demographic aggregates' (Marshall 1997, p. ix). For Jeremy Gilbert (2003, p. 86) celebrity is 'inherent to capitalism from the moment of its earliest emergence', its privileging of individualism and faciality as palpable in the Roman Empire as today. For Nick Couldry (2001) the mediated zones of celebrity culture offer spaces of recognition gravitated towards by the powerless: and so the 'hidden injuries of media power' are tied to broader injustices of financial poverty and cultural neglect. In these terms the gross inequalities between the 'ordinary civilian' and the 'extraordinary celebrity' speak of the social and financial divides between rich and poor, haves and have-nots.[1] Consequently, the proliferation of celebrity discourse over the past two decades can be understood (although this is a point rarely made) in relation to a broader context of the rise of neo-liberal capitalism and its savagely widening global disparities of wealth and power.

This paper examines the currency of such expressions of pleasure in celebrity loss and asks how they operate in relation to neo-liberalism. It argues that *Schadenfreude* represents a negative capacity in socially affective relations, one that *desires* equality, but is primarily unable to think it as anything other than 'leveling through humiliation'. We consider this impasse on several, inter-related levels: social, cultural, political and economic. To begin with, we outline the nature of *Schadenfreude*'s impasse by considering its affective and emotional life. Secondly, we explore the paradoxical centrality and disavowal of equality to the modern 'social imaginary', in particular the contradictory tendencies of rejecting ideas of economic equality whilst embracing the idea of 'equality of condition'. Thirdly, we explore how this impasse correlates with the cultural-political economy of celebrity, its tabloid lives and its turnover of stars.

By considering popular pleasure towards celebrity pain on these different levels, the paper aims to demonstrate that contemporary manifestations of *Schadenfreude* can best be understood in relation to the production of a 'subject of capitalism' (Skeggs 2004, p. 64) in which particular subjective propensities are imbricated with differential logics of property and value. As Skeggs notes, 'capitalism works for the preparation of an individual who might be: endowed with an ultimately self-interested rationality, *convinced of the principle of equality*, [and] *dedicated to the concept of private property*' (p. 64, emphasis added). In this article, we argue that *Schadenfreude* toward celebrities operates at the intersection between such contradictory elements of subjectivized desire which themselves have complex genealogies. In this sense, the paper mobilizes Deleuze and Guattari's model of a political economy of the psyche – thus moving away from notions of *Schadenfreude* as an ahistorical or universal feature of the 'human condition' (Deleuze & Guattari 1977/2004a, 1980/2004b).

In this paper, then, our argument is that this particular reading of *Schadenfreude* as a type of 'blockage' or cultural paralysis also needs to be read in broader terms of its inter-relation with other types of economy beyond that of an individualized ethical or moral economy. What is its relationship to wider social, political and economic ecologies? We are interested in how *Schadenfreude* towards celebrities has predominantly come to emerge, and be encoded, and *why*, by considering its longer-standing discursive genealogies. For it is not simply performed by a few 'bad', transgressive or deluded subjects (see Hills 2002, pp. 8–11) but is a component in a complex affective assemblage – itself formed in relation to particular economies and conceptions of equality – in which most people reading this work, like its authors, have participated.

Schadenfreude's affective and emotional life

In *Celebrity and Power* P. David Marshall (1997) draws our attention to the importance of the affective and emotional intensities circulating around celebrity culture. Marshall argues that the affective domain has important social implications, focusing his discussion on the proximity of politics and affect in the adulation of charismatic leaders. What is of particular relevance for our discussion here, however, is how he describes these flows of affect. He argues that 'there are public forms of subjectivity that are privileged in contemporary culture because they are connected to particular ends and interests in the organization of power' (Marshall 1997, p. 203, see also Hesmondhalgh 2005, p. 122). This is a useful formulation to help us consider the existence and prominence of *Schadenfreude* towards celebrity in popular culture because we might understand it as one such culturally privileged 'public form of subjectivity': a form in which a particular set of feelings towards celebrities are encouraged and travel across public and private domains.

A related means of grasping how such public forms of subjectivity work can be borrowed from Sara Ahmed's conceptualization of 'the sociality of emotion'. Ahmed proposes 'an analysis of affective economies, where feelings do not reside in subjects or objects, but are produced as effects of circulation' (Ahmed 2004, p. 8).[2] Putting these terms together, we might describe *Schadenfreude* as a collectively constructed feeling produced through circulation. This is illustrated for example by the British-based sardonic gossip email newsletter and associated website *Popbitch*, which often features stories about celebrities who have been heckled or attacked by 'the public' for the enjoyment of its readers. One recent newsletter gleefully related how British television star Alan Davies was kicked by a member of the public; another recounted how *Harry Potter* star Daniel Radcliffe 'spent at least one of his schooldays locked in a cupboard as fellow pupils shouted "magic yourself out of that, Potter!"').[3] In the case of *Popbitch*, a collective feeling of *Schadenfreude* towards celebrities is generated on a routinized basis.

But is *Schadenfreude* an emotion or an affect? The classic distinction between these two terms is drawn from psychoanalysis, where it is used to distinguish between the first and third person's representation of feeling (in other words, affect is a state witnessed by an external observer). Recent critical theorists of affect including Brian Massumi have argued that emotion requires a subject, whereas affect does not: emotion indicates feeling given form and function, but affect remains 'unformed and unstructured' (in Ngai 2005, p. 25, see also Massumi 1995). Similarly, for Lawrence Grossberg, it is a contentless state of psychic energy (1997, pp. 145–165). In our case, *Schadenfreude* has a specific object: the celebrity in question. It is also sometimes given 'form' – for example, through the carefully crafted joke at the celebrity's expense. In these cases, *Schadenfreude* can be classified as an emotion structured through an individual subjectivity. Its function, however, is less clear; and it is not always 'strongly structured', shading as it does into a more diffuse, 'transindividual' affective economy of resentment. In this case, *Schadenfreude* would seem to cleave more closely to the status of an affect.

Indeed, the relationship between a subjectively meaningful or self-defining 'emotion' and connection to a transindividual affective assemblage is invariably blurred or even precarious in the occurrence of *Schadenfreude*.[4]

In these terms, *Schadenfreude* is what Simone Ngai calls an 'ugly feeling'. Ngai's work argues that 'bad' emotions, like envy, paranoia and irritation, can be thought of as existing *in-between* emotions and affects, as mediations between the aesthetic and the political that act as knotted or condensed 'interpretations of predicaments'. Ngai is interested in the possibility of recuperating such negative feelings 'for their critical productivity'. In this way she follows in the recent tradition of theorists such as Wendy Brown, and, like Brown, she counsels against the danger of romanticizing them. As Paulo Virno warns, such 'sentiments of disenchantment' which once marked a radical distance and alienation from exploited labour – like anxiety, distraction and cynicism – have, in post-Fordist/late capitalist societies, become 'the very lubricants of the economic system which they came into being to oppose' (Ngai 2005, p. 4).

If they are no longer 'radical', how, then, are these 'ugly feelings' positioned in contemporary culture? Ngai suggests that they often play an ambivalent social role. She points out that they are mainly 'canonically minor,' opposed to the high drama of hatred or passion, and conducts a careful analysis of the workings of these minor emotions across various literary texts. Most interestingly for our discussion here, Ngai concludes that the very 'weakness' of these canonically marginal feelings structures what they can do. She argues that

> [. . .] the unsuitability of these weakly intentional feelings for forceful or unambiguous action is precisely what amplifies their power to diagnose situations, and *situations marked by blocked or thwarted action in particular*. (Ngai 2005, p. 28, emphasis added)

This interpretation of minor ugly feelings as diagnosing 'situations marked by blocked or thwarted action' is particularly applicable to *Schadenfreude* in relation to celebrity downfall. The enjoyment of celebrity misfortune or humiliation fulfils a specific cultural function precisely because it offers vicarious pleasure in the witnessing of the powerful being made less powerful; it is an attempt to address or deal with a severe imbalance of power.

But acknowledging its 'diagnostic' quality and role also raises questions about its effectiveness, its ethical status and the diversity of uses to which it is put. To take the issues of ethics and diverse uses first, it is important to point out that the meaning of *Schadenfreude* and how it can be mobilized is neither guaranteed nor fixed. In his book-length study of the subject, *When Bad Things Happen to Other People*, John Portmann argues that *Schadenfreude* most often appears in minor situations of suffering where it tends to be of a comic nature, 'help[ing] us withstand the difficulties of living' (2000, p. 41). By contrast, he argues, responses to more serious suffering tend to get couched in abstract, Kantian terms of justice. Portmann's study is primarily concerned with the degree to which *Schadenfreude* given its proximity to both comedy and malice, can be said to have a more properly ethical basis.

Portmann's analysis, which draws heavily on John Rawls's concern with the ethical potentialities of envy, is useful in that by avoiding any simple blanket moral castigation of the subject it is able to highlight and provide a more variegated account of its sources and manifestations. Yet, the formal abstraction of Portmann's schema is less helpful on the question of 'effectiveness' or at understanding what *Schadenfreude* actually *does* in relation to that 'equality' towards which it gestures. Here it is useful to return to Ngai's understanding of *Schadenfreude* as acting primarily 'to diagnose a situation marked by blocked [and] thwarted action'. For in one significant sense, the scale and the form of contemporary manifestations of *Schadenfreude* in relation to celebrity can appear to bespeak a social imaginary that is profoundly limited. These manifestations do not appear to offer a substantial or ongoing challenge to the structural inequalities so roundly personified by the 'celebrity-class'. They appear unable to regard the notion of equality as anything other than the experience of levelling through personal humiliation. In these terms, *Schadenfreude* can be understood as a kind of 'individualized' outlet for thwarted desires of equality.

This is not to say that *Schadenfreude* might not be articulated in a number of different directions. As Lawrence Grossberg has pointed out in a discussion of affective charges in popular culture, the link between cynicism and wider forms of social cruelty is not guaranteed, and similarly neither is the link between *Schadenfreude* and wider forms of social cruelty (Grossberg 1997, p. 153). So, for example, Charlie Brooker's caustic journalism in his BBC television show *Screenwipe* extends his hatred of celebrity privilege into an excavation of the media processes which create or augment such privilege. Similarly, it is perfectly possible to imagine that the *Schadenfreude* of a blogger or tabloid-reader might co-exist with political activism, because *Schadenfreude*, like any other subjective propensity can be articulated in different directions. Nonetheless, we aim to show that it is inflected, produced and encoded by both long-term discursive geneaologies and contemporary neo-liberal discourses of 'meritocracy'. In the next section, to explore this issue in more depth, we consider *Schadenfreude*'s relationship to social economies; and in particular, because of its dependence on the theme of 'levelling', we pay attention to the extent to which it can be thought to address the issue of *equality*. This section is a fairly lengthy discussion of the different 'languages' of equality, which we discuss in order to help understand the social processes that are productive of *Schadenfreude,* in which equality figures as both desire and as foreclosed possibility.

The persistence of equality: consciousness and social being

> ... relations of community and equality are themselves but a never ending settling of accounts. (Ranciere 1995, p. 65)

Equality 'as a concrete social and political demand' has tended to be thought of as 'the child of the great revolutions' (Callinicos 2000, p. 20). However, what constitutes 'equality', and how demands rooted in ideas of equality might be made within the broadly liberal polities that emerged from the 'great revolutions' needs to be explored if we are to understand issues of its potentiality, persistence and 'thwartedness'.

The classic account of the form of equality that emerged out of the ('bourgeois') revolutions is delineated in Marx's work. In *On the Jewish Question*, Marx sketches the contours of a particular type of relationship between the post-revolutionary citizen, the state and civil society (Marx 1975). The essay comprises a critique of Bruno Bauer's polemic *The Jewish Question* in which Bauer argues that, with the abolition of the religious character of the state, the formal opposition between *particular* identities (Jew and Christian in his polemic) would be abolished and that particularity within the secular state is therefore dissolved into a formal and universal 'equality'.

Marx sees in Bauer's argument a key problem which relates directly to the way sociality is experienced in liberal capitalist states. As he argues, 'particularities' (of wealth, status or condition) are not abolished by 'political emancipation', but rather banished to the 'private' realm of civil society. Thus, citizens who are formally equal to one another in legal-political terms nonetheless retain their 'particularities' within civil society and a firm distinction is retained between (abstract) citizens and (concrete) private individuals. Equality is, therefore, experienced as a 'property' of the citizen, and the experience of the self as a 'communal being' (as an equal among equals), is, Marx argues, possible only within the 'phantom' realm of abstract citizenship. This version of equality, Marx argues, is profoundly disjunctive, contradicted as it is by the parallel experience of profound *economic* inequalities that such an abstract-universal notion of citizenship cannot elide.

Marx's analysis offers a compelling account of disjuncture and contradiction in the formation of subjectivities through which we can begin to locate the historical specificity of *Schadenfreude*. Something of the powerfully *affective* dimension of this 'contradictory' subjective experience can be seen clearly articulated in de Tocqueville's 1830s account of democratic society in America, which figures 'equality of condition' as a 'fundamental fact' of emergent democratic society. Here equality and affect are intimately linked. From the quotidian (in which equality 'daily gives each man in the crowd a host of small enjoyments') to the grandiloquent ('men pounce on equality as their booty and cling to it as a precious treasure they fear to have snatched away') the 'passion' for it 'seeps into every corner of the human heart, expands and fills the whole' (de Tocqueville 1994, p. 505). However, crucially, there is again a disjuncture between economic equality and 'equality of condition': whilst equality of condition is experienced as 'booty' and a 'precious treasure' which must be preserved at all costs, wealth itself is experienced as a form of ephemeral 'circulation', as a 'wheel of fate'. De Tocqueville also notes that 'I know no other country where love of money has such a grip on men's hearts or where stronger scorn is expressed for the theory of permanent equality of property ... wealth circulates there with incredible rapidity and experience shows that two successive generations seldom enjoy its favours' (1994, p. 54). For de Tocqueville, the passionate attachment to equality of condition, 'scorn' for equality of property and 'love of money' are central to the affective experience of democratic sociality. This affective assemblage, with its paradoxical language of property, is subjectivized in its production of individualities that must bind together elements of *contradictory* desire. As we will demonstrate, *Schadenfreude* comes to be experienced as a levelling process that both compensates for, and enacts, these central tensions.

A further dimension of the centrality of equality to the modern social imaginary is provided by radical democratic theory, which can help us understand more about how *Schadenfreude* functions. Claude Lefort, for example, argues that 'the democratic revolution' is not simply a set of political institutions rooted in formal equality (1988, p. 183). Rather, it is a complex of factors that influence all aspects of the social field whilst having profound consequences in terms of individual modes of subjection. For Lefort, social space and division are always already mediated through discursive modalities particular to an overall type of social form, a form which has a generative dynamic of its own beyond its putative infrastructural determination.

According to Lefort the 'revolutionary and unprecedented' feature of democracy lies precisely in the fact that the 'locus of power becomes an empty place' (1988, p. 17) which cannot be filled with a single collective agent. This indeterminacy is exacerbated with the emergence of capitalism and its continual upheaval of social and political institutions. Divisions between dominant and subordinate groups in contemporary societies are always potentially fragmentary and antagonistic, and the immediate consequence of this is that 'natural determination' is replaced by a purely 'social society' in which '*any individual or group can be accorded the same status*' (p. 18, emphasis added).

In radical democratic theory, the 'social' is regarded as an open field of permanent antagonism with the subject of this antagonism figured as a subject of 'lack', a subject for whom the plenitude of full self-presence is always thwarted by the agency of an antagonistic 'Other' (Laclau & Mouffe 1985, Laclau 1990). The 'form' of democratic society therefore produces and sanctions a proliferation of points of contestation, an endless staging of conflict on its groundless ground. Demands for 'equality' clearly figure as central within the proliferation of open-ended sites of contestation that make up contemporary sociality but as has frequently been noted these themselves tend to be routed through identity claims and concomitant desires for 'recognition' rather than 'redistribution' (Fraser 1995, 2000, McNay 2007).

We would argue that in its contemporary manifestations *Schadenfreude* to a large extent endorses radical democratic notions of the proliferation of antagonisms and evinces the collapse of a 'natural' order and its replacement with ontological indeterminacy. *Schadenfreude* towards celebrities is significantly different to notions of the temporary reversals of naturalized, hierarchical order in the carnivalesque, for example; its negative affect proliferates across the social field through multiple and ubiquitous forms of mediation that are not delimited by the circumscribed spatial and temporal specificity of 'carnival'. However, as we will see later on, it can simultaneously function to sediment power relations, rather than to radically disrupt them, and the privilege and position of its targets are 'naturalized' in albeit highly complex and unstable ways.

The work of Ranciere gives us a further language to help understand *Schadenfreude*'s relationship to equality. Ranciere's work is suggestive for its framing of the question of equality in terms of both its persistence as the 'only universal axiom of politics' (Ranciere 2004, p. 86) and in terms of the profound and persistent opposition that it faces. Tracing the tension between equality and its opponents back to Plato's political philosophy, Ranciere argues that we must distinguish between two discrete logics: that is, the logic of equality (the absolute and unconditional equivalence of any body with any other body) and the logic of police (Ranciere 1995, 1997, 1999, 2004, 2006). By 'police' he means the managed, ordered field of the 'social' and what this field legitimates as its perceptible, 'natural' elements, the places and positions which subjects and identities occupy within it. These can be straightforwardly 'hierarchical' in terms of a law of 'essences' (as in Plato's ordering of the city in *The Republic*) or 'naturalized' in more complex ways through notions of a hierarchy of 'intelligence' or 'merit'. In either case they account for and legitimate rule by the 'best'.

For Ranciere, the essence of demands for equality is not so much to unify as to declassify: to undo the supposed naturalness of 'police' orders and replace it 'with the controversial figure of division' (1999, p. 30).[5] As Ranciere argues:

> . . . a political subject is not a group that 'becomes aware' of itself, finds its voice, imposes it weight on society. *It is an operator* that connects and disconnects different areas, regions, identities, functions, and capacities existing in the configuration of a given experience – that is, in the nexus of distributions of the police order and whatever equality is already

inscribed there, however fragile and fleeting such inscriptions may be. (1999, p. vi, emphasis added)

For Ranciere, subjectivization does not emerge in awareness of the gap between a 'political illusion' and 'social/economic reality' (as in Marx's 'praxis'). Rather, the egalitarian polemic itself 'invents' an always *insubstantial* community 'determined only by the contingency and resolve of its enactment' (1995, p. 87). This cannot simply be reduced to 'the immateriality of egalitarian communication' ('the political' in Marx). It exists as a permanent possibility which can erupt in 'heroic' form in ('subjectivized') demands for equivalence to be taken seriously in its case (civil rights movements and feminism being classic instances). Clearly *Schadenfreude* does not achieve 'subjectivization' in Ranciere's terms: it is neither a demand nor a polemical statement of equal worth and thus not an 'operator'. But it does evince a much more *dynamic* relationship between subject formation and equality as an inherent possibility than either Marx or radical democratic theory are able to capture, positing as it does a permanent conflict between egalitarian demand and police order which is immanent to politics as such. From our perspective, the transient and highly mobile nature of subjectivization in its 'heroic' or properly 'political' mode is subtended with a more diffuse and more quotidian experience that both challenges and reinforces police logics. The levelling desire which in *Schadenfreude* expresses as the cruel laughter of humiliation at the individual mis*fortune* of those who have got 'above' their station therefore become caught up in new 'naturalizing' economies of worth and value.

The tension between inequality of property and capacity for political subjectivization which concerns Ranciere (2006, p. 95) is also at the core of Etienne Balibar's argument about the efficacy of 'equaliberty', the conflation of equality and liberty which are 'identical in practice', precisely because in their declaration in the founding documents of political modernity neither one can exist without the other (Balibar 1994, p. xii). Balibar highlights how, historically, liberalism has insisted on the foundational and 'mutually exclusive' tension between the two poles of the revolutionary demand, equality and liberty (1994, p. 39). This tension is nowhere more apparent that in the encounter between 'equaliberty' and differing conceptions of property and community. Thus for liberalism, 'liberty' functions as the guarantor of a right to 'unconditional private property' (p. 216) which equality has most often been figured as dangerously antithetical because of its encounter with traditions insisting on the transcendence of this property form and the institution of collective mechanisms for its distribution. Liberalism, which figures the individual as essentially 'possessive' (in McPherson's term) and thus as a subject of the juridical 'right' to unlimited property, simultaneously casts property itself as *outside* 'politics'. As we have seen in de Tocqueville, such liberal discourse enters the domain of subjective experience through its negative attitude towards 'equality of property'.

'Politicized' property has been central to modern understandings of individual *value* either as the subject of private possession or through arguments concerning the equitable allocation of resources. Indeed, if the latter option was frequently decried as adjacent to 'totalitarianism' in liberal thought, it has increasingly been foreclosed as a possibility at all. Consequently, the inscription of *individual* value in relation to an aggressively naturalized 'private' property is subjectivized through the codes of political economy itself:

> Every property [of the person] is inscribed in the codes and equivalences formalised in the knowledge of political economy; every individual is a proprietor and measured by his property insofar as he understands the practical and theoretical science of the exchange of value, or is recognised by it (that is, is himself inscribed in its account books). Individuals ... only have a relation to their being or their having by the mediation of this abstract knowledge ... (Balibar 1994, p. 58)

But this 'mediation' of the individual is always already a 'transindividual' (Balibar 1994, p. xii) phenomenon, a sculpting of the interiority of the subject which is a 'folding' of the outside in the production of an 'inner self' (Deleuze 1988). In this sense the 'psyche' is at the intersection between the materiality of social relations (the 'inegalitarian weight of bodies') and the 'semiotics of power' (the signifying systems of ideological justification) (Due 2007, p. 79). The double gesture that inscribes self and others within schemas determined by exchange value means that individual *being* and *having* are always experienced in relation to others and, more precisely, to the *value* of what others have and what they are. Equivalences are therefore always also comparisons of net worth.

However, although exchange values *appear* (as in the broader economy) to be related to transcendental properties which determine value absolutely, their worth is entirely immanent to the vagaries of the market. In terms of the 'ordinary' relationship to celebrity our individual worth is therefore experienced as *relative* in comparison to that of the celebrity in so far as the celebrity is thought (like the 'highflyer' or the precociously 'gifted' individual in other walks of life) to possess properties that are *intrinsically* more valuable; those of a 'natural' or hard-won 'talent', for example. But this is not the same as the absolute determination of place, which is experienced as a *natural* hierarchy of value in pre-modern societies and the relative difference in worth established through exchange value is inherently unstable.[6] The self, for example, is experienced as possessing an 'intrinsic' value of its own in a relational sense whereby this is measured against that of the other in a system of presumed meritocratic worth governed by an abstract justice that allots places accordingly. However, the apparent stability of the system of relative 'meritocratic' value collapses at the point at which value is shown not to be based on intrinsic worth but that of arbitrary exchange value. The celebrity who is recognized as simply 'famous for being famous' for example effectively abolishes the artifice of distance that notions of a meritocratic or intrinsic 'worth' must work to maintain through continuous performance or display of a distinctive 'talent'.

In terms of subjective experience, *Schadenfreude* therefore enacts the process of levelling whereby value is reinscribed in the other in line with a radical reappraisal of its supposed 'intrinsic' worth. But a full recognition of the arbitrariness of value based only on its *market* rather than its intrinsic worth would radically undermine the self's belief in its *own* intrinsic worth, which is foundational to modern self-hood. *Schadenfreude*'s revelling in falls from grace is therefore a compensation for the slippage between these systems, underwritten by a righteous and accusatory apportioning of *blame* at the other's apparently *willed* de-valuation (the drugs, drink or sexual excesses which *destroy* a 'natural talent') or at the other's exposure as 'talentless' after all. Even apparently 'natural' (rather than volitional) catastrophes such as the signs of ageing or of bodily imperfections serve to reinforce the sense that the properties of the person are *property* in a quite literal sense. Intrinsic and market exchange value blur, as the conception that properties must be maintained and protected in order to retain their value in a system of exchange comes into direct conflict with the somatic limits of the life-span itself. The value of an intrinsic property (such as 'beauty') is not tied to the person as such but is a 'part-property' alienated from the individual in the temporal continuum of the life-course and of worth only in so far as its upkeep can be guaranteed. An uneasy tension therefore opens up between a sense of self that is underwritten by notions of the inherent integrity of the person and its worth, and the value-giving marketability of discrete aspects of it.

Ranciere argues that

> One enters the community of one's equals not by being useful to them but only by being like them. There is no way of being counted one of them without reflecting their own image: an equal is someone whose image is that of an equal. (2006, p. 70)

A 'celebrity', on the contrary, is experienced as an 'image' through the complex mediation of discourses of worth and value which seek to maintain distance through the social fiction of an absolute differential 'talent'. Even the much-cherished characteristic of celebrity 'ordinariness', which appears to announce an equality of condition, underwrites inequality of property at the same time through 'the merit' of deserved success. The tension between such performances of being 'one of us' and conspicuous displays of wealth is held in check so long as worth is *earned*, and so long as the celebrity functions as an emblem of 'making it'; in other words, as emblematic of *aspiration*. Losses of wealth, health, looks, career collapses, everyday misfortunes can be celebrated and enjoyed in direct proportion to their apparent deservedness. This is because enjoyment at such levelling poses no challenge to the delicate balance of an economy in which equality is both expected and desired but also feared lest its infinite regress put one's own property in question.

To conclude this section, we have, in some senses, come full circle from Marx's position in which formal political equality is illusory in comparison to the 'real' positions occupied within 'civil society'. Attempts to highlight the determinate effectivity of political 'form' themselves require a theorization of the transindividual subjective consequences of a 'form' in which equality is present as permanent but foreclosed possibility. The 'democratic form', the ontological insecurity experienced by those for whom power is an 'empty place', the exigencies of 'equaliberty', and the constitutive effectivity of antagonism are all at odds with what Ranciere describes as 'post-politics' (1999, see also Crouch 2004). Furthermore, the neo-liberal order has further closed down the political possibility where politics is understood as the claim to equality against the naturalized order of 'police'.

> We are no longer in an age of expert judicial constructions designed to inscribe the irreducible 'power of the people' in oligarchic constitutions. This figure of the political and political science is behind us. State power and the power of wealth tendentially unite in sole expert management of monetary and population flows. Together they combine their efforts to reduce the spaces of politics. (Ranciere 2006, p. 95)

Desiring economies: mediating *Schadenfreude*

The sensibility of *Schadenfreude* can be related to both this longer political landscape and to the contemporary cultural conjuncture. In this final section, we explore what is at stake in the business of laughing at celebrity downfall at the present moment in the context of the reduced democratic space of neo-liberalism. In more detail, paying particular attention to both the mediation of its contemporary affective dynamic and the economic logic it is bound up with.

Of key importance in contemporary culture, as we have already indicated, is the myth of meritocracy. The dream of unlimited social mobility, that driving narrative of the post-Fordist era, has magnified very tangible and important examples of social movement in order to justify and push forward a system of deregulated flexibilized capitalism that entails a very limited and circumscribed amount of social mobility alongside increasingly stark divides between rich and poor. Thus, as David Harvey puts it, the hallmark of neo-liberalism has been 'the restoration of power to an economic elite [. . .] in the advanced capitalist countries' by means of that 'series of gyrations and chaotic experiments' which only really converged as a new orthodoxy in the 1990s: the expansion of deep pockets of poverty emerging alongside 'the rise of extraordinary concentrations of wealth and power, with the top 1 per cent of income earners doubling their share of national income from 6.5 in 1982 to 13 per cent in the UK and rising to 15 in the US' (Harvey 2005, pp. 21, 16–19, 29–31). Alongside this, as Christopher Holmes Smith has written in his discussion of hip-hop moguls, those that 'make it' need 'the spectacle of the more impoverished masses for they give him the raw material, the literal human canvas, for which, and upon which, his ascent can be made emblematic' (Smith 2003, p. 85). The cultural desire for meritocracy or 'making it against the odds' exists simultaneously with desires for degradation and humiliation of those 'above themselves' or deemed to be at the end of their celebrity lives. It is in such a social and political formation that *Schadenfreude* functions: as the flip side of meritocracy whilst imbricated in its logic. For in this framework of understanding, just as people 'go up', so too do they 'fall down'.

The phenomenon of 'knocking celebrities down' does not merely resonate *symbolically* with this new meritocratic order, or with the genealogical inconsistencies of the discourse of equality: it also operates as part of political economy through the 'rise and fall' of celebrity stock. Taking pleasure in the 'fall' of a celebrity, in other words, is not only related to the individual celebrity concerned, but to a larger 'game' of celebrity, a wider system of multiple rises and falls in which the 'death' (in terms of demise in status and media coverage) of one particular celebrity makes space for the rise of a new one. This structure is dramatized quite literally by the BBC online game *Celebdaq*, an online celebrity stock-exchange game where participants can buy and sell imaginary stock in particular stars (a cross between *Fantasy Football* for celebrity culture and *Nasdaq*).[7] Equally, a 'fall' does not need to indicate the 'death' of a particular star but rather the death of their current image and the launch of another, a celebrity 'rebirth'. Laughing at Paris Hilton's jail sentence, for example, both helps generate further stories about the star and the later 're-invention' of Paris as 'good citizen'. As P. David Marshall has pointed out, to achieve longevity as a celebrity, the initial limitations of the presented personality must be transgressed. In addition, most internal celebrity narratives themselves also need to contain some element of 'triumphing over adversity' (Marshall 1997).

The 'downslide' of celebrity therefore enables it to fit into a political-economic cycle: fame, downfall, to potentially be followed by re-invention and the restitution of fame (and from then on: to be repeated). On a broader level *Schadenfreude* works to mobilize celebrity longevity and acts as a means to enable celebrity culture to feed ever more inventively off its own carcass. The phenomenon of celebrity reality TV (like *Celebrity Big Brother* and *I'm a*

Celebrity, Get Me Out Of Here!) is a particularly good example here. These programmes often play on *Schadenfreude* by encouraging ironic laughter over the 'washed-up' nature of the former stars and D-list celebrities who are subjected to various degrees of debasement (whether being made to act as 'servants' for other contestants or eating bugs). Watching and laughing at celebrities 'debase' themselves, however, serves to pump up their celebrity profile and invent it anew. In terms of the political economy of celebrity, *Schadenfreude* towards 'failing' stars is an integral part of the cycle of celebrity culture: it has become part of the raw material of capitalist accumulation that is used to create further celebrity profit.

The popularity of the D-list celebrity is particularly interesting because it is a new cadre of celebrity in which *Schadenfreude* is 'built-in' through media commentary to their very persona. Gareth Palmer has suggested that D-List (sometimes termed 'Z-list') celebrities are a new phenomenon that has risen to prominence over the past few years. The D-list are a mixture of 'wannabees who never were' (such as reality TV rejects) and those whose star is deemed to have faded; both groups are depicted as 'still struggling' for fame even though their moment has apparently passed. Palmer (2005, p. 42) links the construction of this new subject to a wider 'meritocratic' celebrity context including reality TV (through its 'spectacles of shame' and celebration of the talent-hungry) and to the decline of deference in its replacement of a 'privileged peek into high society' with 'a new fascination with celebrities from a seemingly classless world' (Palmer 2005, p. 39).

Even though the D-list celebrity merely engages what we are all encouraged to do in these individualistic, post-Fordist days – constant self-branding – they are roundly mocked as 'getting above themselves', partly because they are often perceived as having relatively low social origin and because they lack 'proper' PR. Palmer speculates that 'perhaps the venom so often directed at D-listers represents revenge for having to "kow-tow" to the demands of the micro-managers employed by the properly famous'. Here, mocking the D-list becomes a way of ramifying class distinction in an ostensibly 'classless' realm and an opportunity for journalists to express both their frustration at a wider celebrity 'system' and their role within it. Significantly, by presenting the D-list celebrity as dumb or stupid for striving too much, for being 'misplaced' and not following the rules, they are being mocked for 'failing to grasp their true economic value in the system' (Palmer 2005, see also Dickinson 2008).

The popularity of the desire to see celebrities fall down as well as rise up clearly indicates how this form of *Schadenfreude* is structured through contemporary discourses of meritocracy. It functions as both its flip side (in that people move down as well as up) and as integral to the continuation of its logic (there is a reciprocal and a 'balancing' fall for every rise of the 'wheel of fate' if there is to be room at the top). But as we have seen in the previous section, contemporary *Schadenfreude* and meritocracy are *not only* structured through the disparities of neo-liberalism (although this is of course crucial) but also, at the very same time, to longer-standing cultural discourses. *Schadenfreude*'s affective desire to seek punishment and levelling can itself help to explain how meritocracy works by sedimenting new logics of 'police' order against equality in Ranciere's terms. It is structured through these modes of being – the very ones we see at work in de Tocqueville's account of nascent liberal-capitalist sociality – in which we are taught to desire equality of condition but scorn equality of property. *Schadenfreude*, in other words, is in its dominant form an expression not simply of a thwarted desire for equality, but also a state which contains a conservative expression of delight in the uneven landscape of human material resources which it presents as 'natural'. The emergence of a D-list star is therefore a moment that threatens the logic of 'meritocratic worth', highlighting as it does the absolute arbitrariness of exchange value within the system. The idea that 'anybody can make it' is central to the logic of 'equality of condition' which underpins meritocracy. But the emphasis here is on the active process of 'making it' and the 'anybody' in the expression is always qualified in terms of its capacities for hard work: 'anybody can make it *so long as* . . .' What the 'D-lister' represents is a troubling reversal of emphasis: '*anybody* can make it'. Here 'making it' appears to involve nothing other than the elevation of an arbitrary 'anybody' whose 'worth' relates only to its immediate bankability within the 'celebrity economy'. However, both the trenchant *denunciations* (they are rewarded for 'nothing'! how dare they!) and the very *generation* of these parodic celebrities specifically *to-be-scoffed-at* works to defuse the systemic limitations it makes apparent.

We can see some of the workings of these discourses in the realm of tabloid culture. Pleasure in celebrity humiliation connects to studies of tabloid culture in two ways: firstly, because demonstrations of *Schadenfreude* towards celebrities feature prominently within tabloid newspapers themselves (think, for example, of the *Daily Mail* or the *National Enquirers'* propensity for glee in female celebrities looking off-par or in the throes of breakdown); and secondly, because an entire cottage industry of programming in the kind of entertainment-based media that is today often defined as part of the broader domain of 'tabloid culture' or as indicative of 'tabloidization' is devoted to the celebration or dissection of celebrity collapse (Biressi & Nunn 2007, pp. 1–2, Gripsund 2008, pp. 34–44).[8] The Sky One TV programme *50 Best Celebrity Meltdowns*, which ranked celebrity outbursts and breakdowns in terms of how flamboyant and shocking they were deemed to be, is one example of the expansion of this genre.

Tabloids, in a similar way to the carnivalesque, have often been read as launching populist challenges to privilege (Bonner 2005, pp. 86–92). As Anita Biressi and Heather Nunn put it, 'tabloid culture thrives because its rhetoric, attitude and posture (with two fingers stabbing the air in a vulgar salute to high culture and its advocates) consistently speak to the majority of ordinary people and hold our attention' (Biressi & Nunn 2007, p. 1). For Ian Connell, tabloids bust through the politely acceptable discourse of the bourgeois public sphere. They

> break the boundaries that have been drawn between that which can and cannot legitimately be discussed in public, by drawing to their readers' attention that which the bearers of public office have deemed private. [...] They are rude and raucous intrusions into the sphere of rational public discussion and debate. Their contribution is like someone shouting from somewhere near to, but not at, the centre of the action; 'Stuff the sophisticated arguments, the effete excuses and the labyrinthine qualifications – these ba ... rds have been caught with their pants down.' (Connell 1992, p. 74)

In this way, Connell writes, tabloid stories 'bash the "power-bloc" and aim to 'not only [to be] revealing tales, but also tales which set out to teach moral lessons by exposing unworthy and unbecoming actions' (Connell 1992, pp. 74, 77).[9] Tabloids work by articulating as antagonistic the relations between three different groups:

(1) powerful elites (from which are drawn the tragic heroes and heroines of the tales);
(2) narrators who are by a variety of means in touch with the goings on of the elites, but who are not at one with them;
(3) the rest of us, the powerless ordinary people on whose behalf the stories are told (Connell 1992, p. 81).

Connell's analysis resonates with but also complicates more avowedly populist accounts of the 'anti-establishment pleasures' to be found in tabloids (Hartley 1992, Fiske 1987). However, Connell is not uncritically celebratory, arguing that

> In a particular light the stories can be read as the expression of outrage on behalf of the 'have nots'. This can be powerfully and pleasurably engaging. [...] Like much populist ranting, however, these stories are quite conservative. They are not against privileges being granted, *merely angry that they have been granted to the wrong people* – to 'them' and not 'us', not to 'me'. (Connell 1992, p. 82, emphasis added)

Interest in how these populist and demotic sentiments are channelled to conservative ends is shared by James Carey and Graeme Turner, whose work on the cultural-political economy of tabloid culture has similarly highlighted how boisterous tabloid addresses are often directed towards anti-democratic populism and 'increased commodification rather than enhanced political enfranchisement' (Carey 1988, Turner 1997, p. 499).

This should not, however, blind us to the populist potential (see Laclau 2005) of the tabloid, demonstrated recently in the UK by the *Daily Mirror*'s support for the anti-Iraq war movement (see Freeman 2007). At the same time, studies of tabloid culture and in particular Connell's salient account provide us with one useful set of references for understanding how *Schadenfreude* or delight at celebrity downfall is mediated. They supply us with an account of how relationships between three sets of groups ('elite' celebrities, outraged narrators and 'ordinary people') are managed (often, although not always, in the *interests* of the outraged narrators, in the *name* of the 'ordinary people'). This formation is not confined to tabloids, but is also the province of the 'highbrow' or 'serious' media. (For instance, in British broadsheet newspaper *The Guardian*, Marina Hyde recently reflected on her 'increasing *Schadenfreude* dependency'; her sense of glee that Princess Beatrice had her new car stolen and that Ronaldo's Ferrari was a write-off [Hyde 2009].)

In Ngai's terms, ugly feelings have a 'diagnostic' quality, an ability to express a situation marked by blocked or thwarted action. *Schadenfreude* towards celebrities clearly falls into this zone. It expresses a reaction to the blocks 'ordinary' people face in relation to social mobility and recognition and the forms of inequality which are rightly perceived to constitute the celebrity economy. However, at the same time, *Schadenfreude's* diagnostic basis is profoundly limited. This, as we have seen, is most apparent in the increasingly dominant trend by which *Schadenfreude* is routinely mobilized in ways which appear to critique the celebrity economy but is also central to that very economic turnover of celebrity capitalism that it critiques (as in *Celebrity Big Brother*). However, *Schadenfreude*'s diagnostic basis is also profoundly limited in other fundamental ways. And as we have argued, in order to understand why – as with the economic system 'itself' – we need to draw not only on contemporary analyses of divisions of wealth and power under so-called 'meritocratic' neo-liberalism but also longer historical discourses which can help to contextualize them. For whilst *Schadenfreude* registers the graphic divisions of wealth under neo-liberalism, its economy of adulation and abjection is also related to long-standing historical codings of personhood and property which form a 'subject of capitalism'. Since the advent of industrial capitalism we have been taught to scorn equality of property as much as we have been taught to assume an equality of condition, 'personhood' or being. These divergent value systems cohere in our cultural economy, finding both their resonant expression and a dramatic space in which to play out their contradictions in popular delight over celebrity downfall.

In this cultural economy, the reported glamour of the celebrity 'lifestyle' (through which massive disparities of wealth are coded) is deemed 'worthy' so long as relative notions of intrinsic value, which are mediated through the apparently 'natural' (though unequal) apportionments of 'talent', 'beauty', or 'charisma', can be maintained. Tabloid obsessions with 'meltdowns', bad behaviours, sudden signs of weight gain, the appearance of cellulite or visible evidence of ageing all signify a collapse in distance and of the 'natural fairness' between these two economies of worth and value. This collapse in distance is necessary to the distinction's construction: most often linked via discourses of fault and blame to apparent 'failures' to maintain the value of those properties deemed worthy of adulation (and therefore of all the rewards of the celebrity 'lifestyle'). The free floating and ubiquitous feelings of scorn and outrage are therefore subjectivized in highly specific ways. The collapse of the hierarchy of value bespeaks a volitional squandering of individual talent which allows the subject of tabloid mediated *Schadenfreude* to feel justified in its desire for a humiliating levelling, a forfeiture of rewards no longer justified. Scorn and outrage are channelled into specific 'feelings' against named individuals whose just desserts underwrite feelings of pleasure at graphic accounts of their misfortune. It is the apportioning of blame for *volitional* misfortune[10] that makes *Schadenfreude* such a powerful instrument in sustaining an economy of worth in which unequal reward is both celebrated and (safely) despised within the same moment.

Schadenfreude, then, might be mobilized as a sentiment for progressive social change (i.e. to actually produce some form of equality of property alongside equality of personhood) but there are powerful historical reasons why it is most often encoded within and reproduced as a more stultified and paralysed form of cultural economy, one which serves to reproduce its own terms. Whilst here might conceivably be some popular, progressive potential in the delight over the demise of figures like NASDAQ chairman and serial fraudster Bernie Madoff, it can only too easily lend itself to propping up a conservative *status quo*. In the UK, for example, two of the most recent high-profile manifestations of *Schadenfreude* towards celebrities were the Member of Parliaments (MPs) expenses scandal and the media storm over radio hosts Jonathan Ross and Russell Brand's on-air indiscretions. In both cases scorn at celebrity humiliation worked not so much to draw attention to cuts or inadequacies in public provision as to fuel further undermining of the public sector: the media calls for the BBC license fee to be scrapped, and the further deepening of 'post-democracy' disillusion with all things political.

Such paralysis resonates with the characterization of neo-classical economics itself as an 'autistic' system by the post-autistic economics movement.[11] As Edward Fullbrook and others have argued, neo-classical economics as a discipline and practice has been codified in phenomenally blinkered form, from its early template which borrowed from Newtonian physics and worked with the idea of 'an immutably given human nature', through its mechanistic nineteenth-century model that envisioned a economic universe which 'exists in a void rather than an ecosystem', shaped by the 'forces of individual agents', to the resurgent, post-Keynesian neo-liberalism of the 1970s (Fullbrook 2007, pp. 14–15). The 'autistic' internalism of neo-classical economics justifies itself through a closed system: it is autistic because it cannot position itself in relation to wider social formations or cultural ecologies. In this manner it correlates with the autistically limited nature of the critque of *Schadenfreude* towards celebrities. 'Set 'em up and knock 'em down' relationships to celebrity gesture towards a levelling impulse between the 'ordinary' and 'extraordinary'. But such relationships not only fail to actually reach this 'levelling' process (locating the 'ordinary' in a perpetual state of *resentment*, and failing to achieve anything like 'subjectification' in Ranciere's terms) but also contribute to the marked *un*-levelling process of creating celebrity and thus of actually widening a celebrity /non-celebrity divide. In these terms *Schadenfreude* towards celebrities overwhelmingly becomes a logic of not only incorporated criticism but, as we have seen, a form of cultural-affective fuel for the longevity of celebrity. And as the process entails a continual looping, as it happens again and again (as institutionalized through magazines like *Closer*, websites like *Popbitch* and programmes like *Top 50 Celebrity Meltdowns*) it exemplifies a kind of autistic repetitive system. The narratives of 'making it' and 'losing it' can be entirely complementary rather than contradictory, imbricated with one another in a cyclical process of rising and falling, like the operation of the mythical 'wheel of fate'. Indeed, in its subjective apprehension this process is itself experienced as something like fate: as an internalized desiring economy in which adulations and humiliations are routinized and follow apparently inevitable logics: those of 'life itself'. The very repetitions at work in these economies evince an inability to break with a cycle that is predicated in resentment of the adulation it gives while compelled to offer it again and again, even as it humiliates and seeks to destroy the objects of its adulation.

Notes

1 'Civilian' is the term used by celebrities for 'non-celebrity' members of the public.

2 Here Ahmed follows one convention in cultural studies/the humanities of using 'economies' as a descriptive term to indicate the circulation of something other than money. (If we apply this to the recent growth of analysis of 'the economy' using other frames of reference than that of neo-classical economic theory, or, in Fullbrook's (2005) terms 'post-autistic' economics, then such work in these terms functions to analyse economic economies, or economies of economics.)

3 http://www.popbitch.com/home/category/latest-issue/ (accessed 24 April 2009).

4 If relationship to the celebrity is experienced through the subjectivizing property of 'emotion', the relationship can become 'personal' and take on a 'pathological' quality marked by forms of over-identification or fantasies of

personal familiarity. In its pathological over-investment however adulation is equally prone to reversal as the obsessive fan morphs into the murderous stalker. This operatic intensification of the more depersonalized economy of affect in relation to celebrity nonetheless highlights something of affect's own disavowed negative potential; a potential that is manifest in *Schadenfreude*.

5 The discourse of equality is something which emerged in the contingent circumstances of the Greek polis:

> . . . ever since Solon had abolished slavery for debt in Athens, all cities had included a mass of poor people who, though unsuited to the practice of law or leadership, were nonetheless present in the city as free men, possessing the common name, the common title of the political community: freedom. (Ranciere 1995, p. 13)

6 This instability is the essence of Lefort's characterization of the 'democratic form'.

7 http://www.bbc.co.uk/celebdaq/ (accessed April 2009).

8 Itself originally an 'industry' rather than an academic term.

9 Connell cites sex outside marriage, an example which now dates the piece given that celebrities' extra-marital sex is today usually taken as the norm than the exception.

10 Naturally, 'volitional' here is itself entirely arbitrary. This might range from classic narrative tropes of talents squandered, getting 'above oneself' in acts of hubris that misread the scale of one's talent, being 'found out', or simply being a woman where this is deemed to require a permanent and often contradictory set of vigilances around personal appearance etc.

11 The post-autistic economic movement began in 2000 when French students created a petition lambasting their curriculum, stating that, instead, they wanted a curriculum based on a pluralistic approach to the subject, and has since influenced a wide range of critical approaches to economics from a variety of viewpoints. Such paralysis also resonates with David Harvey's account of how today the political left predominantly exists in a state of 'cultural paralysis' at the current recession and of articulating ways beyond the dominance of neo-liberal economics (Harvey 2008, ICA talk).

References

Ahmed, S. (2004) *The Cultural Politics of Emotion*, New York, Routledge.

Balibar, E. (1994) *Masses, Classes and Ideas*, London, Routledge.

Biressi, A. & Nunn, H. (eds) (2007) *The Tabloid Culture Reader*, Buckingham, Open University Press.

Bonner, F. (2005) 'The celebrity in the text', in *Understanding Media: Inside Celebrity*, eds J. Evans & D. Hesmondhalgh, Buckingham, Open University Press.

Callinicos, A. (2000) *Equality*, Cambridge, Polity Press.

Carey, J. (1988) *Media, Myth and Narrative: Television and the Press*, London, Sage.

Connell, I. (1992) 'Personalities in the popular media', in *Journalism and Popular Culture*, eds P. Dahlgren & C. Sparks, London, Sage.

Couldry, N. (2001) 'The hidden injuries of media power', *Journal of Consumer Culture* vol. 1, no.2, pp. 155–177.

Crouch, C. (2004) *Post-Democracy*, Oxford, Polity.

Deleuze, G. (1988) *Foucault*, trans. S. Hand, London, Athlone.

Deleuze, G. & Guattari, F. (2004a) *Anti-Oedipus*, trans. R. Hurley, H. R. Lane & M. Seem, London, Continuum. (Originally published 1977.)

Deleuze, G. & Guattari, F. (2004b) *A Thousand Plateaus*, trans. B. Massumi, London, Continuum. (Originally published 1980.)

Dickinson, K. (2008) *Off Key: When Film and Music Won't Work Together*, Oxford, Oxford University Press.

Due, R. (2007) *Deleuze*, Cambridge, Polity Press.

Dyer, R. (1986) *Heavenly Bodies: Film Stars and Society*, London, BFI.

Dyer, R. (1998) *Stars*, 2nd edn, London, BFI.

Fiske, J. (1987) *Understanding Popular Culture*, London, Routledge.

Fraser, N. (1995) 'From redistribution to recognition: rethinking justice in a post-socialist age', *New Left Review*, vol. 3, pp. 107–120.

Fraser, N. (2000) 'Rethinking recognition', *New Left Review*, vol. I, no. 212, pp. 68–93.

Freeman, D. (2007) 'The media and the war on Iraq', in *The Tabloid Culture Reader*, eds A. Biressi & H. Nunn, Buckingham, Open University Press.

Fullbrook, E. (2005) 'Post-autistic economics', *Soundings*, issue 29, pp. 96–109.

Fullbrook, E. (ed.) (2007) *Real World Economics: A Post-autistic Economics Reader*, London, Anthem.

Gilbert, J. (2003) 'Small faces: the tyranny of celebrity in post-Oedipal culture', in *Mediactive 2: Celebrity*, London, Lawrence and Wishart.

Gripsund, J. (2008) 'Tabloidization, popular journalism, and democracy', in *The Tabloid Culture Reader*, eds A. Biressi & H. Nunn, Buckingham, Open University Press.

Grossberg, L. (1997) *Dancing in Spite of Myself*, Durham, NC, Duke University Press.

Hartley, J. (1992) *The Politics of Pictures*, London, Routledge.

Harvey, D. (2005) *A Brief History of Neoliberalism*, Oxford, Oxford University Press.

Harvey, D. (2008). 'David Harvey on the Communist Manifesto', talk at the ICA, London, 20 November 2008.

Hesmondhalgh, D. (2005) 'Producing celebrity', in *Understanding Media: Inside Celebrity*, eds J. Evans & D. Hesmondhalgh, Maidenhead, Open University Press.

Hills, M. (2002) *Fan Cultures*, London, Routledge.
Hyde, M. (2009) 'I may be a *schadenfreude* junkie: But at least I'm not a banker in denial', The Guardian, 10 January [online] Available at: http://www.guardian.co.uk/commentisfree/2009/jan/10/marina-hyde-ronaldo-bankers (accessed February 2009).
Laclau, E. (1990) *New Reflections on the Revolution of our Time*, London, Verso.
Laclau, E. (2005) *On Populist Reason*, London, Verso.
Laclau, E. & Mouffe, C. (1985) *Hegemony and Socialist Strategy*, London, Verso.
Lefort, C. (1988) *Democracy and Political Theory*, trans. D. Macey, Minneapolis, MN, University of Minneapolis Press.
Littler, J. (ed.) (2003) 'Celebrity' *issue of Mediactive*, vol. 2, London, Lawrence and Wishart.
McNay, L. (2007) *Against Recognition*, Cambridge, Polity Press.
Marshall, P. D. (1997) *Celebrity and Power: Fame in Contemporary Culture*, Minneapolis, MN, University of Minnesota Press.
Marx, K. (1975) *Marx: Early Writings*, Harmondsworth, Penguin.
Massumi, B. (1995) 'The autonomy of affect', *Cultural Critique*, vol. 31, pp. 83–109.
Ngai, S. (2005) *Ugly Feelings*, Cambridge, MA, Harvard University Press.
Palmer, G. (2005) 'The undead: life on the D-list', *Westminster Papers in Communication and Culture*, vol. 2, no. 2, pp. 37–53.
Portmann, J. (2000) *When Bad Things Happen to Other People*, London, Routledge.
Ranciere, J. (1995) *On the Shores of Politics*, trans. L. Heron, London, Verso.
Ranciere, J. (1997) 'Democracy means equality', *Radical Philosophy*, vol. 82, [online] Available at: http://www.radicalphilosophy.com/default.asp?channel_id=2190&editorial_id=10429 (accessed July 2009).
Ranciere, J. (1999) *Disagreements: Politics and Philosophy*, trans. J. Rose, Minneapolis, MN, University of Minnesota Press.
Ranciere, J. (2004) *The Politics of the Aesthetic*, trans. G. Rockhill, London, Verso.
Ranciere, J. (2006) *Hatred of Democracy*, trans. S. Corcoran, London, Verso.
Redmond, S. & Holmes, S. (2006) *Framing Celebrity: New Directions in Celebrity Studies*, London, Routledge.
Redmond, S. & Holmes, S. (2007) *Stardom and Celebrity: A Reader*, London, Sage.
Skeggs, B. (2004) *Class, Self, Culture*, London, Routledge.
Smith, C. H. (2003) '"I don't like to dream about getting paid": representations of social mobility and the emergence of the hip-hop mogul', *Social Text*, vol. 21, no. 4, pp. 69–97.
De Tocqueville, A. (1994) *Democracy in America*, London, Fontana Press.
Turner, G. (1997) 'Celebrity, the tabloid and the democratic public sphere', in *Celebrity and Power Fame in Contemporary Culture*, ed. P. D. Marshall, University of Minnesota Press, Minneapolis, MN.

Randy Martin

THE GOOD, THE BAD, AND THE UGLY

Economies of parable

The recent financial crisis has shattered lives and spread misery far and wide. The magnitude of damage has produced the desire for the economic equivalent of a truth and reconciliation commission. Yet the efforts to get the story right have pointed as much to a crisis of narrative, of theory, even of facticity among the standard-bearers of monied matters, public punditry and policy self-justification. If the underlying parables by which the larger trinity of economics, politics, and culture remains undisturbed by cataclysmic events, we should wonder whether systemic shock is sufficient to re-order habits of mind. We could also worry that what is presented as an exceptional circumstance of suffering for some is the business-as-usual experience for so many who are forced to live by the market's vagaries through what are considered to be by its chief beneficiaries, both good times and bad. If there is an opportunity for cultural studies in all of this, it may lie most of all in a refusal of the neat partitions, the intellectual division of labor by which both normal times and aberrant patches are understood. Cultural studies may benefit from a supple rapprochement with the critique of political economy that yields a different account of valuation and exchange. What follows is an effort to think the condition of cultural studies in the aftermath of financial attention beyond parabolic convention.

The great financial meltdown of 2008 promised to succeed where all other disasters of the dismal science had failed to produce the ultimate parable – a succinct and decisive story by which a world run wild might be understood and its moral accounts settled. But whether in staying the course or requiring a sea change, ignoring the problem, scolding it for making such a mess, promising swift punishment or immediate reward, the words spoken by those at the helm offered neither calm nor solace, illumination or explanation. Expert knowledge and economic growth seemed to be failing one another after so many years of being the perfect couple. It was as if the prescriptive subtext by which economy would engender faith ceased to be a deliverable good, the demand for telling suddenly unmet by narrative conventions of the field, making legible the reliance upon parable in the first place.

Of course this link between knowing well and doing good is the foundation from which economics itself arose. Adam Smith's double vision of political and moral economy joined at the hip the two senses of value – measurable good and ethical bearing – that continue to haunt all contemporary renderings of the human sciences. Adam Smith's parable was that doing well by oneself would ultimately do good for others, a tangled logic or fallacy that Duncan Foley traces as a key lineament of economic thought. 'The moral fallacy of Smith's position is that it urges us to accept direct and concrete evil in order that indirect and abstract good may come of it. The logical fallacy is that neither Smith nor any of his successors has been able to demonstrate rigorously and robustly how private selfishness turns into public altruism. The psychological failing of Smith's rationalization is that it requires a strategy of wholesale denial of the real consequences of capitalist development, particularly the systematic imposition of costs on those least able to bear them, and the implacable reproduction of inequities that divide people from one another in society' (Foley 2006, p. 3).

Foley here nails the arrogance by which economy imagines culture to be its paled reflection, a faith in rationalization that is itself impermeable to reason. But the collective anger targeted at the bankers and their bailers-out suggests that the denial of capital's unreason is not always plausible. From what might be called a cultural-take, popular outcry against public goods for self-interest was an equally long time in the making. And just to complicate that story, the congressional opposition that voted down the initial bank bailout package (on September 29, 2008), mixed right-wing populism against any form of government intervention in markets with skepticism about the bill's soundness and the propriety of this iteration of wealthfare.[1] The denial earlier that month on the part of then Republican presidential candidate John McCain that crisis was nigh and high, his subsequent discovery that crisis was his to suspend his campaign, were subsequently treated as enactments of unpresidential volatility that marked a tipping point in the race. The thing called the economy was refusing to manage itself or be managed. Those who would be its handlers seemed to be suffering the same fate. Both the object and the agency attached to economy were experiencing a volatility that no narrative could tame.

Neither before nor since a crisis has been proclaimed in the land has the challenge of telling the tale gone unanswered. Joe Nocera is one of business's more formidable raconteurs. He was responsible for an early diagnosis of 'how the middle class joined the money class' and has been there to describe what it means to lose club membership (Nocera 1994, 2008). While presidents have offered assurance that 'there is plenty of blame to go around,' Nocera has tried to parse responsibility within the dens of professional economic practice itself. Indeed, contemporary finance would seem to be the influence-minded academic's dream, a world where theory is practice, where abstract mathematical modeling that garners professional respect gains widespread application. The model in question is called Value at Risk (VaR). Its virtue is to take all manner of financial instruments (stocks, bonds, securities, derivatives) held by an individual or firm and translate the net exposure to loss in terms of a single dollar amount. A latter-day alchemy this, VaR promised the ability to spin information into gold. From the mid-1990s into the better part of the next decade, risk was spread not simply through a firm but throughout all manner of financial services including, notoriously the subprime real estate market, through the expansion of what amounted to insurance-against-loss called derivatives. By June, 2008 contracts covering over one quadrillion dollars ($1,140,000,000,000,000) of credit and over the counter derivatives were issued with the confidence that continued hedging of risk would defer unmanageable outcomes indefinitely and the economy would be all good or what was called a virtuous cycle.[2] As is the case in business, what is all good for some is quite nasty for many.

Nocera shares the tale of the one that got away, the success among failures lionized in management studies as a 'best practice.' For a while, at least, that was Goldman Sachs, the investment bank that Henry Paulson had led two years before he became Treasury Secretary.

> Reporters wanted to understand how Goldman had somehow sidestepped the disaster that had befallen everyone else. What they discovered was that in December 2006, Goldman's various indicators, including VaR and other risk models, began suggesting that something was wrong. Not hugely wrong, mind you, but wrong enough to warrant a closer look.
>
> 'We look at the P&L of our businesses every day,' said Goldman Sachs' chief financial officer, David Viniar, when I went to see him recently to hear the story for myself. (P&L stands for profit and loss.) 'We have lots of models here that are important, but none are more important than the P&L, and we check every day to make sure our P&L is consistent with where our risk models say it should be. In December our mortgage business lost money for 10 days in a row. It wasn't a lot of money, but by the 10th day we thought that we should sit down and talk about it.'
>
> So Goldman called a meeting of about 15 people, including several risk managers and the senior people on the various trading desks. They examined a thick report that included every trading position the firm held. For the next three hours, they pored over everything. They examined their VaR numbers and their other risk models. They talked about how the mortgage-backed securities market 'felt.' 'Our guys said that it felt like it was going to get worse before it got better,' Viniar recalled. 'So we made a decision: let's get closer to home.' (Nocera 2009, p. 27)

Subjective feeling that inhabits experienced managerial judgment trumps cold-hearted reliance on quantification. The early warning system worked perfectly. The alarm sounded and all escaped safely. The risky exposures (later to become toxic assets) are shed and the partners find comfort and safety back at 'home'. A hard day spent, the good men put the good tools to rest. An effective oikos entails sensing what belongs to art and what to science, of giving subject and object each its due, of building a marriage of anima and animas. Before leading us to this unmarked gender of the gift – of each knowing their place, contributing to the commonweal of the bonus pool from their distinct ability – Nocera tours us through the ethical incompleteness of those who cannot recognize this golden mean.

While mathematical models are attributed with powers of seeing the future, in practice they operate in the moment of their available data streams. More, what they see in the present is what they take to be most likely to happen. Accordingly, the meltdown was not so much unforeseeable, but improbable, when probabilities were being forged out of institutional investors adhering to their own forecasts. While this has been derided in studies of investor psychology as a herd mentality that makes for animalistic 'irrational exuberance,' the lesser charged term, clustering around the mean, describes that most normal of statistical figures, the bell curve. The VaR model slayer that Nocera brings into his picture is Nassim Nicolas Taleb, a long-time trader who becomes a professor in a newly formed and funded university department of finance and risk engineering. Taleb has made his fortune, 'a killing' as Nocera describes it (2009, p. 31), betting on the statistical outliers that make for disaster capitalism. His term for these unforecasted earth-shattering events is 'black swan,' the dreaded unknown unknown. 'Because we don't know what a black swan might look like or when it might appear and therefore don't plan for it, it will always get us in the end. "Any system susceptible to a black swan will eventually blow up," Taleb says. The modern system of world finance, complex and interrelated and opaque, where what happened yesterday can and does affect what happens tomorrow, and where one wrong tug of the thread can cause it all to unravel, is just such a system' (Nocera 2009, p. 29).

Systems blowing up as opportunities for making a killing, can remind one more of the war on terror than of rational economies until it becomes apparent that both rely on the derivative logic of making much from the outliers, of capitalizing on a high risk environment that others have made, of passing through quickly rather than holding ground. Professor Taleb has set out to convince the risk modelers that they are all wrong but it is not clear how he could normalize his own model so that all could be right. This would seem to be the bane of a profession where 80 percent of paid investors cannot outperform the broad market average (which they are helping to create) but those few who do get all the attention. And yet these exceptional talents are naturalized in a way that justifies among other things uneven compensation and pursuit of same. If the present debacle had a cautionary instance it would have been the implosion of the hedge fund Long Term Capital Management (LCTM) a decade before. LTCM applied the complex mathematical formulae of 1997 Nobel prize winners Myron Scholes and Robert C. Merton, to exploit small differences between expected bond prices and leverage just under $5 billion to cover debts of over $120 billion (Lowenstein 2000). The problem was that they could not image that others would use these same arbitrage techniques unbeknownst to them and amplify both the risk and the opacity to detect it. But the bigger conceit here is to suggest that capital accumulation is but the statistical volatility of markets. If the issue is not what to do with the vast sums of wealth that are produced and what life is like amidst its production, then the story can be managed as one of trust in those with the best judgment to set prudent rates of return to investors, those who would 'be ever vigilant for the dragons' (p. 51). When the news arrives that there is $700 billion of social wealth that can be used to save the day, a very different vigilance rears its head and sees dragons where expert judgment lay safe in its lair. Anger bears the prospect that public good might get re-attached to promise social expenditure.

Perhaps this is why the parable of the good meets its undoing in the telling. A two-hour telecast of 'explanatory journalism' *House of Cards* aired on CNBC on February 16, 2009, the day before newly elected President Obama was to sign the $789 billion economic stimulus bill. The show wove together stories of individual foreclosures, predatory lenders, merchants of collateralized debt obligations, and the ultimate federal (de)regulator, Alan Greenspan. Greenspan admitted that he did not grasp the mathematics in the esoteric derivatives, but at the end of the day it did not matter. Regulation was pointless in the face of greed. 'The flaws of human nature are such that we cannot change that.' J. Kyle Bass, also featured in the program, had made 600 percent returns betting on the real estate crash. For him as well, the catastrophe was part of a state of nature, and all would be set to right after a 'Darwinian flush' wiped out the unfit. In the end, economic modeling has little to say to such convictions.[3]

The parables by which blame is apportioned may demonize greed as it describes our underlying nature, or those excessive ones whose nature got the better of them. But the toolkit of economic thought and practice is indemnified against culpability. When it comes to the question of government attention, who deserves rescue and what requires regulation is another matter altogether. If nature got us into this mess, politics must pull us out. While the former can resume the equilibrium that restores good, the political must go away as soon as possible lest help turn to hindrance and the bad exposes the state as an underlying evil. The declaration of crisis serves to delimit these exceptional conditions in anticipation of the return to normalcy that proper regulation and subvention provide.

Crisis also lays bare the twin morality tales that underpin what it means for labor and capital to live their normal lives. Capital gets moral hazard, and labor, moral panic. Moral hazard, the worry that government bailouts of big business will encourage more bad behavior, is typically a form of fretting after the fact. Government rescue seems condemned to get it wrong no matter what it does. On March 16, 2008 when Morgan Chase was handed Bear Stearns to feast upon, in an early deal engineered by the Treasury Department and the Federal Reserve Board – which issued a $29 billion credit line to the new owner and took hold of another $30 billion of collateral at taxpayers expense, it seemed that the government was whimsically deciding who missed out on being too big to fail.[4] When the same agencies stood by and watched Lehman Brothers drown in its debt, their inaction was said to spark the global meltdown. The spectacle of bailout money being at once too little and too much, too constraining and too flexible, has done little to clarify what might count as a proper fix, but it does serve to assure that government would not be the source of redemption – even as it continues to dole out the funds.

Moral panic is the anxiety of contagion when publicly designated bad subjects are allowed access to the pen of good conduct. Developed famously by Stuart Hall and colleagues in an analysis of racialized crime waves as a displacement for crisis mongering, the term retains its utility for the present plague anxieties (Hall *et al.* 1978). Here is *The New York Times* describing the fear that the foreclosure disease might spread. 'Until recently, people with good credit, who tend to pay their bills on time and manage their finances well, were viewed as a bulwark against the economic strains posed by rising defaults among borrowers with blemished, or subprime, credit' (Bajaj & Story 2008). Note that subprime here refers not to jacked up interest rates, but to a type of borrower, one who is discolored, disfigured, or cannot make the grade. The specter of subprime is that the bad will haunt the good, and that the nearly two million mortgages at low introductory rates set to expire in the next year will unleash more waves of collective nausea. Contrary to arbitragers who bet for a living on interest rates going up or down and deserve a rescue operation, those who had little to begin with and are forced to abandon their homes are considered 'speculators' by former US Treasury Secretary Henry M. Paulson, Jr. Said he, 'Washington cannot create any new mortgage program to induce these speculators to continue to own these homes, unless someone else foots the bill' (Bajaj 2008). While securitized bundles of mortgages are being discounted and repriced to appeal to lenders (the 'somebody else' Paulson is willing to subsidize), the 'speculators' are not those who originated mortgages but those who imagined they deserved to be homeowners. Months later, when plans were announced to stave off imminent foreclosure of nine million homes, but leave aside another 15 million whose mortgages exceeded the value of their residences, the White House announced that its aid would only go to 'responsible homeowners' (Healy 2009).

Subprime was all about getting people to move up to property. Like the wages of whiteness, whereby immigrants were invited to trade in their swarthy particularities of ethnicity to huddle with the master race, this might appear to be another saga of becoming unblemished. Indeed, home ownership in the United States peaked at the end of 2006 at 69 percent before sliding down to its current rate of 67.8 percent after the recent waves of foreclosure. Positing a natural drive to ownership omits the coercive thorn in the heart of the market organism said to grant all their rightful emancipation. The carrot for ownership was doubtless the 66 percent gain (controlled for inflation) in home prices between 1998 and 2005. The stick was declining real wages. At the same moment that ownership spiked, workers' collective share of national income was the lowest since such figures began to be kept, while corporate profits hit a 40-year high. This decline in real income during a time of economic expansion and increasing productivity was a first, and one that affected nine out of 10 workers.[5] The 20-dollar an hour wage – a benchmark for the affluent worker has fallen in every sector of the economy but seen a 60 percent decline in manufacturing (Uchitelle 2008). In the 1980s and 1990s wage inequality was on the rise both across industries and within individual companies. During the same period, unionization fell from 20 percent of the workforce in 1983 to about 13 percent in 2003 (excluding governments workers of whom 37 percent are unionized, the private sector rate is lower still at just over eight percent). Without expanding unionization, the value of the minimum wage declined, at the same time that lower paid immigrants increased to 15 percent of the workforce (Aboud *et al.* 2007).

Economist Rick Wolff ties the decline of wages to the advent of a credit economy. He observes that the 'solution' when longer work hours did not generate enough money to increase consumption – was to borrow. Multiple credit cards per family and increasing mortgages added to vehicle financing to generate historically unprecedented levels of total consumer debt across the last 25 years – and especially since 2000. March and April 2006 saw negative real savings rates for the public of 1.5 percent. Nor do these stark statistics count the vast sums that adult children increasingly 'borrow' from their parents' savings (Wolff 2006). The promotion of a credit economy through direct and indirect government policy accompanied all manner of initiatives that replaced welfare state security with individual's capacity to assume and sustain financial risk. When this works, the person reaps the rewards of self-management, when it fails people become speculators who can spread terror and place good subjects at risk. The new economy gibberish which tried to convince potential investors that the business cycle was over and they could find safe harbor in stocks that would go up forever in a virtuous cycle, simply got transferred to the real estate boom. Who needs unions (or politics) to induce higher living standards when ownership of a home whose value expands forever does the same thing and is so much more comfy. So buy today.

Now, some nine million US households (more than one in 10) owe more on their single family home than it is worth. In exchange for not having any money to put down (and therefore no equity to walk away with), the subprime set simply get charged more for the privilege of being in debt. As such, it is a crafty reinvention of the nasty practice of redlining, whereby certain neighborhoods are excluded from bank services because of their risk of default. Redlining had suppressed ownership rates among workers and people of color and left financial services a cottage industry for loan sharks, pawnshops and other local entrepreneurs. Like the discovery of some new native population, mineral rich land, or underexploited environment, the blemished credit of the working impoverished became fodder to large returns in the hands of subprime, microcredit, and other enclosures of the hitherto unbankable. The 1977 Community Reinvestment Act (CRA) required banks to lend throughout communities where they previously had not. Thirty years later, in response to such regulations (and abetted by others, i.e. deregulation) mortgage initiating and other financial services had taken flight from conventional banking institutions in an institutional free-for-all known as 'disintermediation.' By the time that the crunch came along, half of the subprime loans came from companies not covered by the CRA and another quarter from subsidiaries banks spun off to be free of it (Gordon 2008).

The bait and switch of subprime is that it is a way to market social pain. The move from exclusion to enclosure signaled by the deregulation of redlining carved up the unevenness by which greater gain could be extracted while punishment falls to the newly speculative. Just to take New York City as an example, Jamaica Queens, with a black majority and $45,000 median income, subprime lenders issued 46 percent of mortgages. For mostly white Bay Ridge in Brooklyn, the corresponding rate is 3.6 percent, for a population with a median household income of $50,000. Even for more affluent households the racial divide is sharp. For non-Hispanic whites, 24 percent took out a subprime mortgage in 2006 while for blacks 63 percent did (Fernandez 2007). The typical profile of foreclosure is that it is concentrated among lower income housing stock, disproportionately multi-family, among those who put no money down to buy their home and have owned it for a short period of time. Also typical is withholding information to new purchasers about how the adjustable rates work and how first time buyers can receive assistance (Kirchhoff & Kean 2007). Whereas the last time mortgage defaults erupted when home prices fell (12 percent between 1990 and 1996) 15 percent of those in arrears owned their homes less than three years. In 2007 (during a one year period when housing prices went down six percent), nearly half owned for three years or less. One in four subprime mortgages ended in foreclosures as opposed to 7.3 percent for all mortgages (Willen 2008). The ambivalent consequences of moral panic have left public remedy in a bit of a muddle.

Home ownership is meant to be the pillar of private life and an impregnable partition between the public realm of social goods and claims, and the domain of personal affairs. Of course tax codes, deregulation of financial services, monetary policy are all government measures that help to engrave this separation between the political and the personal. Just as home ownership was a salve to declining wages that claimed to give labor a stake in expanding capital markets, the subprime fiasco displaces the political into the hallowed realm of the private. Even in a progressive formulation, housing is no longer simply a human right, but has now raised the question of how best to steward massive accumulations of social wealth. Whatever repairs are administered to get subprime lending on the move again, the shift from personal holding to social wealth will continue to mark future housing struggles. To see what these politics bring, we need to move beyond the twin moralities of hazard and panic – unearned reward and undeserved punishment – and embrace a more speculative stance toward our lives together where mutual indebtedness heightens a sense of interdependence. The speculative claim is that great wealth can be amassed in our midst out of what we have to hand and invested anywhere for any purpose. Perhaps it is time to demand that speculators get their just rewards, but also to redefine who gets to participate and what gets to be defined as the benefits. Crafting such a parable would hinge upon an embrace of the political where it is otherwise seen as an object from which we must take flight.

By now it may be apparent that the good, the bad and the ugly is not simply a reference to the film, directed by Sergio Leone (*The Good, the Bad and the Ugly*, 1966), that offers a parable for the end of the west and its genre, but also a nod to that holiest of trinities in the human sciences – the economic, the political, and the cultural. As with the eponymous characters in the film, these three ride an ambivalent partnership. With economics, bad science is continually rescued from its predictive reality to do good another day. For politics (at least that cast as the state), the helping hand, whether as regulated intervention or agitating punishment, only seems to make things worse. And then there is culture, where all that was supposed to be beautiful (in the film literally getting the gold, unearthing buried treasure, riding off into the sunset), quickly turns ugly. The struggle to free culture to its own realm of resistance, critique, and alternative, gets dragged back into the grave of uneasy partnership with the other two. Such, at least, has been the staging of this relationship under the sign of finance, which has partitioned economy into the real and the fictitious in a manner reminiscent of the divide between base and superstructure from which cultural studies itself sought a break. The irony here is that at least one genealogy of cultural studies is as an elaboration of Marxism to valorize labor's agency while a certain cultural Marxism would share with a particular political economy an evisceration of this political efficacy of the cultural.

Consider the following by leading Marxist critic Fredric Jameson:

> But that is precisely what finance capital brings into being: a play of monetary entities that need neither production (as capital does) nor consumption (as money does), which supremely, like cyberspace, can live on their own internal metabolisms and circulate without any reference of the older type of content. But so do the narrativized image fragments of a stereotypical postmodern language; they suggest a new cultural realm or dimension that is independent of the former real world, not because as in the modern (or even romantic) period culture withdrew from that real world into an autonomous space of art, but rather because the real world has already been suffused with culture and colonized by it, so that it has no outside in terms of which it could be found lacking. Stereotypes are never found lacking in that sense, and neither is the total flow of the circuits of financial speculation. That each of these also steers unwittingly towards a crash I leave for another essay and another time. (Jameson 1997, p. 265)

As prescient as Jameson is of the Fall, and as acute as he is in his observations regarding the seemingly independent operations of circulation from reference, finance, far from sorting real and imaginary value, fuels a riot of production and consumption along with ways of knowing and being. These emergent ways of life and modes of association, affiliation and identity are sure-fire entailments of the cultural – whereby the future is brought into an anxious present as life is rendered into risk. The temptation is to see risk as mere speculative activity, something epiphenomenal to production. Marxist political economy, in a potent line of critique that stretched from Hilferding (1910/1981) and Luxemburg (1913/1951) to Magdoff and Sweezy (1987), and Arrighi (1994), identified the salience of finance to a destabilizing link between accumulation and imperialism. Yet in this work, the divergence between circulation and production is central. John Bellamy Foster, taking up this legacy in tribute writes, 'this financial superstructure has been the creation of the last two decades. This means that its emergence was roughly contemporaneous with the return of stagnation in the 1970s. But doesn't this fly in the face of all previous experience? Traditionally financial expansion has gone hand-in-hand with prosperity in the real economy. Is it really possible that this is no longer true, that now in the late twentieth century the opposite is more nearly the case: in other words, that now financial expansion feeds not on a healthy real economy but on a stagnant one?' (Foster 2007).

Here too is the sense that finance is capital unmoored from reality, that speculation, phantom value, superstructural effects feed upon ugliness, stagnation and decay. Clearly there is no indication that what is called economic prosperity manifests social development, or why industrial commodities like armaments are intrinsically superior to financial services. More pointedly, finance has driven unprecedented production and consumption, and the financial meltdown proved so disruptive to the lives of so many because of the way that populations have been rendered mutually indebted and their material circumstances thoroughly infused with conditions of credit. If finance is intrinsic to current arrays of productive capital, it is equally forceful in its impact on labor. Two Marxist political economists, Mike Rafferty and Dick Bryan see in derivatives the social operations of making disparate commodities commensurate in value that was performed by such mechanisms as the Bretton Woods financial architecture (until dismantled in the 1970s). This socialization of capital meets its equivalent number in its pressing together measures of labor. 'Where capital is not achieving this rate of return, pressure reverts to the sphere of production, and particularly labour to deliver higher profitability, be it by higher productivity, longer working days, or lower wages' (Bryan & Rafferty 2006, p. 162).

So finance stands for an ungainly request – more is to be asked from everyone. It bears no respect for what might separate the real from the imaginary, the useful from the speculative, the aggregate from the outlier. A refusal to hold beauty in the lap of truth spreads ugliness far and wide. What might once have been read as a story firmly planted in the terrain of the economic is now being retold as an ambivalent partnership. Doing so requires a shift from a conception of the cultural as one of three steady horsemen riding in non-reductive tandem to a capacity to inscribe shifting allegiances, inflections, and effects in the accounts by which we live and the means we have to embody the telling. The older economy of parable rested upon a neat Trinitarian subtext that preserved the partition between barely concealed disciplinary domains. Cultural studies would revert to its place in granting autonomy to its domain at the expense of leaving the others alone. The blankness of narrative that opens a chasm in the present financial crisis, suggests a very different principle for parable-making. Finance will not remain in its vault, its promiscuity ranges from rarefied precincts of expertise to the most quotidian quarters. A good, bad and ugly cultural studies would draw a parable of the economic for every occasion and keep an eye cocked for the potential partnerships that lay within reach. It would of necessity accumulate its critical knowledge and register its means of production as resources that could circulate elsewhere, economies of parable that are fruits of its own labors.

Notes

1 Amy Goodman's *Democracy Now* show of October 3, 2008 gives a nice flavor of these various currents. Transcript available at: http://www.democracynow.org/2008/10/3/wary_of_public_outcry_revised_800b (accessed February 16, 2009).

2 *Global Derivatives Market Now Valued at $1.14 Quadrillion!* Jutia Group Thursday, July 24, 2008 http://www.istockanalyst.com/article/viewarticle/articleid/2432853.

3 Excerpt of interview with Greenspan on *House of Cards* premiered February 16, 2009. Available at: http://www.cnbc.com/id/15840232?video=1029053619&play=1

4 Treasury details key role in Bear Stearns bailout. Agency involved in all aspects of transaction, signed off on Fed move, Greg Robb, *MarketWatch, Wall Street Journal*, April 2, 2008. Available at: http://www.marketwatch.com/news/story/treasury-forced-detail-extensive-role/story.aspx?guid=%7B79C94AFF-EC37-44AC-A93C-721E276B8495%7D.

5 Report: Most not seeing real wage gains. Employee pay lowest share of GDP [gross domestic product] since 1947, when government started tracking data. Corporate profits highest share of GDP since the 1960s. August 28, 2006. Available at: http://money.cnn.com/2006/08/28/news/economy/real_wages/index.htm

References

Aboud, J., Haltiwanger, J. & Lane, J. (2007) *Wage Structure and Labor Mobility in the United States*, Cambridge, MA, National Bureau of Economic Research.

Arrighi, G. (1994) *The Long Twentieth-century: Money, Power and the Origin of Our Times*, London, Verso.

Bajaj, V. (2008) 'Mortgage holders find it hard to walk away from their homes', *The New York Times*, 10 May, pp. C1 and C4.

Bajaj, V. & Story, L. (2008) 'Mortgage crisis spreads past subprime loans', *The New York Times*, 12 February. Available at: http://www.nytimes.com/2008/02/12/business/12credit.html

Bryan, D. & Rafferty, M. (2006) *Capitalism with Derivatives: A Political Economy of Financial Derivatives, Capital and Class*, Houndmills, Palgrave.

Foley, D. (2006) *Adam's Fallacy: A Guide to Economic Theology*, Cambridge, MA, Harvard University Press.

Fernandez, M. (2007) 'Study finds disparities in mortgages by race', *The New York Times*, 15 October. Available at: http://www.nytimes.com/2007/10/15/nyregion/15subprime.html

Foster,, J. B. (2007) 'The financialization of capitalism', *Monthly Review*, April.

Hall, S., Critcher, C., Jefferson, T., Clarke, J. & Roberts, B. (1978) *Policing the Crisis: Mugging, the State, and Law and Order*, New York, Holmes and Meier.

Healy, J. (2009) 'Obama plans $75 billion outlay to fight foreclosures', *The New York Times*, 18 February. Available at: http://www.nytimes.com/2009/02/19/business/19housing.html?_r=1&hp

Jameson, F. (1997) 'Culture and finance capital', *Critical Inquiry*, vol. 24, no. 1, pp. 246–265.

Gordon, R. (2008) 'Did Liberals cause the subprime crisis', *The American Prospect*, 7 April.

Hilferding, R. (1981) *Finance Capital: A Study in the Latest Phase of Capitalist Development*, Boston, MA, Routledge and Kegan Paul. (Originally published 1910.)

Kirchhoff, S. & Keen, J. (2007) 'Minorities hard hit by rising costs of subprime loans', *USA Today*, 25 April. Available at: http://usatoday.printthis.clickability.com/pt/cpt?action=cpt&title+Minorities+hit+hard+by+rising+costs+of+subprime+loans

Lowenstein, R. (2000) *When Genius Failed: The Rise and Fall of Long-term Capital Management*, New York, Random House.

Luxemburg, R. (1951) *The Accumulation of Capital*, New Haven, CT, Yale University Press. (Originally published 1913.)

Magdoff, H. & Sweezy, P. (1987) *Stagnation and the Financial Explosion*, New York, Monthly Review.

Nocera, J. (1994) *A Piece of the Action: How the Middle Class Joined the Money Class*, New York, Simon and Shuster.

Nocera, J. (2008) *Good Guys and Bad Guys: Behind the Scenes with the Saints and Scoundrels of American Business (and everything in between)*, New York, Portfolio.

Nocera, J. (2009) 'Risk mismanagement: were the measures used to evaluate Wall Street flawed? Or was the mistake ignoring them?', *The New York Times Magazine*, 4 January, pp. 24–33, 46, 50–51.

Uchitelle, L. (2008) 'Wage erosion cuts deeper in U.S.', *International Herald Tribune*, 21 April.

Willen, P. (2008) *Federal Reserve Bank of Boston*, Presentation at Furman Center Roundtable, 2 May. Available at: http://furman.center.nyu.edu/events/documents/subim1.Willen.pdf (accessed 20 February 2009).

Wolfe, R. (2006) 'The fallout from falling US wages', *MRZine*, 12 June. Available at: http://mrzine.monthlyreview.org/wolff120606.html

Stefano Harney

CREATIVE INDUSTRIES DEBATE

Unfinished business: labour, management, and the creative industries

In what follows I am going to argue that the rise of the creative industries has in general been understood too narrowly. This narrow understanding has had implications for the way that a politics of management and labour in the creative industries has been framed and contained, and it has held back an analysis of class struggle in the creative industries. To elaborate an understanding of labour in the creative industries I am going to revisit some insights related to the development of British cultural studies, and try to link these insights to what Stuart Hall calls the conditions of possibility for the creative industries today (1973/1980). These conditions of possibility require a different conception of labour, infusing the circuits of production in what Italian post-workerist theorists call the social factory. Such an elaboration of the work of culture allows us to reframe the questions of labour struggle and management control in the creative industries. The method of this article will of necessity be somewhat speculative and its scope broad, but where possible I will try to give examples of what I mean in order to focus on the possibilities for developing a politics of labour under the expanded conditions considered here.

Overview of the creative industries

I will begin with an overview of how the rise of the creative industries is commonly described. That description breaks into two views, views which ultimately complement and reinforce each other. In the first view, the rise of creative industries is understood as an invasion of the arts not just by business, but specifically by management. To say that the arts have been invaded by business is to join a long conversation about the fate of art in what Walter Benjamin (1969) famously called the age of mechanical reproduction. It is to look back at least to the Frankfurt School, if not to Nietzsche, and extends to recent works like Sara Thorton's *Seven Days in the Art World* (2008) or Tricia

Rose's *The Hip Hop Wars* (2008), where art and the artist are stalked or seduced by capital. In this view the commodification and the marketization of art changes both its innate character and its social character. But while this is a vital conversation in the background of any consideration of the rise of the creative industries, its chronology does not correspond to the more recent and stark expansion of these industries. This is why it is important to insist that this rise be understood not as the invasion of business, or capitalism as these authors would have preferred, but as the invasion of management. Because management implies labour, and not just any kind of labour but organized labour, massified and industrialized in some form.

So the first way that a broad view of the creative industries is established is by tracking the arts not through their own commodification, but through the commodification of those whom produce them. The arts move from the workshop to the workplace. Some of this movement is technological; where once one designed a plate in a workshop, today one designs a computer game in a workplace. But the movement from workshop to workplace most especially designates a new condition of labour, and new tools are only an aspect of this new condition.

There are those who regard this movement into the workplace within a tradition of critique stressing exploitation, a tradition which, at its best, also stresses the historical specificity of that exploitation. Thus the best of the recent ethnographies of the creative industries, *No Collar* by Andrew Ross (2004), focuses on the harnessing of the persona of the artist to a workplace culture of overtime and total commitment in Silicon Alley firms, understanding the new economy as a forerunner of the creative industries but also as management's term for an emerging regime of work. And a series of articles and talks by Angela McRobbie (2007) on fashion, feminism and creativity point to the paradox for workers of the pleasures of making art even in the workplace. These scholars as well as others represented in the recent reader *MyCreativity* (Lovink & Rossiter 2007) stress the unique quality of the exploitation taking place in the creative industries. They often stress the precariousness of work in the creative industries, echoing the Marxist exploration of the un-freedom of free wage labour and the struggle over labour time. Andrew Ross's latest collection of essays *Nice Work if You Can Get it* (2009) and Ned Rossiter's *Organized Networks* (2008) exemplify a new understanding of this labour as deriving from the artistic life but bred with the precarious life, the migrant life, life in the reserve army of labour at the sharp end of responsibility for survival, a responsibility for reproduction almost entirely abdicated by state and capital.

Other authors focus on the kinds of productivity opened up by the organization of the arts into the creative industries. Most visible here is the work of Richard Florida (2003) who sees not a new precarious worker in the creative industries, but a new labour aristocracy he calls the creative class. Florida's work is nonetheless important in the way it makes the link to economic development, and especially gentrification explicit. In this way, Florida offers us the broad view of the creative industries as a new engine of the economy, as before him prophets of internet technology or for that matter plastics and chemicals had privileged a new workplace and class formation within the emerging regime of accumulation. The emphasis on new forms of production as well as new forms of investment, is perhaps more comprehensively analysed by Neil Smith in his book *New Urban Frontiers* (1996). Smith makes the link not only between the emergence of the creative industries and gentrification, but also to the new role of finance in powering this partnership and policing in enforcing it.

However, Florida's work is also anticipated by another body of scholarship emerging in the UK and Australia in the early 1990s on cultural policy. Scholars like Tony Bennett (1995) sought to counter the combination of accumulation by dispossession, new workforce discipline, and reinvestment by advocating a new science of cultural policy that would make a governmental virtue of this revanchism. In its critical registers, as for instance in the vast assemblage of analysis in the work of Toby Miller, cultural policy studies not only situated the emerging cultural industries within the larger scale of political economy but linked these industries critically to the popular struggles and subjectivities stressed by cultural studies (see Miller & Yudice, 2002, Miller, 2006, for examples.) Indeed Miller (2008) recently extended this critique in a fluent response to an article by Daniel Mato (2008). Mato reasserted the notion that all industries would benefit from examination through cultural studies, and that the term cultural industries risks restricting our analysis to only certain sectors. Miller countered by noting that Mato was right, and that indeed numerous cultural studies of industries cited by Mato had been carried out. But for Miller the question remains why we speak so confidently right now, at this moment in history, about something called cultural industries, and increasingly creative industries. For Miller, the answer has to do not with the way cultural aspects of commodities can be recoded, but the way they can be marshalled by forces of management to sort populations and accomplish the complex differential inclusion of labour now required by global capitalism. Miller spots this new managerial class emerging from the humanities, eager to prove itself in this new factory.

Overall this understanding of the creative industries as the coming of management to the arts, the move from workshop to workplace, is a rich vein of analysis. I do not mean to suggest anything less. For instance, Andrew Ross (1997, 2007, 2009) has linked his perceptive study of small software firms to other studies of the fashion industry and the sweatshop and the new labour militancies of China. Angela McRobbie (2007) draws our attention to the struggle over pleasure as a pressure point of politics, tracing this struggle from its highest levels of analysis in feminist thinking, to its re-emergence around the question of art as a labour of the workplace. By doing so she allows us to link her analysis to the workerist tradition I will sample later, where the emergence of affect as paid labour by feminist in relation to this tradition including Leopaldina Fortunati (1995) and Silvia Federici (2004).

Another overview?

Nonetheless we can see why we must try to exceed this framing of the creative industries as the movement from workshop to workplace, as the coming of management into the arts, when we consider its opposite and complementary vision. In the second view of the rise of creative industries, we find the vision of the coming of creativity into management. Such a vision has perhaps been most succinctly if hyperbolically summarized by Daniel Pink (2006) who announced that the Masters in Fine Arts (MFA) is the new Master of Business Administration (MBA). That a MFA should now be the ultimate qualification for today's manager might not surprise those artists who experience the degree as the professionalization of their practices. But it was really a phrase aimed at the business school and designed to shock it into a certain recognition about the new qualities of managing. Again, with this view we have to distinguish what is happening now from a long history of management thinking about the labour process as a kind of artwork to be, if not created, then certainly arranged, orchestrated, recomposed, and of course redesigned. Many a business school student has had to sit through the tendentious introduction to management as both an art and a science. And early writings in management often aestheticized the labour process and the labourer even as these writings sought to establish the scientific, or at least social scientific basis, of management. Even Taylor's pig iron worker was stylized. And Mary Parker Follett is today recovered in part for her attention to sensibility and interpretation in the workplace (Graham 1996). Such interpretation takes the subjective form of intuition in subsequent work on muddling managers by Charles Lindblom and Woodhouse (1993), and limited information by Herbert Simon (1997). In more recent times we have seen the growth of a massive literature on innovation and creativity in the disciplinary journals of business and management, and even more specific attention to the arts as a lens on the organization of work as for instance in the 'Art of Management and Organization' group at Essex University.

Of course much of this history need not be seen within the frame of the arts. Intuition or innovation fit into human sciences in other ways too. What interests me more here is the movement from art as a trope for management activity, to art as the objective of management – because what seems to characterize the historical moment of the creative industries is precisely the latter. Toby Miller (2008, p. 8) is certainly right to note that any industry where creativity can be said to be an input is designated a creative industry, but the ambition may extend beyond new levels of extraction of labour-power to new levels of property rights in all commodities. This is to say that more than just a management tool for exhorting or demanding more labour going into all kinds of services and commodities, this notion of creativity also marks a problem for management of how to track what is coming out, how to attach and detach this creative labour from what it creates without the traditional management prerogatives at hand, and indeed whether to do so. Chris Bilton's *Management and Creativity* (2006) is emblematic of management's temptation and weakness. Now it is not just that creativity is required to manage the worker, or even that creativity is required to innovate the product, but that creativity is the end, not just the means, of the labour process. In other words, something like art is to emerge as the final product, a product open to interpretation and aesthetic judgement, a product in dialogue with other products, a product that is not used up in use but instead produces new versions of itself, a product that will be coded differently by different users, a product that will in a sense have both audiences and critics. And, of course, a product that retains through the class relation, certain property rights, and certain rental properties. This tendency achieves a recognizable schizophrenia in a book like *The Art Firm* (Guillet de Monthoux 2004), a kind of lives of the artists re-imagined by McKinsey and company. In this view, creative industries lead not from the outside as they do with Richard Florida, drawing older economic formations into their orbit, but from the inside transforming production bringing the promise of all production being the production of brands.

In other words, what marks the creative industries in these two complementary views of their development is, on the one hand, the arts as the object of management and, on the other hand, the arts as the objective of management. Seen from the 'outside' perspective of the arts, the creative industries mark the transformation of the arts into something not made for themselves but made specifically for management. Seen from the 'inside' perspective of management, the creative industries mark the vanguard of management's new objective: to make the commodity into art. Of course one can draw a distinction within each view, within the arts as the object of management and the arts as the objective of management, between those who see the benefits of such tendencies, and those who highlight the perils.

The presumed benefits of the arts produced as an object of management and the benefits of management aiming to produce art are of course chiefly the same: economic growth, expanded circulation and distribution, access and participation, and profit. The perils are also the same. The arts are said to be further degraded by the degradation of the artist, they become an invidious technique for getting at the souls of workers and consumers, with possibilities of exploitation lurking in both conditions. At any rate, what seems clear is that the two broad perspectives are really one, from different angles.

Management sees art as its objective, and art sees itself as management's target. What this bifurcated view cannot tell us however is why this is happening, and why now – the question Miller raises in his critique. Here it is no accident that theorists emerging from cultural studies to confront the creative industries point repeatedly to the expanded domain of labour, not culture or the arts, in their analysis.

Ross, Miller, Rossiter and McRobbie all focus on the deepening and the widening of interdependencies of work witnessed in the creative industries, from the depths of affective labour to distances of outsourced labour. This attention by these figures in cultural studies to the expanded domain of labour in the creative industries helps us to rethink the famous cultural turn provoked by that intellectual movement. We can turn to cultural studies briefly then to begin to answer the question of why the creative industries have come to prominence now, and what problems this might pose for managing in the creative industries.

Back to cultural studies

Cultural studies itself can be understood as a kind of proliferation, a proliferation whose principle of expansion was to find new value where before none was acknowledged. Indeed, cultural studies found new value both by a kind of deepening of itself and by a widening of its attention. Cultural studies reached across disciplines (like literature, sociology, and communications) and across genres (from television to music to fashion) and across theoretical terrain (from psychoanalysis to deconstruction to Marxism), as well as across social class and race and gender to locate value in the popular. But cultural studies also deepened the stakes of its encounters, insisting on the critical quality of its work, on the transgressive effects of its analysis, and the links between its imperatives and political movements.

Whatever one's assessment of the current efficacy of this project the condition of possibility of cultural studies, and in particular British cultural studies from which we will draw some insights, is worth recalling. These were the expansion of the university, the expansion of popular culture through new technology, the redefinition of nationhood and identity produced by post-war migration, the resistance to social time that would become neo-liberalism, and the collapse of representative democracy under the weight of new social movements. Again, the interpretation of these sweeping changes in society will be a matter of debate but what seems beyond contest is the obvious but often neglected result: populations today are more deeply involved in creativity, judgement, opinion, aesthetics, and social and cultural re-evaluation than at any time in history. This is a result grasped by British cultural studies first, though today cultural studies itself rarely claims its own record of discovery. Art is closer to people than at any time in history. People make and compile music. They design interiors and make-over their bodies. They watch more television and more movies. They think deeply about food and clothes. They write software and surf the net for music videos and play on-line games together. They encounter, study, learn, and evaluate languages, diasporas, and heritages. There is also a massive daily practice in the arts, from underground music, to making gardens, to creative writing camps. And with this, there is production of subjectivities which are literally fashioned, which are aesthetic, which are created. When people are not working, they are doing this other work (or the work renewing their capacities to work, in the gym or the classroom, but that is another story). The point is there is a massive daily register of judgement, critique, attention, and taste. Cultural studies in some ways responded to this deepening and widening of cultural activity in populations.

But more importantly for my argument, cultural studies also brought into focus the new raw material that would form the basis of the creative industries. If one is to look beyond the phenomenal aspects of the creative industries and to ask why these industries have arisen, if one is truly to develop the kind of vision that can contextualize labour struggle in the creative industries, it is necessary to start with the massive daily activity in populations. Cultural studies gave us a sense of the vast wealth at stake, of the value latent in popular culture, a value that would soon be realized in the creative industries. Re-reading cultural studies in light of the creative industries serves to reminds us that the creative industries, much like cultural studies itself, are a response to this new value in society.

But cultural studies still does not tell us how the creative industries managed to capitalize on this value. While we owe a debt to cultural studies for seeing the value in all this activity, for investing so heavily in it and bringing theory to bear on it, we can also see now with the rise of the creative industries that, if anything, cultural studies did not value this activity enough. Or rather perhaps we should say cultural studies did not value it accurately because cultural studies, despite its investment, tended to focus on this massive daily activity in the population as matters of circulation, consumption and distribution.

For cultural studies, the struggle was principally over the forms of consumption, the way cultural commodities were recoded and appropriated, as famously in Stuart Hall's work on television. This politics of consumption both made possible and drove onward a broader circulation of cultural commodities, which in turn became subject to new readings in the expanded circulation of cultural forms, as in the studies of soap operas and their adaptations and receptions globally. But it was also a struggle over the hierarchical qualities of this circulation and was thus tied to the struggles over the distribution of cultural value, to the circuit of distribution, most famously the valorization of popular cultural commodities, as for instance in the case of Black British cultural expressions. Here the question of who had the power to value culture and who held the means of cultural production provided a sober response to the popular expansion of cultural assessment. This politics of distribution led cultural studies to other sites in search of this valorization, to communities, clubs, homes, and subcultures (and away from workplaces, schools, factories and offices that had occupied their predecessors in Marxist literary studies or industrial sociology). It also led cultural studies to value different subjectivities for the way they consumed, circulated, and distributed cultural forms, and to open fronts of new recognition among these subjectivities in an effort to redistribute cultural value. In short, cultural studies, in the main, focused on three of Marx's four circuits of production.

Some of this emphasis on circulation and consumption was intended to blunt the productivist tendencies cultural studies encountered on the Left, as for instance in labour process studies, and some of it was designed to recast older notions of reception and education in the arts, mostly on the Right, as for instance in Leavisite criticism. And indeed there were always attempts to balance the circuits, as for instance in the Sony Walkman study (Du Gay *et al.* 1996), a study that often finds its way on to business school courses in Britain today. Some of the emphasis on the politics of distribution had much to do with the university as a site of social welfare where resources and knowledge could be allocated differently, and where the forms of property rights and embodiments of free labour appeared to slacken. And, as I mentioned earlier, some of this shift in political emphasis responded to the new social movements whose most radical, if often unrecognized, stance was to push welfare state politics out of its productivist stance and into the realm of expanded distribution.

But what is already implied in cultural studies, and becomes explicit with the rise of the creative industries, is that the struggle over cultural commodities was not just a struggle about the redistribution of value, but also about its absolute expansion. In other words, what was already emerging was the idea that a cultural commodity could produce value, not just at its point of production as is traditionally understood in Marxist thought, but along the other circuits as well. This is because what cultural studies begins to grasp is that the expansion in circulation of cultural forms appeared to create new value everywhere. If we want to think of this concretely, think of the way cultural studies was caricatured as finding resistance everywhere, or valuing body art or comic books, and thus appearing to lose the ability to make distinctions on value. In fact, this ambition in cultural studies was a symptom of the new condition of value. As the creative industries would soon show us, there was more and more value to be had in body art and comic books, and even in putting resistance to work [as the cultural theorist and activist Franco Berardi (Bifo) suggested in a recent talk at Tate Britain (2008)]. Policy advocates like Boltanski and Chiappello (2007) understand this resistance as grist for the management mill and thus seek a truce in the workplace, but Bifo, influenced by Felix Guattari and the Italian summer of the 1977 emphasized the priority of this resistance and the residual character of the management Boltanski and Chiappello rate as so powerful (Harney 2005).

Part of this shift has to do with the two meanings of value coming together in the cultural commodity, a condition that cultural studies recognized. Value as wealth and value as norm seem to co-exist in the cultural commodity, or perhaps I should say seem to jostle each other, revealing not just the split between them, but the split within themselves. Value as wealth always raises the spectre of surplus value, of wealth created through exploitation but also of the potential for expansion, for more wealth, in this split. Asking whether art should have a price on it always raises the question of what is wrong with a price and thus always brings to the surface the split in value as wealth. At the same time, cultural studies used this first question to raise a second, what is the split in value as norm, what is this norm I use against the spectre of price? Whose norm is it, and how was this norm itself generated, questions which split value as norm as surely as value as wealth was split. But this is not the whole story. Because with the rise of the creative industries we now see that bringing these two ideas of value together did not just provide a critique of each, as cultural studies helpfully insisted, but also increased the potency of each sense of value in a new combination that requires another step in our analysis.

Cultural commodity

In fact I could say bringing these two senses of value together in the cultural commodity did not just open up both senses to critique, but opened up both senses in general. Both ideas of value in the commodity became unfinished, not just in the sense of open to interpretation but open to augmentation, to modification, to development, to redirection, in short, to labour. But not just any labour, not labour in the workshop-become-a-workplace or even creative labour, but labour beyond the workplace, labour in the other circuits. No longer was this labour merely there to keep things moving, or allocate things, or use them up to realize their value. This was labour that did the work of workplace labour, changing the commodity, adding to it, developing its value, and developing the value of its own labouring subjectivity.

This kind of commodity and the labour that attends it is described by Maurizio Lazzarato, the Paris-based Italian theorist, in his seminal and much misunderstood article on immaterial labour. Leaving aside some of the other aspects of this term, here is his discussion of the cultural commodity, which it is necessary to quote at length:

> Immaterial labour finds itself at the crossroads (or rather, it is the interface) of a new relationship between production and consumption. The activation of both productive cooperation and the social relationship with the consumer is materialized within and by the process of communication. The role of immaterial labour is to promote continual innovation in the forms and conditions of communication (and thus in work and consumption). It gives form to and materializes needs, the imaginary, consumer tastes, and so forth, and these products in turn become powerful producers of needs, images, and tastes. The particularity of the commodity produced through immaterial labour (its essential use value being given by its value as informational and cultural content) consists in the fact that it is not destroyed in the act of consumption, but rather it enlarges, transforms, and creates the 'ideological' and cultural environment of the consumer. This commodity does not produce the physical capacity of labour power; instead, it transforms the person who uses it. Immaterial labour produces first and foremost a 'social relationship' (a relationship of innovation, production, and consumption). Only if it succeeds in this production does its activity have an economic value. (Lazzarato 2003)

I would say what is distinct here is not a new kind of labour, called 'immaterial' by Lazzarato and characterized by communication, but the dominance of a new kind of labour process characterized by the unfinished quality and condition of the cultural commodity that is the object and objective of this labour process.

Again it was cultural studies that first helped us to focus on this idea of an unfinished commodity and its labour process because it was cultural studies that first introduced the idea of a commodity that could be coded and recoded by those who take it up, and it is cultural studies that located this process of unfinishing the commodity (and the subject) in society at large, in the social factory and not in the workplace. It is also cultural studies that first gives us a sense of the magnitude of this social factory, and consequently of the magnitude of the work going on in this social factory. This post-workerist idea of the social factory – of the realms of social reproduction coming under the searchlight of paid work without penetrating all the shadows of unpaid work that remains in those realms – is thus first posited by Italian Marxism, but first felt, explored, lived by British cultural studies.

And lastly, residually, it is grasped at by management. Because where there is work, even unpaid work, can management be far behind? (Harney, 2005). This, then, is the real call of the creative industries – not the coming of management into the arts, nor of arts into management, nor even the advent of brand as art work, but the sound of police sirens in a new hunt. The dogs of this hunt chase not the artist but society itself. And the struggle is not for authorship, wages, or authenticity, but to use the distance, the ground still open between hunter and hunted, to plan something different (Moten & Harney 2009a).

Managing cultural commodities?

Management may be residual and thus behind, but it is not far behind. Focused on the twin conditions of the arts as the object of management and as the objective of management in the movement from the workshop to the workplace, management in the creative industries has yet to come to grips with all this work out in the social factory, all of this unfinished business. The focus is still mainly on the workplace and its more traditional labour process, still productivist, still stuck in one circuit. But this is not to say management has not noticed all this potential value, and tellingly this tends to come in those parts of the management sciences more attuned to the other circuits, in marketing and in operations.

Two examples here would be viral marketing, and advanced distributed learning through game simulation as a form of operations management, the former is supported by the murky corporate intelligence community and the latter by US and UK military, both as promising methods of investigation into the social factory. The latter, also known as massive multiplayer online gaming (MMOG), offers a model of what is called network centric warfare where contributions can be made (work can be done) anywhere in the circuits, and not just in the command and control environment of military units (Bonk & Dennen, 2005). But most importantly simulations, unlike games, have no finish, and the efforts here are to bring the motivational advantages of gaming, a way of describing the effort bargain, under conditions without end. This work provides a model of operations where work would never be completed at any point, and where the product, whether conceived as training, intelligence, or war, is developed all along a distributed network, perpetually. Endless property, endless rent, endless work.

Viral marketing has recently been discovered by the Society of Competitive Intelligence Professionals and also is beginning to make an appearance in journals like *Marketing Intelligence and Planning*. Viral marketing, like experiential marketing and relationship marketing hint at a consumer who is already organized and indeed the latest thinking on viral marketing assumes this condition. It seeks to data mine competitors and then releases negative information into the bloodstream of these organized consumers. But even more interestingly, the latest thinking in experiential marketing emphasizes not just the participation of the consumer but the development of the experience through the work of that consumer. In that sense experiential marketing is prospecting the same territory as simulation, the territory of the unfinished cultural commodity.

There are of course more innocuous examples of this fitful interest in the social factory, examples that often make it into the curriculum precisely because students are hard at work on them. One thinks for instance of the viral marketing campaign of *Snakes on a Plane* (2006), or the online simulation game *Second Life* (2003), both of which are commonly cited in the business school lecture halls today. But even these can been seen as they are by Tiziana Terranova (2004) as examples of free labour exploited by the network culture. And beyond these straightforward examples of management at work outside the workplace in the social factory, where to place the assembling of audiences, attentions, states of affect, that begin with the exhibit or the CD or the layout of the coffee house, but cannot capture all the value of these assemblages in moment of performance, the moment of the show? Is management to let all this wealth making capacity slip away, or into the hands of competitors?

Concluding questions

This is the real condition of labour struggle in the creative industries, a condition in which much of what management seeks is beyond its traditional grasp in the legal sense. Much of the labour the creative industries requires does not work for it, and will not remain with it. Of course there are other ways to view this larger picture of the creative industries, both from an orthodox business and economics perspective around such issues as intellectual property and indeed from a Marxist perspective around such issues as exploitation. It is possible to keep the circuits in their place. Laikwan Pang (2009) makes a powerful argument for keeping creative and traditional industries together. She argues that creativity should be understood as an input into production in the same way as raw materials, which for Marx were already social, already the product of the labour that harvested, mine, or farmed them. In this way, what the creative industries mark is a greater social intensity of labour fed through the production process, social intensity produced by traditional industries, and all the more powerful in her view for not knowing their own origins.

But I think it is worth thinking about these circuits today as intensely laboured, thinking about the social intensity of these circuits, and thinking about the creative industries as the effort of management to reach along these circuits. At very least this perspective credits management in the creative industries with some ambition. After all, before the advent of the creative industries who but the state had the vision to imagine that the population as a whole, and not merely one's own workforce, could be the object of management? And indeed from this point of view this precedent of the state's management of populations helps explain the growing number of management techniques that come to echo the techniques of state, and hint at the general productivity of the population now being available not just at the level of the workplace, but at the level of society, at the level of the social factory. The rise of strategy, of governance, of social responsibility and citizenship, of intelligence gathering, of brand loyalty do not just echo qualities of governmentality, they also borrow the techniques, like data mining, that were the disciplinary and security underpinnings of these ambitions (Moten & Harney, 2009b). To manage in the creative industries is to enter into this contemporary statecraft, where the stakes are far greater than whether an artist can be supervised. And the stakes for labour in this social factory could not be higher. The social factory comes to subsume civil society and transform the struggles over neo-liberal governmentality outlined in Foucault's late lectures. The creative industries raise an even more sinister alarm. Civil society in all its morals, tastes, attentions and opinions becomes the site not only of control but of direct expropriation, all the more sinister because it does not collapse into categories of the economy but expropriates from the distance of governance. Occupying or sabotaging such a factory is no simple matter. But cultural studies distinguished itself in this space between economy and politics, in the hidden abodes, finding value and finding organization long before the creative industries. Now would be the time to remember this history.

References

Benjamin, W. (1969) *Illuminations*, New York, Shocken.

Berardi, F. (2008) *Conjunction/Connection*. Available at: http://www.tate.org.uk/britain/eventseducation/symposia/11586.htm (accessed May 1, 2009).

Bennett, T. (1995) *The Birth of the Museum: History, Theory, Politics*, London, Routledge.

Bilton, C. (2006) *Management and Creativity: From Creative Industries to Creative Management*, London, Wiley/Blackwell.

Boltanski, L. & Chiapello, E. (2007) *The New Spirit of Capitalism*, London, Verso.

Bonk, C. & Dennen, V. (2005) *Massive Multiplayer On-line Gaming: A Research Framework for Military Training and Education*, Washington, DC, Office of the Under Secretary of Defense for Personnel and Training.

Du Gay, P., *et al.* (1996) *Doing Cultural Studies: The Story of SONY Walkman*, London: Sage.

Federici, S. (2004) *Caliban and the Witch*, New York, Autonomedia.

Florida, R. (2003) *The Rise of the Creative Class: And How It's Transforming Work, Leisure, Community and Everyday Life*, New York, Basic Books.

Fortunati, L. (1995) *The Arcane of Reproduction*, New York, Autonomedia.

Graham, K. (ed.) (1996) *Mary Parker Follett: Propher of Management*, Cambrige, MA, Harvard University Business Press.

Guillet de Monthoux, P. (2004) *The Art Firm: Aesthetic Management and Metaphysical Marketing*, Stanford, CA, Stanford University Press.

Hall, S. (1980) 'Encoding/decoding', in *Centre for Contemporary Cultural Studies*, Culture, Media, Language: Working Papers in Cultural Studies, 1972–1979, London, Hutchinson, pp. 128–138. (Originally published 1973.)

Harney, S. (2005) Why is management a cliché?, *Critical Perspectives on Accounting*, vol. 16, p. 5.

Lazzarato, M. (2003) *Immaterial Labour*. Available at: http://www.generation-online.org/c/fcimmateriallabour3.htm (accessed May 1, 2009).

Lindblom, C. & Woodhouse, E. J. (1993) *The Policy-making Process*, New York, Prentice Hall.

Lovink, G. & Rossiter, N. (2007) *MyCreativity: A Critique of the Creative Industries*, Amsterdam, Institute of Network Cultures.

Mato, D. (2008) 'All industries are cultural', *Cultural Studies*, pp. 1–18.

McRobbie, A. (2007) *British Fashion Design: Rag Trade or Image Industry*, London, Taylor & Francis.

Miller, T. (2006) *Cultural Citizenship: Cosmopolitanism, Consumerism and Television in a Neoliberal Age*, Philadelphia, PA, Temple University Press.

Miller, T. (2008) 'From creative to cultural industries', *Cultural Studies*, pp. 1–12.

Miller, T. & Yudice, G. (2002) *Cultural Policy*, London, Sage.

Moten, F. & Harney, S. (2009a) 'Policy and planning', *Social Text*, vol. 100.

Moten, F. & Harney, S. (2009b) 'Blackness and governance', in *Beyond Biopolitics*, ed. P. Clough, Durham, NC, Duke University Press.

Pang, L. (2009) 'The labor factor in the creative economy: a Marxist reading', *Social Text*, vol. 99, no. 27:2, pp. 55–76.

Pink, D. (2006) *A Whole New Mind: Why Right-brainers Will Rule the Future*, New York, Riverhead/Reed Elvesier.

Rose, T. (2008) *The Hip Hop Wars*, New York, Basic Civitas Books.

Ross, A. (2007) *Fast Boat to China: High-tech Outsourcing and the Consequences of Free Trade: Lessons from Shanghai*, New York, Vintage.

Ross, A. (2004) *No Collar: The Humane Workplace and its Hidden Costs*, Philadelphia, PA, Temple University Press.

Ross, A. (1997) *No Sweat: Free Trade and the Rights of Garment Workers*, New York, Verso.

Ross, A. (2009) *Nice Work if You Can Get it*, New York, New York University Press.

Rossiter, N. (2008) *Organized Networks*, Rotterdam, NAi Publishers.

Simon, H. (1997) *Administrative Behaviour: A Study of the Decision-making Processes in Administrative Organisations*, New York, Simon & Schuster.

Smith, N. (1996) *New Urban Frontiers: Gentrification and the Revanchist City*, New York, Routledge.

Terranova, T. (2004) *Network Cultures: Politics for the Information Age*, London, Pluto Press.

Thornton, S. (2008) *Seven Days in the Art World*, London, Granta Books.

Zizek, S. (2007) *Enjoy Your Symptom: Jacques Lacan in Hollywood and Out*, New York, Routledge.

Mark Hayward

Afterword: After Austerity?

The essays in this volume were originally published as a special issue of the journal *Cultural Studies* in 2010, having been written over the course of the preceding year. At that time, talk about the end of the economic crisis was starting to circulate, suggesting that it would only be a matter of months before things got back to "normal." However, it was already clear that the post-crisis "normal" was only going to make more visible and widespread the contradictions and cruelties that had defined the economic transformations of the previous decades. While a few suggested that the end of neoliberalism (or at least its humbling) was still a possibility, it soon became clear that it would be public services and the infrastructures that help to shape and maintain communities that would be the hardest hit as the effects of the collapse of credit markets that had been a central factor in the initial crisis were shifted from banks onto the states that had bailed them out less than two years earlier.

As noted in the introduction, the essays in this volume emerged at a moment when it was necessary to contextualize the crisis in such a way that it would be possible to recognize and develop the potential for radical and egalitarian social change, potentials that were often explained out of discussions about how to best respond to the situation at hand. The narratives of crisis, bringing together explanations of how it was caused and what would be necessary for it to end, posited the economic downturn as a discrete series of events. This denied the degree to which these occurrences were part of broader systemic crises within capitalism. The mainstream media and elected officials repeated the mantra that there was no need to acknowledge or address the long-term erosion of the rights, services and protections that were the true legacy of the crisis.

In many countries, the language of austerity emerged as a way of justifying these rounds of reductions in healthcare, education and other social services. The need for austerity measures, however, was not merely a way of expressing the perceived necessity of the cuts, but also as a way of asking individuals to contribute to the ongoing restructuring of social services by doing (and giving) a little more of their own time and labour as well as expecting less from institutions and each other. Hard times and hard choices, the logic went, required everyone to tighten their belts a little. In this way, the beginning of a period of austerity was part of a broader shift in language and practices of representation that took shape as the crisis ended and the grey morning after started to take shape. In the northern hemisphere, a wave of elections bringing conservative and reactionary parties to power highlighted how fears and anxieties about the future coupled with a sense that there was no other way forward except for cutbacks and massive job losses fueled a powerful wave of post-crisis populism. Popular xenophobia and state-endorsed racism moved to the center of political platforms as a politics of exclusion came to be seen as the only way to protect jobs, property values and the community from the dangers of the global financial crisis, externalizing a threat that was very much home grown. Even as banks and corporations profited from attempts to stimulate the economy, appeals to 'ordinary' people continued to ask for more sacrifice.

While the attempt to redefine a leftist politics has continued in South America and the popular uprisings across North Africa in 2011 should give hope that there remains the possibility for radical and revolutionary change, the forms of populism that have taken hold in many of the world's most developed economies should serve as a reminder of how collective energies for social change can be marshalled in regressive and self-destructive ways. However, the fact that these forms of populism have stifled and exhausted many egalitarian programs and initiatives ranging from the reconstruction of infrastructure in the United States to a global and co-ordinated attack on organized labour, is more than simply the naked exercise of power by the planet's political and financial elites. Rather, as Stuart Hall wrote more than thirty years ago in his attempt to document and analyze the rise of authoritarian populism under Margaret Thatcher, the success of the discursive and material formation that constituted this populism, "is no rhetorical device or trick, for this populism is operating on genuine contradictions, and it has a rational and material core. Its success and effectivity does not lie in its capacity to dupe unsuspecting folk but in the way it addresses real problems, real and lived experiences, real contradictions—and yet is able to represent them within a logic of discourse which pulls them systematically into line with policies and class strategies of the Right." (Hall 1979, 20).

Thus along with justifying the immediate actions of governments as they slash their budgets, the language of austerity is also the most explicit and concrete way of structuring the popular imagination for social change. In this way, drawing on Hall's insights into the rise of Thatcherism, it is important to analyze how many forms of expression and participation have been reorganized in the contemporary moment to produce this experience of austerity. This is a reorganization of the material and representational spaces in which millions of people live, shaping not only attitudes towards financial capitalism (and its unshakeable importance to the production and organization of wealth) but the texture of everyday live in a number of different areas.

There have been a number of attempts to make sense of this particular conjuncture, recognizing that it is not sufficient to simply map the economic determinants of the crisis and its aftermath, but to also examine the management of representations and affect that have played such a key role in defining how this crisis has 'felt' on the ground. In *Capitalist Realism: Is There No Alternative?*, Mark Fisher describes this expansive notion of capitalism as "a pervasive *atmosphere*, conditioning not only the production of culture but also the regulation of work and education, acting as a kind of invisible barrier constraining thought and action" (Fisher 2009, p.16) At the end of his paper in this volume, John Clark refers to the idea of "disaffected consent," introduced by Jeremy Gilbert to explain the affective and material organization of the atmosphere which defines life after the crisis. This is a particularly appropriate way of characterizing our contemporary moment. It is not that most people do not know what is happening (and are therefore duped into following manipulative leaders.) Rather, even as we come to understand better the extent of collusion and corruption that structures the relationship between the financial elites and elected officials, the rationalities which underwrite the turn to austerity effectively block the translation of knowledge into sustained and strategic action.

For this reason, the post-crisis moment is a particularly difficult moment for many engaged in the struggle against exploitation and for scholars interested in analyzing practices of dissent and resistance. The struggle for social change, taking place in a number of arenas ranging from the re-organization of the global political economy to the nature of labour to the popular representation of economic knowledge, seems to have been successfully colonized by the ideologically and economically regressive project that has gone by the name neo-liberalism for the past four decades. Therefore, while the issues raised by the essays collected in this volume remain of vital and urgent importance, it must be acknowledged that we have entered a different moment in which the tensions sketched out in the preceding pages have been normalized and, perhaps more worrisome, expected.

Randy Martin, in his contribution to this volume, concluded by arguing that it would benefit work in cultural studies to seek out narratives which would "keep an eye cocked for the potential partnerships that lay within reach." Such an attitude, which seeks out solidarity yet its not naively optimistic about programs for social change, is an important one for researchers in Cultural Studies to cultivate in the contemporary moment. The fog of austerity is not absolutely stifling and it is worth working to developing relationships with those movements and practices that have proven successful in challenging hegemonic ideas about the economy and the structure of society. Looking to these movements would be to recognize some of the possibilities open to Cultural Studies as a hybrid intellectual project that straddles the institutional boundaries that demarcate the university, the state and everyday life.

At the level of how research might develop this relationship, there are two directions in particular that seem necessary and important to develop further which draw upon the long history of work that has been identified with that name Cultural Studies. The first relates to those practices of representation which characterize the post-crisis landscape, representations ranging from popular, mainstream media to activist organizations who make use of spectacle to draw attention to the contradictions at the heart of the contemporary moment. The second relates to the radical transformation in the structure and organization of information and communication networks; this transformation and its consequences for individual and collective action has been characterized as 'convergence culture' by Jenkins and others. While much has been made of the democratic potential of these new technologies, there is much more than could be said about the radically de-stablizing effects that they might have for political practice and the institutionalization of power.

The analysis of representations of the economy is a field which has been argued for most extensively by David Ruccio as part of a call to investigate what he calls "economic representations" (Ruccio 2008). In many ways, this is a program that is consistent with the long history of research in Cultural Studies that has shown the significance of representations in framing and organizing political and social struggles. However, as Lawrence Grossberg has argued, it is no longer sufficient to believe that the critique of representation is sufficient to constitute a political program (Grossberg 2010). The power relations which define the contemporary moment, particularly the concentration of media power in the hands of an increasingly small number of global corporations, means that strategies for dissenting through the production of symbols need to pay greater attention to the material context from which they emerge. It is along these lines that we should pay greater attention to the practices developed by groups such as UK Uncut or the Not An Alternative group based in New York City. Through a series of highly inventive and representationally sophisticated protest actions, groups such as these have brought into the light the ways in which the material contradictions which constitute the post-crisis moment are lived, yet remain undiscussed.

Playing an important role in providing a language and a space to speak out about the popular discontent with the current predicament, these groups seek to show that "there is anger at these cuts, that the idea of mass apathy is a myth and that people are willing to do more than just join a Facebook group to stand up and defend what they believe in" (www.ukuncut.org.uk). The strength of these coalitions is their interest in reconnecting representation and action. As much as the above quotation suggests a skepticism with the usefulness of contemporary media for social protest (i.e. Facebook), they explicitly court and encourage the production and circulation of media texts as part of protest actions. As mainstream media coverage of protests against austerity cuts in Greece in 2011 make clear, the curation of representations of protest is essential as cameras are drawn to the most spectacular (and often most violent) images, flattening the complex networks and practices which define resistance to neo-liberal orthodoxy into street riots.

The work of Cultural Studies in association with such movements is not merely to show support nor is it to do the work of these movements itself. Rather, it would be to think in a more extended way about the relationship between the circulation of representations of the economy (and representations which themselves perform the act of protests) and the sensibilization and mobilization of communities. While there is a long tradition in Cultural Studies of studying the way that media intersects with everyday life, this has often remained at the level of interpretation. The rise of mobile media as well as the exigencies of the present moment ask us to think more explicitly about the relationship between text and action or, in equal measure, the complex ways in which particular configurations of media networks and practices of representation inhibit or block engagement and response. This would be to draw upon the historical strengths of Cultural Studies adoption and hybridization of both hermeneutic and ethnographic methods.

Mapping the circulation of representations and their relationship to modalities of economic empowerment and disaffection must also entail an engagement with the changing organization of information and communication networks often referred to, using the language of Henry Jenkins, as 'convergence culture'. Jenkins argument posits that the structural changes in the organization of media network as well as the changing opportunities for participation in vernacular media production translate directly into a democratic political project. Jenkins argument is strongest in dealing with the way in which the changes have affected mainstream media culture; it is less explicit in its discussion of how these changes might affect other areas of society. In much the same way that contemporary practices of protest look to bridge the connection between representation and engagement, an analysis of these transformations would also need to consider how institutional formations such as the state or the actors that make up the financial sector are themselves being transformed as media convergence spreads across society. How, for example, have mobile media technologies and the increasingly rapid circulation of media texts and other information across various platforms changed the ways in which the economy is regulated?

We need to know more about the way in which government agencies as well as those who work in the financial sectors are being transformed through their use of new information and communication technology. This might seem like a straightforward question about the diffusion and adoption of new technologies, but it is a question for Cultural Studies as it will point directly to the intersection between practices of representation, consumption and the particular configuration of material resources that structure power in the age of financial capitalism. Take, for example, the periodic scandals around the consumption of pornography by financial workers and regulators while on the job. This is an example that draws out attention both to popular attitudes about the financial sector and those who work there, but it also says something about the permeability of these institutions to the circulation of media content and their continuity with other cultural dynamics at large.

These are only two tentative suggestions about possible directions cultural studies research might take as it develops its engagement with the world after the economic crisis. It is a project that moves beyond straight forward analysis and is guided by a desire to improve the dire situation in which many find themselves. Drawing attention to the movements and practices that have proven successful in mobilizing coalitions and making visible the structures of power which work to take away rights and concentrate wealth must continue to be the main goals of critically oriented intellectual work. The essays gathered in this volume offer many insights into how such work might develop and the ways in which scholarly research might contribute to broader social struggles.

References

Fisher, M., 2009. Capitalist Realism: Is there no alternative?, London: O Books.

Grossberg, L., 2010. Cultural studies in the future tense, Durham [NC]: Duke University Press.

Hall, S., 1979. The Great Moving Right Show. Marxism Today, pp.14-20.

Ruccio, D.F. ed., 2008. Economic Representations: Academic and Everyday, London: Routledge.

Index

Page numbers in *Italics* represent tables.